To Liz and Alice for helping me with my homework.

The Social Worker Speaks
A History of Social Workers Through the Twentieth Century

DAVID BURNHAM

ASHGATE

Published by
Ashgate Publishing Limited
Wey Court East
Union Road
Farnham
Surrey, GU9 7PT
England

Ashgate Publishing Company
Suite 420
101 Cherry Street
Burlington
VT 05401-4405
USA

www.ashgate.com

British Library Cataloguing in Publication Data
Burnham, David.
  The social worker speaks : a history of social workers
  through the twentieth century.
  1. Social workers – Great Britain – Attitudes – History –
  20th century. 2. Social case work – Great Britain –
  History – 20th century.
  I. Title
  361.3'2'0941'0904-dc23

Library of Congress Cataloging-in-Publication Data
Burnham, David Michael.
  The social worker speaks : a history of social workers through the twentieth century / by
David Michael Burnham.
     p. cm.
  Includes bibliographical references and index.
  ISBN 978-1-4094-3638-6 (hbk)—ISBN 978-1-4094-3639-3 (ebook) 1. Social
workers—Great Britain—History—20th century. 2. Social service—Great Britain
—History—20th century. I. Title.
  HV40.8.G7B87 2012
  361.30941'0904—dc23

2012029489

ISBN 9781409436386 (hbk)
ISBN 9781409436393 (ebk)

MIX
Paper from
responsible sources
FSC
www.fsc.org
FSC® C018575

Printed and bound in Great Britain by the
MPG Books Group, UK.

Contents

Acknowledgements

No book is created by one person alone and many have helped produce this one. People have responded to calls for help, but others have helped inadvertently just by being themselves and saying what they thought. But I'll start by thanking people I never met: some of whom died before I was born; the people who set me onto this task – Mary Haslam, Alice Kearsley, William Payne, Cyril Bustin, Jo Harris and Walter Watkinson among others – people whose example is still an example decades after they did their work.

My primary thanks are to those who agreed to be interviewed for the book and this includes the many who agreed, but who, for various reasons, I did not interview. I ran out of time and also realised once I had interviewed over forty people that I was getting close to the amount of material I could reasonably handle; but thanks again to Annie Hollows, Ros Thorpe, Malcolm Jordan, Keith Bilton, David Jones, Olive Hammersley, Helen Bramley Burgess, Hilary Mercer, Sheila Whipp, Chris Gardner, Don Rowbottom and Joe Slater.

Thank you too to the people I interviewed who practiced in the 1940s and 1950s: Nora Cooper, Mary Mason, Barbara Totton (who I only met through her daughter Julia Pither) and Brian Fox. I am grateful too to the representatives of the next generation: Joyce Rimmer, helpful in so many ways, Marian Penny, Hilary (Clare) Makepeace, Maurice Ffelan and his eye for detail, Marie McNay, Isobel Groves, Peter Hewitt, Keith Hiscock, Hilary Corrick, Sheila Ives, Jack Preston, Ron Standring, Mary Hartley and Val Burnham.

Representatives from the generation which started out in the 1970s include David Custance, Carol Clark, John Dunkerley and Dinah Dunkerley, Lynn Baxter, Amanda Brown, Judith Niechcial who has been immensely supportive, Jennie Polyblank, Hannah McCarthy, Wendy Leach, Nirmal Singh, Sue Moya, Howard Syddall and Tom Daniels.

Penny Hindle, Eileen Gallagher, Julia Pither, Wyn Haslam, Elizabeth Mannion, Brenda Ryan and Heather Cameron represent the youngest generation of social workers I interviewed. They are thanked for their openness, despite the vague pressure on them of still working with or close by the organisations where they gained their formative experiences as social workers. In fact candour was a universal feature in the responses of the people I interviewed. As pleased as I was by this, it did necessitate careful subsequent consideration of the text with all the interviewees to ensure the appropriateness of what was included in the final text. Necessary as this has been it has imposed a further burden on those I interviewed which I recognise and for which I thank them.

Ian McHugh, Dave Seaber, Michael Murphy and Ciaran Rafferty have helped immensely over the years as has Stirling Smith, unusual in an Anglican as he sometimes played the role of Devil's Advocate. Barbara Lewis and Peter Shorrock both helped as did Kev and Irene Lynn and I am indebted to Don Rowbottom for his forgiveness when I left his precious copies of *Case Con* on a train. Howard Davies returned to me material from a course he and I had both been on the 1980s, as well as a copy of *Probe*, which stimulated further thinking.

Michael Stewart and Brenda Mallon gave up their time to talk to me as did Robin Hobbes, who is forgiven for the brutal cycle training. Alan Calvert, Kathy Brown, Ted Perry, Ciaran Rafferty and Dawn Butterfield all read sections of the draft for which I am grateful, and many others have been encouraging: Joan Rapaport, Patsie Law, Viv Cree and Michael Burt as well as all those who, when told of the project, said 'Oh, what a good idea'. Ruth Mills was very generous with photographs of her father Cyril Bustin and Shirley Malin, Milo Drury, Robert Lake, Annie Skinner, Edwin Coope and Paul Wilding all opened up new avenues of enquiry. Clare Barker and Harry Venning gave and continue to give constant inspiration.

Thanks too to the British Library – unsurpassed in the efficiency of its catalogue, helpful staff and the delightful oak finished environment. But why not have more pencils? I also sought help from York Library, the archive in Bury Library, St Bartholemew's Hospital Archive in London, Birmingham Library Archive, Manchester University Library and Lancashire Archive in Preston, where special thanks are due to Jacquie Crosby. I would also like to thank Joyce Rimmer for allowing me access to her extraordinary collection of social work literature. I have made considerable use of material in Bolton History Centre from the collections of Bolton Library and Museum Service, whose copyright I acknowledge. The people working at Bolton History Centre have been constantly helpful over the several years it has taken me to gather material – so thanks are due to them, and their pencils, and to Caroline Furey for being so accommodating. And my life as a researcher has been much eased by the availability of the services of Amazon, Wikipedia and Ancestry.com. Finally I owe a great deal to Kirstie Clegg for her cool, orderly and reassuring organisation of the final stages of the project.

And Linda Drury has been there, as ever, interested and calm, offering constant support and advice.

List of Abbreviations

ACCO	Association of Child Care Officers
ACO	Association of Children's Officers
APSW	Association of Psychiatric Social Workers
BASW	British Association of Social Workers
BBS	Bolton Benevolent Society
BHC	Bolton History Centre
BPPS	Bolton Poor Protection Society
CAB	Citizen's Advice Bureau
CCO	Child Care Officer
CD	Children's Department
CETS	Church of England Temperance Society
CO	Children's Officer
COS	Charity Organisation Society
CQSW	Certificate of Qualification in Social Work
CYPA	Children and Young Person's Act
DAO	Duly Authorised Officer
DH	Department of Health
DHSS	Department of Health and Social Security
FSU	Family Service Unit
FWA	Family Welfare Association
IA	Institute of Almoners
LCC	London County Council
LGB	Local Government Board
LSE	London School of Economics
MOH	Medical Officer of Health
MWO	Mental Welfare Officer
NAB	National Assistance Board
NAPO	National Association of Probation Officers
NISWT	National Institute of Social Work Training
PAC	Public Assistance Committee
PO	Probation Officer
PSU	Pacifist Service Unit
PSW	Psychiatric Social Worker
RO	Relieving Officer
SAO	School Attendance Officer
SAWO	School Attendance and Welfare Officer
SSD	Social Services Department

TB	Tuberculosis (or Consumption or Phthisis)
WD	Welfare Department
WO	Welfare Officer

Introduction

This book is about social workers; the ordinary men and women across the twentieth century who toiled on society's front line. The account describes their motivations, work practices and interventions, wherever possible in their own words, set against social and cultural developments, legislative changes and practice requirements. To allow the narrative to flow, the tale returns regularly to the social workers in one town. This is no history of 'Social Work' the profession, it is about individual social workers. This is an unusual approach so I shall explain what I have done.

Aim

Most histories of social work are partial, concentrating on particular aspects of the profession such as practice theories, professional training, organisational changes and the introduction of legislation. And such histories often concentrate considerable attention on events which were perceived as contributing to the development of social work as a profession rather than paying detailed attention to what actually happened (Woodroofe 1962, Younghusband 1947, 1964, 1978, Rooff 1972, Payne 2006, Pierson 2011). Some, alternatively, have concentrated on grand characters in social work, pioneers such as Octavia Hill (Moberley Bell 1942) or Eileen Younghusband (Jones 1984). Other histories have a clear focus on a particular field of activity or organisation. hospital social work (Barraclough et al. 1996), psychiatric social work (Timms 1964), the Children's Society (Stroud 1971, Bowder, 1980). Finally, some histories of social work published towards the end of the twentieth century focus on various crises in social work, from the mid seventies onwards, when social work's status and role was questioned from the left and its very purpose questioned from the right. At the same time widely publicised child deaths and the perceived failing of social workers to protect children brought very unwelcome public attention (Butler and Drakeford 2005).

Read any of these histories and look for individual social workers and the reader will not find them – very few mention front line workers or discuss their day-to-day experience. The partiality of such histories, histories without people, is akin to the way histories of the Great War were presented until Martin Middlebrook's *First Day on the Somme* (1971) was published with its direct quotes from 500 ordinary soldiers involved. When Middlebrook submitted his manuscript Penguin asked Corelli Barnett to review it. A fine historian of the Great War in the traditional vein, Barnett commented that Seigfried Sassoon and Henry Williamson had already told the tale from the trenches so Middlebrook's book was not necessary. But Sassoon and Williamson were both middle class, both writers, both educated and had been officers. Barnett just did not get it. Penguin published Middlebrook's book and it has sold 40,000 copies (Middlebrook 2004). Subsequently, first class scholars like Lyn McDonald (*The Roses of No Man's Land,* 1980; *1914,* 1987) followed Middlebrook's lead and now no account of the Great War would be considered complete without observations about and from men in the trenches.

This gap in the history of social work has broader connotations. Consider the idea of the social worker available to the general population. There are, I would contend, three broad public images. There are those unfortunates caught up in child deaths or other failings: real people involved in thankfully short-lived media storms, but as silent and furtive on TV news bulletins as murder suspects as they scuttle into buildings holding enquiries. Then there are the fleeting, ill-drawn but invariably wooden figures who occasionally appear in TV soaps, interviewing the main characters who want to become foster parents, or whose dad can no longer cope. The third example is *Clare in the Community.* Compare this stilted, demeaning set of images with the idea the general population has of teachers for instance or doctors, priests, nurses or police officers. Novels, radio and TV dramas offer us scores of examples – Jane Tennison, Gene Hunt, James Herriot and so on. These may be inaccurate or idealised, but they breathe; they live. Anyone who has done the work understands that life as a social worker can be fascinating, scary and rewarding; offering horrendous insights into the way people suffer, granting flashes of achievement. But only social workers know this. Social workers have not told their stories.

Who Were These Social Workers?

I have to be clear about who I claim to have been a social worker. The major difficulties this presents are threefold:

- Those who regarded themselves as social workers has changed, developed and narrowed over the century.
- Some of the work associated with social workers has disappeared, while new tasks and types of workers have taken their place.
- The focus in histories and records has been on some types of social worker while others have been completely ignored.

In 1904 at the beginning of our narrative the term 'social worker' was less widely used than it is today. Voluntary workers were as often referred to as philanthropic or charitable workers (Kirkman Gray 1908), while at the same time the term 'social worker' was used to describe a very wide range of philanthropic activity. Clement Attlee, in his influential book *The Social Worker* (1920) defined a range of activities under the term social work which included, among other things, district nursing and housing management. Attlee himself, a lawyer, carried out his social work largely by giving legal and housing advice to local tenants of private landlords. Legal advice workers would not consider themselves social workers today, but Attlee did. At the same time Poor Law workers, undertaking tasks such as visiting boarded out children, would neither have classed themselves as social workers nor been considered as such.

As welfare and public service occupations developed in the 1920s and 1930s some aspired to professional status which, among other things, set occupational groups apart. Then as legislation identified more precisely which organisations should lead and manage specific state responses to poverty, health, unemployment and disability, some groups of workers – previously referred to as social workers – took another path. In the 1950s, for instance, Health Visitors were described without controversy as 'medico-social workers' (Williams 1956). Between the wars women with a midwifery qualification considered themselves qualified for roles we would, today, unhesitatingly regard as social work roles. Sanitary Inspectors and welfare supervisors in factories applied for child welfare worker posts without comment. Some roles just disappeared; tuberculosis visitors for instance. Outworkers in Moral Welfare Associations appeared in the 1920s and disappeared in the 1970s.

It is hardly surprising therefore that, throughout the century commentators attempting to define who social workers were have produced lists of roles considered to fit their particular criteria. The most constant list maker was Elizabeth Macadam who offered three such lists between 1925 and 1945 (1925, 1934, 1945). The roles included the traditional elite groups such as almoners, probation officers and latterly psychiatric social workers, but she also included school attendance officers, personnel officers in industry and relieving officers. In this she broadly agreed with the list offered by Clement Attlee in 1920. Her successor as doyenne of social work education, Eileen Younghusband, produced a list in 1947 which excluded more or less all but the elite groups (1947). As I have argued elsewhere one of the purposes behind Younghusband's work was to establish social work as a profession, so her selection was understandable (Burnham, D. 2011). Rodgers and Dixon's list compiled in 1959 was more inclusive again counting staff of the National Assistance Board (often former relieving officers) who visited claimants in their homes and the considerable number of unqualified people referred to as welfare officers.

My aim here is to be inclusive and draw from the inter-war analysis of the Wickwars (1936), who included as social workers people who assessed, proposed and intervened; the post-war proposal of Rodgers and Dixon who considered social workers to be workers in personal touch with consumers of social service who could understand and interact with people in their social setting and family group (1960) and the broad congregation proposed by Vivien Cree (1995). So principally I include people who worked in the community rather than those working solely in an institution. I embrace people whose task was to assess social need of some sort, who offered some response or support to those in need, which might include but was more than simple financial help, but might consist of practical help.

This approach makes the boundaries of those who are regarded as social workers fuzzy, but it does mean that groups of workers who have been ignored in previous considerations of social work history get a mention.

Approach

Timeline

Most social work histories attempt to dredge the depths of the nineteenth century to find evidence of the beginnings of social work. I have not done that but instead I concentrate on the twentieth century. This is for four reasons.

Firstly it is neat and gives a definite beginning to the narrative. Secondly there is a huge literature about the origins of social work activity as we would recognise it, so further investigation would be going over old ground. Thirdly, before the 1890s records available about voluntary organisations, Poor Law Guardians and health activities are much thinner than afterwards – this is at least partly because case papers, superannuation and nationwide recruitment came into practice in public services only with the local government legislation of 1889. After that public service records become more detailed. Finally and most importantly, the start of the narrative is a time of great change (Rose 1971, King 2004, 2006). I start the narrative surveying philanthropic work and Poor Law workers' activities just before the establishment of Guilds of Help in 1905, a network of voluntary organisations infused with a more giving spirit than the stern prescriptions of the Charity Organisation Society. At that time too women and working class men were finding their feet as elected representatives on bodies such as the Poor Law Guardians. The welfare legislation following the liberal election victory of 1906 heralded a more comprehensive state rejoinder to poverty, disease and disability. This period then, when society as a whole began to take more responsibility for poverty and want, is an appropriate time to start.

The narrative ends in 1989 at the time of the Children Act and NHS and Community Care Act. I had intended to round off the tale much closer to the turn of the century but I found myself becoming uneasy in interviews with people who worked in the 1990s. The closer their experiences were to the present day, the more likely the subject matter was to be sensitive and the more guarded the interviewees became. So the period covered is 1904 to 1989.

Research Methods

The methods used have been simple. There are three strands:

1. I undertook a survey of the literature. This included a search for unpublished MA and PhD theses as well as a review of the histories of social work written from 1900 onwards. Part of the literature search included a sub-category exploration for accounts by individual social workers. There are diaries, memoirs, some autobiographies and even a few autobiographical novels.

2. I reviewed a considerable amount of material in the Bolton History Centre (BHC), the public archive in Bolton. There is a good set of Poor Law and Public Assistance records there and records of many voluntary organisations. I have also consulted records in London, Birmingham, Manchester, York, Bury and Preston.

3. I sought out social workers from across England and contacted about 70 people seeking reminiscences. As a result of that I have taken personal testimony from 48 social workers, one or two who started before the end of the war and a few others, at the other end of the scale who are still working. There are of course contributions in the records of social work associations from front line workers, but I have avoided these because I wanted to capture the individual experience, not organisational or political views. Similarly I have interviewed people whose careers culminated in senior positions or in social work education and research but have deliberately not asked them about their years of leadership or their time in academia. In the text I have used the real names of the social workers I have interviewed, subject to their permission, but have used pseudonyms where people have asked not to be identified. The names and circumstances of all the people they worked with mentioned in the text have been changed.

Local Focus, National Observations

In order to more easily focus on individuals, I have chosen to return regularly to how social workers operated in one town. About a fifth of the text concerns social workers and their activities in Bolton. This focus allows a chronological narrative to flow in which careers of individuals can be tracked, family connections investigated and organisations followed. For instance Alice Kearsley worked for the Waifs and Strays Society before the Great War and also volunteered with the Girls Welfare Society. She became the first Lady Visitor with the Poor Law Guardians and resigned after the war, possibly because she was out of favour with her boss and later, in 1929, was appointed as Almoner at the Infirmary. Her career demonstrates the intimate association between work in voluntary and public sectors at the time and also shows how social workers' careers have followed political and social developments.

Her story is available in the unexciting vehicle of a Poor Law personnel record available in Bolton History Centre. There are hundreds of local archives across England and the snapshot here could be replicated for Bristol and Bournemouth as it could for Belfast, Bangor and Brechin. The personal voices of social workers found there and in forgotten memoirs and autobiographies, are waiting to contribute to a richer national picture of the history of social workers.

Another practical reason for returning to the story in one town is that it helps weave the voices from across the country into a patterned whole. I found only a limited number of memoirs, diaries and autobiographical accounts and they are stylistically and geographically diverse. The possibility of linking Dorothy Manchee's gentle tale of almoners in London (1942), with Ken Powls' gritty account of mental welfare in Humberside (2010) and Cyril Bustin's picaresque stories of life as a relieving officer in Bermondsey (1982) without a geographical anchor, would have been beyond my powers. In addition this approach offers the beginnings of a realignment of social work history away from London. This is no clichéd jibe about a North / South divide. Social work histories have, it seems to me, concentrated on characters and activities in the capital to the exclusion of almost everywhere else (Burnham, D. 2011).

Bolton is also a good benchmark because it is an ordinary town and not as complicated to write about as a big city. Bolton was a distinct local government unit throughout the twentieth century, with the full range of health, local government and voluntary organisations: two COS type visiting charities, a workhouse, a District General Hospital, NSPCC worker(s), probation officer(s), Poor Law Guardians / Public Assistance Committee / Welfare Departments / Social Services Department, Waifs and Strays Society, Guild of Help, several District Nursing Associations and a Moral Welfare Association.

So this book follows in the tradition of such texts as *Family and Kinship in East London* (Willmott and Young 1957) and *The Classic Slum* (Robert Roberts 1971) which offer local experiences to inform a general understanding.

Shortcomings and Biases

So the approach I have taken is to attempt to give a voice to front line social workers from the beginning of the twentieth century to near the end. There are several shortcomings with this. First of all I cannot claim complete coverage for this text. For one thing I have had to restrict the account to England and time and geographical constraints have limited the numbers of people I have been able to talk to.

Secondly the voice of social workers has been sought from a mixture of sources. The public records offer a good haul but as they were written for purposes alien to much of what I am trying to achieve there are gaps in what the records can offer. Also this source dries up half way through the century as personnel records are, for good reason, closed to researchers until hoary with age. Memoirs and autobiographies present other difficulties. How trustworthy are they as sources? People might put a positive gloss on their experiences and only write about what they want to reveal, and of course people tend to remember the out of the ordinary more certainly than the mundane. There is the potentially more serious problem of accounts having been written at the end of people's careers. This is also the case with the interviews I have done. It is not that people forget or elide their failings or exaggerate successes; the more serious danger is that what they say or write may not represent what they would have said or written at the time, for there is an inevitable elegiac quality in many of the memories I have encountered or recorded. Thirdly, I cannot claim to have reported on a representative sample of social workers. I issued invitations for interviewees nationally via several channels, but could only interview people who came forward and only a limited number. So coverage is patchy. Education Welfare Officers are not mentioned in the latter half of the book, nor are youth workers after their separate identity was established after the Second World War. There is no proper mention of tuberculosis visitors or the Army Welfare Service. Housing managers and factory inspectors are absent and there is almost no mention of teachers for the blind and social workers for the deaf.

I have also used five novels as sources. All are written by people who had worked as social workers and all have strong autobiographical elements, E.R. Braithwaite (1962) and Bronwen Rees (1965) even using their own names for the protagonists in first person narratives. My justification for this is that if novelists present events more colourfully than they were, they are using no more artifice than was available to the people writing memoirs or those who kindly gave up their time to talk to me.

A more demanding potential charge is my own bias, for of course, I am no cypher. Any historian, especially one personally involved in the area of study, as I have been since 1973, cannot escape the accusation of having some agenda. I trained as a probation officer on a Certificate of Qualification in Social Work (CQSW) course at Leicester University between 1973 and 1975. I worked as a probation officer for three years in Nottingham, then latterly as a child care social worker in Manchester before moving away into training and management in the 1980s. I am married to a social worker. Some of my best friends are social workers. So I have some conscious biases and no doubt unconscious ones too.

Of conscious biases underpinning the approach to this text, I lay claim to three. First of all I offer a vehicle for people to tell their tale and try to report people's views directly. I suppose I am following J.R. Green whose observations of charitable workers are quoted in Chapter One. Green was a clergyman-turned-historian who rejected the Rankian claim that all history is the history of politics and diplomacy, refuting drum and trumpet history as he called it, and wrote instead about people (Green 1892).

Secondly I have tried to uncover the tales of people whose roles have been largely ignored in previous histories. So part of the aim here is to tell the tales of those social workers working before 1948 under the Poor Law (Burnham, D. 2011).

Thirdly I have deliberately attempted to consult a broad and non-traditional evidence base. Using personnel records, memoirs and novels as material for a history of social workers brings to mind R.G. Collingwood's observation that historical understanding develops sometimes with the use of evidence historians have hitherto thought useless (*An Autobiography,* 1939).

Butterworth's admonition to historians to empty their minds is impossible but I have tried to stand outside the system, at a distance looking in, leaving my contemporary baggage at the door (Marwick 1973). One example of how I have tried is in the language I have used. References to Cripples Parlours or Relieving Officers for Lunatics make for uncomfortable reading but I have decided to use language in the text which was used at the time rather than try and ameliorate it. I do this for a number of reasons. First of all much of the language we find offensive today was technical in the past, in the sense that it denoted a particular characterisation of people under legislation. Words such as Idiot and Mental Defective fall into this category. It is also the language people actually used on a day-to-day basis and gives some flavour of societal attitudes. Thirdly, it allows me to chart the changes in language, many of which follow legislation, although some denote changes in practice fashion. Finally, using the language of the day helps us to put our own language into context. We stand all the time at the end of history, sometimes perplexed by the language and behaviour of our forebears and sometimes sneering at them. Our own views and practices are up to date and logical, so we think, and we are unable to see any foolishness in them and are unable to imagine that the accepted language of today will be regarded as oppressive and unhelpful in the future. So we think.

On a less testing note I have used traditional currency notation here. Before 1971 in the UK the pound sterling comprised twenty shillings, each of which was made up of twelve pennies. In written form a shilling was noted as 's' and a penny as 'd'. So six shillings and fourpence was written 6s 4d. Before the Great War a working man would bring home between one and two pounds a week. By 1945 a decent weekly wage was around five pounds and the average wage by 1989 was around £150.

Despite it all I have no doubt brought my own baggage and biases to bear here. But in doing so I hope I have produced a solid and colourful contribution to the debate. While succeeding histories on the same subject may not be cumulative, differing approaches, contrasting views and even conflict is good for debate and increases the readers' ability to reach or reconsider his or her own truth. So partial as this history is, if it offers a different angle on the past or encourages anyone to seek out the history of social workers in their own area, it has done its job.

Dave Burnham

Chapter 1
1904–1914: Visiting Societies, the Poor Law and Local Activists

Mary Haslam Goes to Town

On the morning of 15 June 1904 Mary Haslam made her way from her house, White Bank, into Bolton. She may have used the new tramway or a pony and trap or even walked the two miles to town. At the time around 150 textile mills dominated the town's industry, each belching smoke. All houses used coal or coke for heating and cooking, and smoke from steam locomotives completed a toxic mix, often cloaking the town in a muggy cowl. But Mary Haslam would not have thought twice about the tang of coal smoke in her throat, motes of ash in the air, nor noticed the ammoniac odour of horse dung on the streets; all would have been too familiar (Bolton Evening News [BEN] 15 June 1904a: 3).

In the town centre carts and carriages would have been plying up and down avoiding deliverymen on bikes and messenger boys darting back and forth. The street layout she passed through, as in many towns in Britain, would have been familiar to twenty-first century eyes, but the life in it was very different. If chimneys ruled the skyline, the backdrop at ground level was jerry-built terraced streets with thin walls and one source of heating – the kitchen range. Toilets were outside, by the back yard gate, though water was piped to a single tap in the house and gas was used to light fragile gas mantles. Floors were stone-flagged and usually bare and a two up, two down terrace was the limit of ambition for a cotton worker or miner, no matter that families of six or more children were commonplace (Foley 1973, Hamer 1938).

These houses were small, cold and crowded and were treated like dormitories, with people leaving the house for things we regard as domestic activities. Many used public baths to wash, bakery ovens to cook, or bought plated up meals or fish and chips to eat at home. People went out to pubs, music halls, choirs, missions and societies. Drunkenness was rife, aided by only limited restrictions on pub opening hours, and in 1904 the town had 126 pubs and 225 ale houses, for a population of barely 200,000 (Bolton Directory 1904). Syphilis was common especially in the armed forces, but tuberculosis (TB) was the big killer, taking off tens of thousands of Britons each year. Tens of thousands more died of opportunistic infections such as pneumonia, whooping cough or diphtheria – all of which thrived in conditions where people were undernourished and worn out. And while epidemics of cholera were long past, large-scale infections of smallpox were still a threat. Even the relatively well-off fell prey to such threats as typhus and TB (BHC GBO/28/50, BHC GBO/28/4).

Half the working men in industrial towns were in mass occupations in factories, mills and mines, 36,000 men and women working in mills in Bolton alone. Nearly a million men worked on the railways and a million in mines. An eleven-hour day was the norm; hours often of mind-flattening repetition and constant noise. And the workplace was dangerous, there being a steady procession of fatal and crippling accidents in mills, factories and mines and the occasional disaster such as the Pretoria pit disaster of 1911, when an explosion in a mine five miles from Bolton killed 320 men and boys. Childbirth was probably a bigger killer, with some parts of industrial towns having each family lose one child for every five born. The high death rate of women in childbirth contributed to the considerable number of one-parent families and step-parents, a constant feature in accounts of social workers at the time (Thompson 1992).

Childbirth apart, women's work was safer than men's, with a third of all women who worked outside the home employed in domestic service. Safe perhaps, but their constant task was to defer to their masters. Deference to elders was rigid too, and where children shared space with adults – school, home or workplace – the adults frequently used humiliation, intimidation or the strap to control them. And while the affluent were often condescending about the crudities of those obliged to defer to them, working class women had to develop immense capabilities in managing all the washing, cooking, cleaning, child-rearing and budgeting – often working out of the home as well, or taking in needlework or other outwork. At the same time middle and upper class women in the same station as Mary Haslam did nothing for themselves and, as one historian put it, were almost useless (Marwick 1967, Roberts 1976, Thompson 1975).

As she made her way to her business in town the far from useless Mary Haslam may have pondered these things. She was one of a number of active affluent local women who worked in the Poor Law Union and in voluntary organisations, lobbied for improvements and visited poor families in distress.

Local Activists

Mary Haslam was one of a distinct group of women in Bolton, but there were thousands of such women across the nation whose activities had been supported and stimulated by the Local Government Act of 1894. This extended the franchise, allowing women candidates for Councils and Poor Law Boards. The franchise-widening coincided with the impact of several Education Acts from 1870 onwards, which resulted in a huge increase in literacy amongst working people. At the same time, the reduction in the general working week to around 55 hours and the appearance and popularity of mass circulation newspapers in the 1890s meant that increasing numbers of working class men were both readers and writers – and interested, informed and able to take part in local politics and administration.

All this stimulated debate about the role of the Poor Law, local government and the traditional attitudes which had dominated local affairs. Affluent women came forward as candidates; in some places facing jeers at meetings and in the columns of local newspapers. But a trickle of working men and affluent women were elected to Councils and Poor Law Unions, joining the ranks of professional men, retailers and industrialists who traditionally peopled such bodies. The new members often had a different attitude to poverty and to the role of women than their established male colleagues. In Bolton in 1894 no less than five women had been elected to the Board of Poor Law Guardians, supported by a cross party alliance of clergymen, employers and worker's interests. Of this class of 1894 the most significant figure was Mary Haslam (King 2006).

Mary Heywood was born in 1851 into an affluent Liberal and Unitarian family. She married William Haslam, a mill owner and prominent local Liberal, in 1872. Once her four children were growing, she embarked on a career in public service which spanned a quarter of a century. The 1901 census reveals that, in White Bank, the Haslams had five live-in servants so she had ample time to devote to her wide range of social and political interests. She joined the Bolton Workhouse Visiting Committee (BWHVC) in 1885. Such committees, traditionally made up of the wives of local professionals, visited infirm and older paupers, taking flowers and other petty comforts, laying on treats and days out. Mary Haslam was involved in that kind of work but, from the beginning, she championed a more ambitious agenda. The Guardians accepted BWHVC suggestions such as the classification of mental patients so they could be offered separate care, payment for workhouse inmates who worked in the laundry and the establishment of a halfway house for young women leaving the workhouse as a means of re-establishing friendship groups in the outside world. Steven King suggests that Mary Haslam had an impact because she did her homework, consulted with staff, lobbied Guardians individually and knew how to propose reforms which gave the other Guardians room to manoeuvre (King 2004). Once a Guardian, Mary and her colleagues established a workhouse library, introduced individual ovens to the Cottage Homes for children (hot food previously having been brought over from the workhouse), brought in ordinary clothing for workhouse children and persuaded the Guardians to employ more paid staff in the workhouse, replacing inmate labour. She also proposed, and had accepted, the employment of a married couple as foster parents in one of the Union cottage homes to replace care attendants for children and replicate something closer to family life for them. But like other female Guardians this formal role was far from Mary Haslam's only welfare activity. She was a member of the National Society for the Protection of Cruelty to Children (NSPCC) committee and the Bolton Poor Protection Society (BPPS) – a long-standing local charity for which she herself undertook visits and befriended families.

Although we might not, in the twenty-first century, describe Mary Haslam as a social worker it is clear that, at the time, she was regarded as just that, being referred to in the local newspaper on her death as a *zealous social worker* (BEN 1922: 4). She was, like many others with time, aptitude and determination, what we might call a 'full spectrum' social worker – someone who saw a need, gathered supporters, pulled together a plan, raised money, managed the initiative and was personally involved in supporting the individuals or families who were the focus of the plan. Another 'full spectrum' social worker in Bolton at the time was Mrs Greg, another affluent woman and a Poor Law Guardian. Her primary commitment was to support the local workshop for the blind, which she had set up, taking the longstanding workshop in Liverpool as her model. She found out by chance the plight of blind children:

> I paid the first visit I think I ever made to the Education Offices ... to secure a pair of spectacles for a child ... Mr Hilton, the ... then Superintendent Attendance Officer, pointed out to me how the table was scattered with papers about the deaf and dumb. Each individual case when about to be returned from school was notified to Mr Ayliffe and he undertook to ... make provision for them (Bolton Journal and Guardian 1913a).

Mr Hilton pointed out that nothing was done for blind children and Mrs Greg was horrified. '*They were allowed to sink into the abysmal depths ... simply allowed to degenerate into hopeless wrecks.*'

She learned of 172 such children who had left school in the previous two years. Mrs Greg called together a committee of like-minded women and put in place arrangements to help the children fend for themselves and prevent them from becoming street singers or helpless. The committee investigated practice in Manchester and Nottingham and put in place a training school teaching the children to type, to weave and make clogs and jerseys. The committee also arranged evening classes and free concert tickets. But the core of the work, according to Mrs Greg, was to assure that '*no child was allowed to depart from school unwatched*'. Her ambition was '*that there shall be continuity of care from birth to the time when they shall have been taught to earn their own independence followed by reasonable supervision*'.

The breadth of her commitment is revealed by Mrs Greg's purchase of a building as the centre for activities, her involvement in visiting many families herself and chasing up employment opportunities for individual children (Bolton Journal and Guardian 1913a).

There were several other such women in Bolton: Mrs Mothersole, Mrs Barnes, Miss Barlow and Miss Reddish, who initiated many schemes to improve the welfare of the poor and sick. There were thousands like them across the land. They each had their own specialism and most were involved in the women's suffrage movement. Mary Haslam's special concern was TB and she sponsored what became an annual health week in Bolton, which took place for several years before the Great War.

But her journey into Bolton that June morning in 1904 lay at the heart of her activities. She was travelling to attend the meeting of the Board of Guardians which met every other Wednesday. She tried to contribute to every meeting, save for a month off in August and a winter break in St. Moritz. There were two items on the agenda that morning with which she was particularly concerned. She had recently persuaded the BPPS to appoint ladies to its committee. As Hayworth puts it:

> The most useful work it was felt they could do was to bring to bear their womanly sympathy … to their poorer sisters in distress. A lady was invariably a more welcome visitor to the homes of the poor … where the clumsier efforts of a man could be fatal (Hayworth 2007: 17).

She proposed to ask the Guardians to offer a grant to the BPPS which was having difficulty raising funds for its applicants. The agenda that day also included consideration of a proposal by Mrs Barnes to introduce the Case Paper system – a recording arrangement where each applicant for out-relief had an individual record, a case paper, completed on application and updated as and when necessary. The proposal was to replace the old ledgers, in which the details of each applicant for out-relief were recorded chronologically; necessitating a search through the previous pages of the ledger should the same family or individual apply for help again. The members of the Union agreed to consider this and Mary Haslam was appointed to a sub-committee to look at it in detail (Bolton Chronicle 1904: 3). Support for this clear, helpful change was typical of the sort of move Mary Haslam and her progressive group championed. The proposal to introduce individual case papers was of immense significance. Like the payment to inmates for working in the laundry, closing the workhouse school and sending the children to local schools, it was one of the small changes that shifted the perception of the Guardians. The grand leather-bound ledgers – and they were very grand indeed – were one of the aspects of the Poor Law which implied that people applying for out-relief (payment or cash) were an anonymous mass, an endless, undifferentiated stream of need to be assuaged; the Poor. A separate buff folder about each applicant, a case paper, on the other hand confirmed their status as individuals. It also challenged the informal practice knowledge held by the Guardian and the relieving officer (RO), as a case paper could be used to confirm or deny opinions of the officials. And it required the RO to keep a record of their contacts with families and individuals, necessitating something different of them. As tiny as this proposed change was, it epitomised a shift in the official attitude to those seeking help from the Poor Law.

Philanthropic Visiting Societies and Settlements

What Mary Haslam's and Mrs Greg's activities demonstrate, Jane Lewis identifies as the Edwardian '*mixed economy of welfare*'. Local authority, Poor Law and charitable organisations not only worked together as a matter of course but were often led by the same people (Haldane 1911, Lewis 1995, 1996, Burt 2008). But this day-to-day collaboration masked a politically fraught debate nationally about emerging state intervention into the lives of poor people which confronted the powerful philanthropic tradition of poor visiting. In order to place the emerging role of social workers in both spheres, we'll consider Poor Law functions and charitable efforts to help the poor. Charity first.

In 1876 J.R. Green wrote a skit on charitable work, which still had force at the turn of the century. Green, a Church of England clergyman, was for a while in Stepney, a warren of grim courts populated by earnest dockers as well as drunkards, prostitutes and thieves. So he knew poverty and the poor. In *The District Visitor* (1892) he identifies three sorts of charitable work:

1. General visiting of the poor. Green has in mind here the lady parish visitor, asked by the vicar or his wife to spend, say, an afternoon a week visiting the poor of the parish.
2. Personal efforts of an individual. Committed, romantic young men are Green's model here. Fellows in ones and twos would descend on some dark court, live there and encourage the poor to live decent lives using direct teaching, advocacy and setting an example. Sustainable vehicles for such personal commitment were established when residential settlements were set up in the dingy parts of our great cities. The first, Toynbee Hall in Whitechapel, London, was established by Samuel Barnett in 1884. Most, set up over the next two decades, were associated with and populated by universities.
3. Organised, recorded district visiting with the clear aim of offering help, encouragement, advice and relief, but only to those who demonstrated that they could use it to better themselves. Here Green speaks of the Charity Organisation Society and its ilk.

To these types of activity may be added two more:

4. Immediate time-limited relief in response to some natural disaster. The most common natural disaster in Victorian Britain was winter and time limited Distress Committees were ubiquitous up and down England. They distributed food, cash, blankets and so on more or less indiscriminately because the need was immediate and pressing.
5. Finally came precisely targeted charitable activity for specific categories of vulnerable people: abandoned children, the blind, the feeble-minded, fallen women and so on. Prime examples of organisations which developed from these responses include Dr Barnardo's Homes, Thomas Bowman Stephenson's National Children's Homes, the Church of England Waifs and Strays Society, the Church Penitentiary Association and the NSPCC.

The tradition of Christian alms giving was beating strongly in nineteenth-century Britain and money distributed by charity in mid century outstripped that distributed via the Poor Law (Young and Ashton 1956). The evangelical revival of the early century encouraged such activity and the emancipation of Catholics in 1829 and the strength of non-conformist churches added rivalry to the charitable efforts of different sects. More than this, with the industrialisation of Britain, the emergence of cities, the size of which were unprecedented, and which were teeming with people introduced a new phenomenon. The census of religious worship of 1851 revealed low attendances in cities, especially amongst the poor and of course their numbers and degradation overwhelmed what religious infrastructure there was (Mann 1853). It was in these circumstances that the general duties of the vicar's wife and her lady friends to visit the sick and needy developed into something more determined and, in the form of organised visiting charities, something new.

Although the evils of drink, gambling and immorality fired much charitable effort, a more subtle and pervasive threat was pauperism – a word which in nineteenth-century Britain carried a precise meaning. Paupers were thought to choose a way of life which depended on handouts, either from gullible lady visitors, as Green describes, or from the Poor Law. If people were pauperised by handouts, it was thought, they would not take responsibility for themselves. Pauperism was not so much a description of poverty as state of mind that middle and upper class interests thought many of the poor aspired to. This social analysis underpinned the 1834 Poor Law Amendment Act, whose aim was to make help from the state so unpalatable, in the form of stigmatising, regimented workhouses, that only the meanest and most desperate would accept it. This unpleasant strategy was described as 'less eligibility'. But it was also the logic underpinning the work of many voluntary visiting societies which sprang up across England in the latter third of the nineteenth century (Young and Ashton 1956).

The accusation that the charitable activities of the middle classes were a means of policing and controlling the poor, has validity. Many of the philanthropic leaders were open about wanting to educate and civilise the poor, to make poor people accept their lot with genteel acquiescence. And some affluent charitable visitors were sometimes baffled or disgusted by the people they worked with (Lewis 1991). But some contemporary observers regularly criticised what they saw as oppressive attitudes and hypocrisy in organised charity (Green 1876, Attlee 1920). And as early as 1860 Ruskin, in *Unto This Last,* offered an analysis of society which honoured poor people. However most people at the time, rich or poor, active or complacent, did not have imagination wistful enough to envisage the majority of people being able to gain access to decent housing, good sanitation, regular well-paid employment and an expectation of good health. That being the case, it is understandable that religiously motivated charity workers, understanding that in this world the poor were condemned to an uncomfortable lot, should do their best to ensure the poor took up the offer of better things to come, and therefore be encouraged to make their own efforts to seek both spiritual salvation and economic independence.

One tactic used by charitable workers from the 1860s onwards was the use of practical relief – money, bread, a roof – as a way of getting alongside the poor person so that her soul could be saved. Such activity was accompanied by the fear that the helper's good will might be abused by deliberate fraud on behalf of the poor, or what became known as overlapping – giving money or relief twice over, or giving it where it was not necessary. The corollary of these anxieties was the practice of many of the poor: to get as much out of this process as they could. This is encapsulated in a petty but precise way by the tale in William Woodruff's memoir of a poor upbringing in 1920s Blackburn, *The Road to Nab End* (2000). Woodruff describes Sundays when he and his pals would sit through Sunday school sessions of three different sects just to get the bun on offer at the end of each. The instrumental approach adopted by many of the would-be saviours and the instrumental response of many of the would-be-saved was neat if nothing else.

Many charities operated on these twin principles; help was offered to those who could use it, and therefore deserved it, and help was denied to the feckless. In addition the latter third of the century saw the appearance of what was called the scientific method in these organisations; the word scientific here meaning organised and discriminating, a countervailing practice to the indiscriminate giving associated with winter distress committees. The Charity Organisation Society (COS), established in London in 1869, while by no means the oldest of its type, came to represent the brand. COS pre-eminence rested upon a precise philosophy articulated by powerful carefully managed publicity, influential supporters and clear leadership from the long-standing secretary Charles Loch. By these means the COS stayed at the forefront of debate about philanthropic visiting until the Great War. An example of the way COS visitors worked is found in surviving case records of the Fulham and Hammersmith (F&H) committee from around the turn of the twentieth century.

The COS by 1904 had something like 30 separate committees across London and while each operated to COS principles they directed operations in their own area. It is worth at the outset recording the *Methods of Work* adopted by the F&H committee, set out in 1886:

> The members of the Committee ... meet together on Wednesdays and Fridays, at 11am 'to consider cases' ... This means to talk over sympathetically ... the circumstances of distress which have come to their knowledge the previous week, and to ascertain how matters are progressing with any persons who may have been visited ... on former occasions. The 'modus operandi' is as follows: The individual in trouble ... comes to the office and has a good talk with one of the Members of the Committee ... Their story in all its particulars is taken down in writing, and a printed form is invariably sent to the Clergyman of the parish, with a special request for his advice, and asking for any knowledge at the disposal of the Parochial District Visitor, if there is one. The enquiry is first put into the hands of a competent enquiry agent ... who by degree has obtained a useful and exact knowledge of the neighbourhood, and, when possible a Member of the Committee calls to see what can be done. In this way an endeavour is made to gather ... all the information possible to be obtained ... Nothing becomes

plainer to those who work amongst the poor, than that this remedy is not easy to find, and when found, that it is often difficult to apply. One person alone cannot find the remedy – it needs the laying together of many heads and the taking council *(sic)* one with another (Whelan 2001: 27).

Once the committee agreed to help a family money had to be raised to fund whatever support had been agreed.

Anyone volunteering to help from the right station in life became a committee member, so numbers on the committee give an indication of the strength of local support. In the 1870s there were over 50 committee members in Fulham and Hammersmith, by 1909 there were only 19. Whelan suggests that the reducing number of clergymen involved between 1880 and 1910 may be because of a growing reluctance by clergyman to be seen to be associated with the COS's increasingly controversial stance on poverty, which included opposition to old age pensions and state sponsored sickness insurance. As striking is the considerable increase in the numbers of women on the committee, from two per cent in the 1870s, to over 50 per cent by 1910.

The committee employed a paid agent to undertake the investigatory work, but the members of the committee were personally involved with the applicant families. The committee attempted to direct help to those who needed a short-term boost, or had fallen on hard times, whose remedy, as the Methods of Work suggested, looked straightforward. Those who had chronic diseases or were, through illness or perpetual drunkenness, unlikely to work again, were advised to seek the help of the Poor Law relieving officers. This was as much to do with the limited availability of funds as much as it was with the COS philosophy. Thus most help sanctioned was short term. This might include a grant for a man to buy tools to obtain work or work clothes, a stay in a convalescent home, or funding for training for the blind or lame. Regular grants were given for leg braces and special boots for children affected by rickets or with club feet. Female members of the committee might offer sewing or embroidery work to unemployed women.

But despite the aim of the F&H committee to help only those who had the commitment and wherewithal to reclaim an independent life, there are records of work done with families which go on for years, where the families concerned seemed, in COS terms, to be completely hopeless.

An example of this is the case of Mr and Mrs Manley, with whom there was contact between 1887 and 1895. The COS first of all helped Mr Manley to redeem his pawned clothes to enable him to seek work. To prove his clotheslessness at the time of the first application, Mr Manley appeared dressed in only a blanket. Subsequent enquiries however, after Manley had deserted his family, revealed that he was a drunk, who frequently beat his wife. As his whereabouts were unknown and no support could be offered to Mrs Manley, the COS advised her to go into the workhouse – the common fate for abandoned women with no means of support. That allowed the COS to place one of the Manley daughters in service. Once Manley had been found and charged with desertion, he was reprimanded, but was set up with work through help from an uncle and reunited with his family. Later referrals were for support for another of the children (Henry, 16, '*a cripple, easily led astray by bad boys*') to get him into the National Industrial Home for Crippled Boys, for Edith (24, '*anaemic*') and Maude (15, '*enlarged glands*') to get them convalescent home places and for John (23) for a set of tools. By 1895 Mr Manley was long gone and Mrs Manley was forever behind with her rent, a condition exacerbated no doubt by her fondness for brandy, which only seems to have been noted that year (Whelan 2001: 137).

Alice Hodson; COS Visitor

The records contain only sparse descriptions of cases and opinions are expressed only by implication, so the personalities of the visitors do not come across. Alice Lucy Hodson however provides a direct account of a COS visitor's experience. As a young woman she attended lectures at Lady Margaret Hall, Oxford in the 1880s (Hodson 1909). In this she was a trailblazer – women attending university before the Great War can be counted in their hundreds each year. Around 1900 having completed her studies and then in her early thirties, she joined the Lady Margaret Hall University Settlement in South London. So Miss Hodson was, for her time independent minded and socially progressive (LMH Brown Book 1963).

In that sense she was typical of many young people who lived and worked in settlements – affluent, socially aware and determined to contribute to the improvement and education of the poor. Some stayed for very short periods of time, unable to stand the various manifestations of poverty around them. But some stayed and worked for years. Toynbee Hall was the doyen of settlements, ambitious to introduce culture and literature to the East End of London and offering education classes to thousands each year as well as social clubs and financial advice. It attracted the liberal intellectual elite. Residents included William Beveridge, R.H. Tawney, Harold Laski and Clement Attlee, so it was not entirely typical of the settlement movement (Briggs and McCartney 1984). The Newtown settlement for women in Birmingham was more representative. The residents visited crippled children, securing educational and medical support for them, offered Happy Evenings entertainment and weaving and basket making for the older ones. There was a Poor Man's Lawyer service and nearly all the 19 settlement workers acted as collectors for providential insurance societies taking money from 700 families a week by 1913. They ran three girls' clubs, having meetings every evening but Saturday and the workers put on parties for children who had paid back loans for things like spectacles (Rimmer 1980). For all this the residents paid board and lodging, which usually included having meals made for them, their laundry done and their rooms cleaned. This pattern of settlement residents being supported by servants and housekeepers survived the Great War, with Clement Attlee advising would-be social workers to live without domestic servants for six months in order to get a real experience of poverty (Attlee 1920).

Alice Hodson's responsibilities seem to have been typical. She visited a number of courts (tenements arranged around a cul-de-sac); she helped run a boys' club and a Girls Friendly Society (GFS) group which attracted the better sort of domestic servants and young school mistresses, young women in work and cut off from their families. She also ran a club for what she called rough girls and helped with Sunday School treats.

Her visiting role is not spelled out but would probably have included collecting subscriptions for provident society sickness insurance. Her favourite old couple, who she visited every week, both over 70, earned their living by taking in washing – the wife washing and mangling, the husband picking up dirty clothing and dropping off the clean. Miss Hodson referred to their house as spotless and commented that the couple neither had Poor Law relief nor private charity. They earned their own living, did not need help, and did not ask for it. It was not the case for all families and she was cautious about families' interest in handouts and food tickets. In discussing savings arrangements for the annual boys' club holiday, Miss Hodson suggested that all families said they had a smaller income than was actually the case so the committee would be likely to fund a greater proportion of the cost. But she thought this was a natural ploy amongst the poor.

Miss Hodson also made enquiries about people who had made applications for relief. If alerted to a new case Miss Hodson would visit and interview the family using a standard set of questions. A proforma was completed and, should she decide that relief was indicated, the information on the proforma had to be turned into a report which she would present at the weekly meeting of the COS committee. She would by this time have confirmed any claims and assertions made by the family by writing to relatives, employers, clergymen, tradesmen and so on, all of whom seemed generally happy to comment openly about other people's business, and to do so within a day or two of receiving the letter of enquiry. The applicant might be summoned to the committee meeting to be interviewed. Once a proposal was agreed on one of her cases Miss Hodson would have to seek the required funding or materials from whatever sources were available. But Miss Hodson does not seem to have been confident in these investigations. She expressed real anxiety about taking a case, as it was called, having to steel herself to ask applicants difficult questions about income and employment. She also struggled with producing letters to charities, employers or relatives, people who might offer help or contribute to information. The letters were vetted by the head of the settlement and Miss Hodson was terrified of having one of hers rejected.

For practical training she went out visiting with an experienced settlement worker. Theoretical training took the form of lectures, which included information about orphans and the Poor Law. She thought these were interesting but nothing more. There was no attempt to relate theoretical training to practice. A striking feature of her account is that while she at first claimed to accept the tenets of COS teaching, she later pronounced these principles stifling and very difficult to put into practice in the face of horrendous poverty. She mentions this several times: the tension between what was required and what was possible.

It is difficult to discern Miss Hodson's competence from her account, but her sensitivity and naivety in the face of poor families is clear. Those who aspired to settled and respectable lives, like the old couple, she understood and lauded. The others – the drunks and the desperately poor – baffled her completely. She must have understood at one level the paltriness of the offer to the 14- to 18-year-old boys who came to her club in the evenings. She expressed surprise at their surreptitious gambling on the dominoes, irritation at their disruption of discussions and the way they broke things. But she seemed powerless to make the connection with them; boys – like William Woodruff – attracted as much by the warmth, the cocoa and the bun as much as by the childish pursuits on offer. The activities of the poor were astonishing to her because she had no experience of them. She had never been to a music hall or a public house. She described what happened in fried fish shops – the production of battered fish, the use of vinegar as a seasoning and the newspaper wrapping – as if relating some sinister ritual from the darkest corner of the Empire.

Harry Snell, who spent six years as a paid enquiry agent for the Woolwich District of the COS in the 1890s was a less fastidious observer of the poor. The son of a Nottinghamshire agricultural labourer, Snell started his working life as a barman. Always a reader, he began attending public lectures and his heart was soon captured by radical politics. He arranged lectures for socialists in Nottingham and fell in with a rector, C.H. Grinling, who had been one of the first residents at Toynbee Hall with Canon Barnett. Grinling tired of Holy Orders and accepted the post of secretary of the Woolwich district of the COS, inviting Harry Snell along as an inquiry agent. Snell was convinced of the wisdom of the careful collection of information and the precise identification of need which underpinned the COS approach, dismissing criticism that the Society '*always enquired and seldom helped*'. Snell dealt with the full breadth of applicants and listed them, concluding that no single '*diagnosis could be applied because each case presented a special problem and revealed ... physical, mental and moral poverty*' influenced by '*heredity, environment, occupation, habit and training*'. He commented that nearly all attempts at deception by applicants were crude and naïve (Snell 1938: 72).

But commendable as he found the casework, he found the COS social philosophy questionable in equal measure. Snell comments that the '*orthodox COS theory was that anyone seeking assistance should be received by a voluntary helper*' with the enquiry agent's work being restricted to enquiring about the details of the applicant with the clergy, employers and so on and presenting a plain factual report for the committee to consider. Only voluntary visitors '*presented cases*' to the committee. This differentiation was based on the COS assumption that only voluntary workers possessed '*adequate knowledge of human frailties, wise judgement, deep sympathy, tact and insight*' (Snell 1938: 70). Enquiry agents, it was thought, could not be impartial because they were paid for their labours rather than giving their efforts freely. As we have seen, affluent volunteers would have less knowledge of the way the poor lived and their commitment was, of course, variable. Rooff quotes one COS secretary complaining that volunteers were on holiday all summer and ill all winter; ladies being accustomed to long holidays and not accustomed to sustained demands on their time (Rooff 1972).

Mr Grinling took individuals entirely on their merits, so used enquiry agents, including Harry Snell, to present cases to the committee just as volunteers did, diverging from normal practice. The COS was so alarmed at this development, implying that paid workers were as capable as volunteers, that Grinling was forced out and H.V. Toynbee was sent in instead to return Woolwich to COS orthodoxy. Harry Snell would have none of it and left.

No COS existed in Bolton but, as mentioned earlier, there were two similar societies there. The Bolton Benevolent Society (BBS) had been set up in 1837 (BHC NUB/2/6/33). The BBS was for the '*sick and distressed poor*' and was the '*means of keeping them from the workhouse*', to prevent '*pauperising their families*' and operated to a precise formula. '*Recommendations*' were to be placed in the letter box outside the office before 9am each Tuesday. One of the four '*Relieving Visitors*' or a member of the committee, if free, would then visit the '*object*' – the family making the claim – before Thursday evening. The Relieving Visitors were also volunteers but, unusually for this type of activity, were all men. The visitor would complete a form with a set of questions on it referred to as a '*blank*'. This would form the basis of the report to the committee which met each Thursday at 7pm. The Committee considered and decided relief for 11 or 12 cases a week. In 1887, 594 families were visited and 428 people relieved. Only 36 cases were dismissed as '*unworthy*' or '*doubtful*' or where there was '*no sickness*'. One feature is that the subscribers, either by donation or annual subscription, could nominate '*Recommendations*' themselves, which hinted at the practice of special pleading, where subscribers were employers, for their own employees (BHC NUB/2/6/33). Bolton's BPPS, set up in 1840, operated in a similar fashion (Hayworth 2007). The BBS and BPPS both raised money from the rich as it disbursed it to the poor, a hand to mouth approach similar to the COS, which meant there were regular shortages of funds for their activities.

The Poor Law

The Poor Law Amendment Act of 1834 grouped the 15,000 parishes across England, each of which had previously operated its own relief of the poor, into Unions, to allow for a more cost effective approach. The new Unions, around 700 of them, each had a Board of Guardians who had to raise a local rate to fund the operation of the Poor Law. By 1900 the work included registering births, deaths and marriages, vaccinating children against smallpox, care for children boarded-out from the workhouse, medical and hospital treatment for the poor, and care for the feeble minded, lunatics, aged poor and able-bodied paupers. The major expense was always the workhouse and by the 1860s many Unions had built grand multi-purpose buildings, showcasing the forbidding consequences of penury (Crowther 1981). And the familiar clichés are true. Paupers were set to work picking oakum (unravelling old tarred ropes). Married couples were separated from each other, personal belongings were removed and inmates had to wear drab uniforms of grey serge or thick corduroy. Initially there was to be no out-relief – payment in cash or kind to enable the destitute to continue living in their homes rather than enter the workhouse. This was to ensure that only the most desperate people presented themselves for relief. From the beginning some Unions offered loaves, potatoes, blankets and sometimes cash to prevent workhouse admission. This practice, after harsh winters pushed up the numbers seeking help, was confirmed by central order in 1842. Each Union appointed relieving officers and these men – they were all men – interviewed and assessed applicants for relief, reported their findings to the Guardians, paid relief as people turned up to claim it, and arranged escort to and from the workhouse (Crowther 1981).

One account of the work of relieving officers was written by Thomas Wright (1892). He describes the relieving office, a new one in East London, as having a fortress-like appearance, including '*reconnoitring gratings*', making the point that '*it is one of the functions of the relieving officer to thwart the designs of ... habitual charity hunters ... for this he is hated by them, and a bread riot ... is looked upon as an excellent opportunity for executing revenge*' (Wright 1892).

There was a general waiting room with rows of forms as seating, with well scrubbed floors which in periods of epidemic diseases '*is plentifully bestrewn with disinfectants*'. He describes one corner having a weighing machine for calculating quantities of goods and '*sundry little lots of furniture and bedding*', owned by current incumbents of the workhouse who had hopes of imminent discharge, these often being older couples or '*lone lorn*' (abandoned) women. The smaller compartment – the office proper – was dominated by the range of shelves holding two pound weight loaves and drawers which held packs of tea, sugar, oatmeal, sage and other dry goods. There was a corridor separating this office from the waiting room with a counter facing the corridor. The large desk in the office was occupied by the relieving officer and his assistant. Wright found the most startling thing in the office to be the '*strait waistcoat*' hanging on the wall, '*the conveyance of lunatics to the asylum being one of the duties of the relieving officer*' (Wright 1892).

The work of the RO was dominated by order books – for milk, wine, brandy, combination orders of food, orders for admission to the workhouse or workhouse infirmary, orders for the lunatic asylum, orders for the fever or smallpox ambulance and orders for funerals and coffins.

The earliest callers in the day were for those seeking orders for medical attendance. Wright suggests that some played the system in seeking a ticket for the doctor as relieving officers, anxious not to deny the seriously ill, tended to hand out medical tickets with little investigation. '*One chief reason for the run on medical orders is the hope that they may lead to nourishment orders*', doctors having the reputation of being generous with food relief. Wright comments that the '*unpauperised poor would doctor themselves*' (Wright 1892). He was referring to the health insurance movement which developed during the nineteenth century.

Wage earners were exhorted to stump up their penny a week to a provident society as insurance against illness. Regular payment guaranteed a physician to consult or a dispensary bed if the worker fell ill. Every town in England had such insurance arrangements for workers and charitable visitors encouraged everyone to join. Bolton's first provident society was set up in 1813 with regular donations from workers and by 1824 had opened a dispensary with seven beds for those who contributed. In 1877 a huge effort was made by the same organisation to collect enough money for an infirmary. Pennies, collected each Saturday – thus the name Hospital Saturday Fund – added up and led to the building of a substantial medical facility for those wise enough to contribute. This was a national pattern often associated with what became large voluntary hospitals. Such insurance and friendly societies also offered sick pay or payment for funerals. One in Harwood, three miles from Bolton, at its height in the 1880s only had 120 members. Each society appointed a sick visitor to pay out the sick benefit, offer comfort and support and to check on the legitimacy of the payment (Francis 1987). Those who could not or did not pay had to rely on tickets from the RO to see the Poor Law doctor – the lowest of the medical profession.

In Wright's account if new cases presented themselves at the relieving office they were '*put pretty closely to the question*' to find out if they were really destitute and had no relatives who could step in. Deserted wives were investigated thoroughly, as faked abandonments were common. But most new applicants were widows with two or more children, and older women. Widows with only one child under 14 were classed as 'able bodied' as were single women and therefore were not offered out-relief. Destitute men were offered work in the stoneyard before a ticket for the workhouse (Wright 1892).

Wright describes a system riven with misery and suspicion, yet he praises the general attitude and attention to detail of the ROs. In the same vein, George Bartley, writing of the Poor Law in 1876, suggested that relieving officers needed great firmness, coupled with great kindness of manner (Bartley 1876). Mishra, who surveyed the role of the RO from 1834 to 1948, shares this view: '*It seems probable that until 1870 ... the RO was still something of a district almoner: he gave little rather than denied altogether*' (Mishra 1969: 85).

Yet during the last quarter of the century the public attitude to ROs was unremittingly harsh. As Simey suggests, ROs around 1900 were hated (Simey 1951). But she also comments that the Liverpool version of the COS, the Central Relief Society (CRS), had created a service which matched the pattern of the Poor Law. The Poor Law ensured the deserving would not benefit. The CRS made sure the undeserving would not. This jigsaw-like fit from 1870 was the subject of a distinct policy, an understanding between the Local Government Board (LGB) and the COS (Mishra 1969). The secretary of the LGB, Goschen, issued advice in 1869 proposing that Poor Law officers should principally deter misuse while positive efforts for those with some hope of improving their lot should be the preserve of charitable organisations. Part of the logic of this was the increase in numbers of people seeking out-relief during the 1860s, due in large measure to restrictions in trade caused by the American Civil War and a subsequently sluggish economy. This policy, of a return to the original ruthless principles of 1834 was followed right into the 1890s, with ROs expected to apply the rules harshly for the destitute and pass onto charitable visiting societies people thought likely to make good use of short term help. Numbers of people receiving out-relief, especially unemployed able-bodied men, dropped considerably during that period and the stigma attached to the RO hardened.

Pressure from the LGB, Poor Law inspectors and the COS ensured this deterrent approach stayed in place for a long generation, which even included a proposal (which did not come to pass) that those receiving out-relief should have to wear a pauper badge (Mishra 1969: 98). Under this policy it was the charitable workers who were seen to be engaging in constructive work with families, and who saw themselves in that role, thus confirming the gap between the RO and the emerging voluntary society social worker of the 1890s.

Nevertheless, in rural areas, where charitable visiting societies were thinner on the ground, ROs could establish a more positive image. A good example of a steadfast RO was George Dew who worked in Oxfordshire from 1871 until the turn of the century (Horn 1983). Several of his diary entries reveal a preference for keeping old people in the community, supported by out-relief when traditionalist Board members ordered the workhouse. As a boarding-out visitor, Dew showed considerable concern for the fate of children sent out to local farmers and tradesmen, following several of these children up in his own time. He also doubled up as inspector for nuisances for the district sanitary authority, as school attendance officer from 1877, registrar and later vaccination officer.

Relieving Officers in Bolton

But the commitment of George Dew was not universal among ROs. In Bolton RO Jonathon Carrodus was approached one day in 1890 at the paying office by a Mrs Olive (BHC GBO/28/46). She had a problem with her husband, referred to as a '*bad one*' in the record. But Carrodus did not visit her as he was expected to do after such a referral. When brought before the Guardians after a complaint Carrodus said he could not respond because he had been up half the night poorly and was '*not able to go about*' because '*he is threatened with apoplexy*'. The Guardians decided to '*let him go*', on the grounds of '*age, infirmity and inability to perform his duties*' – not a surprising outcome as Jonathon Carrodus was 72. RO posts were not pensionable, so some worked into old age. Also, until the turn of the century, some of their pay was in kind, a beer ration being paid by Bolton Union (BHC GBO 28/50). Neither were ROs paid expenses for their visits to people's houses. Ralph Bates, covering the largely rural Westhoughton District, applied for a wage increase in 1882 on the basis that visiting in such a huge area caused him '*considerable expense*' and he had to employ an assistant to help with the work, whose wages were paid from Bates's own salary (BHC GBO/28/308). Despite the poor status the workload was heavy. That June in Bolton with a population of around 200,000 the seven ROs and three assistants had responsibilities for 3,610 people on out-relief.

So while in 1904 there had been changes in the attitudes to the poor, a more constructive attitude amongst progressive Guardians, and the introduction of a system of individual case papers for Poor Law applicants, the basic structures of the Victorian response to poverty – voluntary visiting societies or relief of last resort through the Poor Law – still obtained. And RO attitudes often reflected traditional values, with applications for RO jobs in Bolton occasionally containing promises to serve the interests of the Guardians before all – this being reference to the classic Poor Law aim of saving ratepayers' money by being parsimonious with relief (BHC GBO/28/300).

Chapter 2
1904–1914: Missionaries, Inspectors, Lady Visitors and Mr Cramp the Almoner

Missions and Missioners

Philanthropic initiatives directed at the poor were often efforts to reclaim people for the church, protect them from the lure of drink or both. Much of this work was carried out by religious missions, set up across urban Britain. In the Edwardian years Bolton boasted several missions, the multi denominational Queen Street Mission (QSM) being the most active. At the annual meeting on 26 October 1904, the President, Major Hardcastle, J.P. referred to the work of QSM as '*most Christlike ... helping those who could not help themselves*' and announced that as unemployment was so bad that '*the distribution of children's dinners and clogs had commenced*'. The previous year had seen the QSM loan out 1,300 pairs of clogs, receive 92 girls and women at the Home for Friendless Girls and Women and distribute 40,000 free school dinners to poor children with around 400 children benefitting. In addition 210 children recovering from illness were sent to the seaside for two week's convalescence, 2,500 went on day trips to Lytham and 80 crippled children received a special tea. There was also a mother and toddler group on a Monday afternoon, to give mothers access to a church service. What is referred to as their '*social work department*' had had a successful year managing a Men's Recreation Club, whose offer included a physical drill programme and regular Pleasant Saturday Evenings; non-alcoholic Saturday evening entertainment (BEN 1904: 2).

The QSM was run by Joseph Popplewell, 47 in 1904, aided by a range of volunteers and his 15-year-old daughter Ethel acting as his clerk. What we don't know is how those receiving help were assessed, or how they presented themselves, but that people preferred to go to the mission for help rather than the RO is obvious: '*The work of the Mission ... did so much to ... help, but there was nowhere ... that sense that they were relieving people*' (BEN 1904: 2).

Mr Popplewell carried his missionary work into his home where he had four beds in his attic to care for neglected or abandoned children, meaning the household saw a procession of destitute children over the years (Bolton Journal and Guardian 1940: 8).

There were hundreds of such missions up and down the country and the numbers of volunteers attracted to mission work dwarfed the numbers of residents in settlements. The primary difference however was that missions were often denominational whereas settlements, while not secular, were set up in the main by universities not churches.

There were also national missions with local branches such as the Salvation Army and the Church of England Temperance Society (CETS). These two missions prided themselves on missioning anywhere – seeking out drinkers at cab-ranks, workplaces, sports stadia and, from the 1870s, in police courts. Famously George Nelson was appointed in 1878 by Southwark Police Court as Police Court Missionary. He still carried on his missionary work in other places but the magistrates agreed, when circumstances were right, to bind over for three months or longer first offenders who had committed crimes while in drink. Mr Nelson would offer advice to try and free them from their attachment to alcohol (National Association of Probation Officers 2007). The idea spread and in 1907 the Probation of Offenders Act encouraged courts to appoint Probation officers. In Bolton the Police Court appointed Richard Burton as Probation Officer in January 1908.

One of the first cases allocated to Mr Burton on 17 January 1908 was Catherine Kelshaw, aged 36. Mrs Kelshaw was a respectable woman with a husband and four children; she had been ill three years before and never really recovered, instead turning to drink. Her husband's attempts to stop her drinking had failed, despite having become teetotal himself 19 months earlier. She was arrested after being seen removing a lamp from outside a shop and taking it home. The police constable, called by the shop owner, had followed her and in her house found other missing and stolen items as well as 31 pawn tickets. Presumably, deprived of money by her husband, she stole and pawned what she stole to buy drink. In court where the sympathy of both magistrates and prosecuting solicitor was palpable even through the constrained text of the newspaper report, she was bound over for six months to the care of Mr Burton. She was also ordered to abstain from drink for that period (Bolton Chronicle 1908a: 8).

Other cases directed Mr Burton's way, just more than one a week through 1908, were similar – first offences, usually of theft, mostly occasioned by drunkenness (Bolton Chronicle 1908b: 3). But all this was grist to Mr Burtons' mill. He may have been freshly-appointed Probation Officer in 1908, but had been Bolton's Police Court Missionary, doing exactly the same work, funded by CETS, since 1894.

There is no indication of how Mr Burton worked, his motivation or successes; but Jo Harris, who worked as a Police Court Missionary then Probation Officer in Lowestoft between 1900 and 1934, left a detailed account of his work and methods (Harris 1937). Mr Harris was motivated by his faith and his account contains many references to '… *fundamental laws of Love, Forgiveness … and Justice … waiting to be applied aright to conquer evil in individuals*'. He saw himself as '*a friend who understands and sympathises and who is ready and able to help the offender back to the right path*' (Harris 1937: 22). He worked from home where probationers reported weekly. He referred to having to report at a given period of time and place every week over a lengthy period of time as being '*no joke*' and had no compunction about returning latecomers to court, as '*a broken rule was broken faith*' (Harris 1937: 24).

His method was to start the relationship with '*one good talk about the whole thing, then we will put it behind us forever and start afresh*'. Mr Harris then went through the court order point-by-point confirming what the probationer had to do '*… this is the surgical part of the interview … perhaps for the first time he has rules*' (Harris 1937: 23). These rules would almost always include a curfew and might include orders to avoid certain people and certain places – the fish market being a favourite to avoid in Lowestoft. Then followed the advisory section of the relationship in which Mr Harris might find work, advise about family relationships or encourage club activity. The last interview was the occasion for Mr Harris to have a '*heart to heart*' with the probationer who – Mr Harris claimed – by then ought to know what '*really counts as a citizen and to have a character to keep*' (Harris 1937: 56).

Mr Harris was also asked by the court to involve himself in '*domestic quarrels and matrimonial tangles*' (Harris 1937: 46), his approach to which was to see the couple separately and then together, then separately again if necessary and once more as a couple. He also carried on informal missioning. Before the Great War he regularly waited outside Norwich prison gates to greet discharged prisoners, taking them for breakfast, befriending them – people he might not know from Adam. He was also active in the Temperance Society, the Pledge Book being an important tool of his trade. This was like a large cheque book, with tear-off certificates for those signing up to abjure drink forever. He also ran a Sunday afternoon discussion session with a group of boys – The Lighthouse Perseverance Class – when as many as 40 adolescents would come into his home, sing a hymn, read a lesson, tell stories, have discussions and go on outings twice a year.

The Children's Man

Social work with children was well developed in the Edwardian years but was, even after the 1908 Children Act attempted to pull aspects of it together, fragmented. There were, in broad terms, five emerging responses to vulnerable children in 1904: child cruelty and neglect, protection from infanticide, the rescue of orphans and boarding-out for workhouse children.

Cruelty to children had been a major social concern since the 1870s and society's formal response lay largely with the National Society for the Prevention of Cruelty to Children (NSPCC). Established for over 20 years by 1904, the NSPCC had nearly 200 inspectors in England one of whom was in Bolton, Mr Hall, whose work was regularly reported in the press. For instance, on 29 September 1904 Frederick Rothwell appeared before the Bolton Magistrates Court and was prosecuted for neglecting his children, Jessie, Fred and Charles, '*Mr Rothwell often being drunk*' (Bolton Chronicle 1904b: 4). He had given his wife only 3s 8d in the first 20 days of the month even though, a book keeper, he earned a good wage of between 35s and £2 a week. Mrs Rothwell had first turned to her neighbours for help and then had to apply to the RO at the Union. She approached the Guardians on 28 September. The RO took Mrs Rothwell's details and sent a messenger to Mr Hall. It so happened that the previous NSPCC Inspector, Mr Fox, had interviewed Mr Rothwell 13 months before, again because he was drinking away his wages. Mr Hall either read in the NSPCC case paper which was Mr Rothwell's preferred alehouse, or Mrs Rothwell told him. Either way, the NSPCC inspector got onto PC Dawson who tracked Rothwell down that afternoon and took him into custody for appearance the following day. This example of fast, multi-agency work was completed when the Magistrates bailed Mr Rothwell for a month to give him another chance – a frequent disposal for such an occurrence.

The 1909 NSPCC Bolton branch annual report (by which time there were two inspectors) noted 515 cases dealt with, 471 of which were identified as neglect and 32 related to ill-treatment (NSPCC 1909). The inspectors made 2,115 supervision visits relating to 1,464 children. Counting Saturday as a working day, this amounts to three per day every day of the year. Yet there were only 12 prosecutions in 1909, indicating that warnings and regular visits had some impact on parents. A detailed account of how an NSPCC inspector worked exists in *The Cruelty Man* (Anon 1912). The author, William Payne, describes himself as the '*Children's Man*' throughout, and gives many examples of the cases he worked on. In an early one he received a post card from a constable which arrived the same day as being sent, calling him to a school where there was a '*very bad case*' (Anon 1912: 15). Payne cycled over immediately and took a statement from the schoolmistress about how a girl, Nell, usually ill-dressed and quiet had been seen that day with bad bruising to her face. The inspector cycled to her home and noticed the poor state of repair of the cottage. Once inside he was direct with the step-mother, asking how the girl got the bruising and swellings. The woman blustered and so he asked to see where the girl slept. An old sack in the hallway was pointed out. Asked how she had received her injuries in front of her mother, Nell said '*I don't know*'. The Children's Man comments: '*I have been told that a tortured child has been known to speak untruths ... in the presence of the offender*' (Anon 1912: 21).

Neighbours confirmed that they had seen the girl sent out early in the morning, ill-dressed, to fetch water. The father, who Payne waylaid on his way home from work, confirmed that his daughter had been badly treated by the step-mother for two years since they had been married. A doctor was called and the inspector decided to remove Nell to a place of safety, the nearest workhouse. William Payne then wrote a report which he sent to London asking for permission to prosecute. This was authorised and both parents were convicted and imprisoned. Nell, once safe in the workhouse cottage homes (homes for workhouse children, often in workhouse grounds), confirmed what the inspector had suspected – the step-mother had beaten and humiliated her regularly. The inspector, though new to his job, was precise in how he went about his task. He gathered what information he could and then confronted the step-mother, making sure the child was present as he did so. He also checked living conditions, bedding and clothing and talked to the neighbours.

Once removed Nell fell ill. She was well nursed and our man took dolls for Nell made by '*Mrs Inspector*'. His wife's involvement is a regular feature of his work, to the extent of accepting complaints brought to their door, putting children up in their home, examining girls where it would have been inappropriate for her husband to do so, and bathing filthy and verminous children.

The informal nature of the help obtained is a constant feature of the inspector's work. After struggling with the conundrum of three children left alone for fifteen hours a day by a labourer, abandoned by his wife, and having tried every avenue to keep the children with their father the inspector literally bumped into a Catholic priest. He relayed the plight of Mr Doolan to his co-religionist and the priest offered some cash and then found a family to care for the children, close by Mr Doolan, so he could both contribute to their keep and stay in touch.

The final tale is extraordinary. The family concerned ran a successful bakery, but the father had remarried and the step-mother did not take to eight-year-old Alfred. He had a useless arm and his step-mother referred to him as an imbecile. The boy was fed crusts and leftovers thrown to him on the floor. Previous bakery employees claimed that both father and mother beat the boy and one occasion when he was dunked, fully clothed, in a water butt in the back yard. The inspector, after calling a doctor '*of the new school*' (Anon 1912: 41) – by which he meant one interested in the mistreatment of children – removed Alfred and had the parents summonsed. The family could afford a solicitor and briefed a lawyer who, at the trial, poured scorn over the evidence of all the previous employees, who were accused of having a grudge against the baker. The defence brought two doctors as character witnesses who suggested Alfred's condition made him impossible to discipline. The father in the witness box described Alfred, who was quaking by the inspector's side, as '*defiant, unruly and cheeky*' (Anon 1912: 43). The recorder, a careful jurist, tested out the defence's claim that a prosecution witness could not possibly have seen the alleged dunking from where he was standing at the time, by taking the jury down the street to the baker's backyard to see for themselves. They could see perfectly. Eventually at 11.30 at night, the jury returned a guilty verdict and the baker and his wife were given fines of £25 each. A crowd outside shouted abuse at the guilty couple as they were hustled out of the side door accompanied by the police. Even so the crowd smashed every window in their shop that night and within three months the pair had to sell up, bankrupted by comprehensive withdrawal of local custom. Alfred recovered the use of his arm and throve at school – nothing wrong with his intellect at all. The inspector had paced the floor of his bedroom the night before the trial, so anxious was he about the defence lawyer, and so determined was he that little Alfred received justice; but he was also '*fearful he had a made a ghastly blunder*' (Anon 1912: 40).

The overall impression given by the inspector is that he entered the NSPCC from the army, like so many of his colleagues, with no particular commitment to children, but soon developed a determination to do all he could. He was compassionate to parents, understanding the desperate plight many were in. His wife and daughters made up a comprehensive back-up team giving practical help in many ways. His advice was to-the-point and his observations implied a sensible approach to domestic management. One set of children for instance were: '*Fed on tinned ... and preserved makeshifts ... scarcely ever tasting fresh vegetables ... what wonder the family were anaemic*' (Anon 1912: 50).

In the Children's Man's experience, four problems were at the root of most of the complaints brought to his attention: drink, step-parents who could not accept their spouse's offspring, cripple children proving too much for their parents to handle and those children dragged around by tramps. But the greatest of these was drink.

Boarding-out

One of the methods of rescuing children from destitution and immorality was the use of emigration. The Waifs and Strays Society, Thomas Barnardo, Thomas Stephenson and others who ran homes for children in the late nineteenth century used it. There were at least two organisations, those of Maria Rye and Annie MacPherson whose whole activity was emigrating children to Canada. These activities were controversial from the beginning, particularly Miss Rye's. In 1875 her practices were investigated by Andrew Doyle, a Poor Law Inspector, and he concluded that many children were removed illegally and were then left to the mercies of people about whom Miss Rye had no knowledge. Her response was that what was good for poor adults who chose to make a fresh start (and until the Great War tens of thousands of Britons did that) must be good for children who otherwise were destined for the gutter (Kershaw and Sacks 2008).

She had a point, especially concerning infants born to unmarried mothers. As the societal rejection of unmarried mothers was total, illegal abortions were frequent and infants were given away or passed off as married women's children. In addition there were baby farmers. This practice was a variant of the then common custom of mothers paying another woman as a wet nurse for her child. Foster mothers placed carefully worded adverts in newspapers, attracting those who wanted rid of unwanted babies. The mother paid a negotiated sum to the foster-mother to keep a newborn infant. No personal information was exchanged, the transaction was completed and the mother knew she would never see her child again (Hendrick 1994). Many children were subsequently cared for in slap-dash fashion or adopted on, adoption being unregulated at that time. The callousness of many foster parents is amply demonstrated in Somerset Maugham's novel *Of Human Bondage* (1915). But some children fared worse. Some were murdered.

The number of commercial foster mothers, baby farmers, caught murdering infants indicates a widespread practice. Amelia Dyer was hanged in 1896, Ada Williams in 1900, Annie Walters and Amelia Sach in 1903 – all for killing children they were supposed to be fostering. The case of Amelia Dyer in 1896 led directly to the 1897 Infant Life Protection Act, which required each Poor Law Union to appoint an Infant Life Protection Officer or Visitor (ILPO or ILPV) to undertake checks on homes where children under five were fostered, checking bedding, food and the capacity and morality of foster parents. From the outset the ILPO had to be a woman. Although some unions like Manchester and Bristol appointed women immediately, many flouted these requirements and the ILPO role was given to male ROs in addition to their other work (Mishra 1969: 139).

It is then not surprising that those connected with the care of children were scathing about the motivation of foster parents. Herbert Preston-Thomas, an erstwhile Poor Law Inspector writing in 1909, comments:

> … all boarding-out cases should be placed under the charge of ladies [Boarding-Out Visitors] … The people who receive such children are not philanthropists, but take them for the profit to be earned; and the worse the treatment in the matter of food, dress and so on, the more profit is made (Preston-Thomas 1909: 122).

But however suspicious people were of fostering, both Poor Law Unions and voluntary organisations used it. There was so much call on their services they had little choice. The LGB permitted boarding-out of children from the workhouse from 1869 and its use grew as the new century approached. In 1885 the LGB appointed a single full-time Assistant Inspector, Miss Elizabeth Mason. Her role was to inspect local boarding-out arrangements. In her first year Miss Mason visited 1,025 children and subsequent annual LGB reports carry similar numbers. Unfortunately the records are simple figures only with no comment from Miss Mason herself about her work (Mishra 1969).

Meanwhile in 1877 ROs were required by the LGB to visit children of families on out-relief where there had been reports of cruelty and produce reports quarterly about the condition of the children. But the ROs visiting, so Miss Mason reported, caused resentment among foster parents both because of what they represented and because they were men (Mishra 1969). So from 1889 that role was removed from ROs and vested instead under LGB guidance, with a Boarding-Out Committee in each Union whose role was to recruit female volunteers to undertake regular visiting of children boarded-out from the workhouse with ordinary families. The final banishment of ROs from any work with children was completed in 1909 when the LGB required the appointment of paid women visitors to undertake such work.

In Bolton Miss Alice Barlow was appointed Honorary Secretary of the Boarding-Out Committee in 1894. In her role Miss Barlow not only had to recruit volunteers but also had to collect their regular reports and present them to the Guardians. She also managed the volunteers who visited children over 13 who had left school, and who had been placed out in domestic service. Elsewhere this task was sub-contracted by Unions to voluntary organisations such as the Girls

Friendly Society (GFS) or the Metropolitan Association for the Befriending of Young Servants (MABYS) (Mishra 1969, BHC GBO/28/527).

The Waifs and Strays Society also decided to have someone checking on the welfare of children boarded-out and in 1893 appointed a female doctor as Inspectress. By 1905 the society had two women doctors, Dr Edith Green and Dr Rose Turner, who undertook the work across the entire nation. They would map out the houses and farms to be visited in an area and, if it were somewhere rural like Norfolk, would hire a trap for a week. The Waifs and Strays Inspectors operated to a set of clear rules, like Miss Mason, which required among other things that children should not be boarded-out with relations or people in recent receipt of out relief; not boarded-out in a house where there was an adult lodger, nor boarded-out at a later age than ten.

> The procedure was to go to the school and ask to see the children – she never notified anyone beforehand of her visit. She always inspected their heads, teeth, ears and eyes … and noticed anything physically that was not as it should be. She always talked to the children as she worked and particularly noted if they seemed happy, cowed or ill cared for. Then there followed a visit to the home: the beds were inspected and she made sure there were night shirts. After the home, [she visited] the [local] supervisor – usually the parson or the lady of the manor, or perhaps a retired school mistress. She wrote up a report on each child at the hotel each night. Many of the foster-mothers had children for years, and were wonderful people, their husbands too, and gave the children warmly loving homes (Stroud 1971: 73).

But Dr Turner did not always find things satisfactory and there are tales of children overworked, subject to little more than cold disinterest from foster parents or victims of ill-treatment. The inspectresses could only be expected to visit infrequently, six-monthly at best, so the system relied on the local worthies being identified as supervisors of the foster-parents. Dr Turner's daughter confirms the level of reliance on the local volunteers:

> I well remember that at one centre my mother found things very unsatisfactory. She discovered that the parson had not visited for about two years. She went in a fury to the parson; but he lied and said he visited them weekly. By the dressing down she gave him she reduced him to head hanging silence (Stroud 1971: 73).

The Guild of Help

Despite, or because of, the anxious introduction of changes to the Poor Law and developments in voluntary responses to charity, there was in some quarters a growing feeling that traditional charitable efforts had failed (Moore 1977). In Bradford, partly in response to rising unemployment, the mayor working with the

Union and voluntary societies set up a new visiting charity (Laybourn 1994). This followed a long-standing German approach to poor relief, the Elberfeld System. Named after a small town in Germany, the idea was simple. The local authority divided the town into divisions. In each division a number of volunteer visitors would get to know the area and take responsibility for anyone seeking aid or support. Financial support was available, but the primary offer was a relationship between the visitor and the family: a friendship. The key to success was a large number of citizen volunteers and the coordination across the town of both voluntary effort and public relief. Bradford's initiative was called the Guild of Help.

Mrs Barnes, a Bolton Guardian, heard about the Guild and sent Mr Cooper to Bradford. She championed the idea for her town, and a Bolton Guild was launched at a packed public meeting on 7 December 1905. As in Bradford, the mayor chaired the Guild and representatives from all charitable groups and the Union were involved. With the motto 'not alms but a friend' the idea took the town by storm. Four divisions were created, containing several districts, each of which had a Head who had to approve proposed support for families and provide guidance for all his or her group of Helpers, as the visitors were called. Each Helper had no more than three families, but was expected to visit them each week, crisis or not. The Helpers befriended their families, advised them and on occasion sought practical aid or financial support. As well as the guidance of the Head, regular support meetings for Helpers were soon established and a monthly newsletter, *The Helper*, was published. The idea spread to Swinton, Eccles, Halifax then within five years all across the North, Midlands and parts of the South, and by 1909 the Guilds were helping more people than the COS (Laybourn 1994).

The Guild of Help in Bolton attracted 400 volunteers immediately. These numbers were sustained until after the Great War and were replicated elsewhere, Sheffield having 1,000 Helpers at one time. These volunteers, the Helpers, were two-thirds women and two-thirds were single, so they were probably relatively young. Addresses of about 25 per cent indicate they lived in terraced houses, so working class Helpers existed in some numbers. As the Guild movement gained momentum, a developing socialist analysis proposed that Guilds were just another means of papering-over-the-cracks in society. Despite that many individual trade unionists were involved. Sarah Reddish was a Helper; so too were Jabez Darricotte and his wife, he being a head teacher and heavily involved in the Municipal Workers Union (precursor to NALGO and UNISON).

The Helpers had a monthly meeting with the District Head and were encouraged to seek advice and support about their cases at other times as well. The Helpers were also obliged to devise '*a systematised plan of action*' with each case; *The Helper* magazine suggesting that no progress could be made without one. The scope of Guild activity was considerable and in 1910 2,100 families (8,000 people) were helped (BHC Guild Annual Reports). And the Guild was always on the look-out for other ways to help. The Guild offered to part-pay for spectacles for children who needed them (42 in 1910). The Guild provided fire guards when the NSPCC drew attention to the number of house fires which injured children. The Guild entered arrangements with the Discharged Prisoners Aid Society to offer after care to young men discharged from prison. The Guild set up a charities register, condemned offering money to street beggars and in 1911 the Guild funded the administration of the new Bolton Council for Social Welfare. Each local Council for Social Welfare, the first being established in Hampstead in 1907, set about coordinating all local philanthropic activity in both private and public spheres (Moore 1977).

The difference between the Guilds and earlier charitable visiting societies has been hotly debated (Kidd 1984, Lewis 1996). Were they different in degree from the COS, something similar with better relationships with public services or were they in effect indistinguishable? The Guilds were ambitious, well-organised and quickly embedded into the fabric of local welfare activity, attracting Helpers from across the religious, class and political divide. Also in the magazine and annual reports regular reference is made to the main aim, which was to offer friendship (BHC Guild Annual Reports). In 1911 the Bolton annual report opined that the real success of the Guild was that '*children have been sent to school better fed and better clothed, homes have been prevented from breaking up*'. And in conditions of war, soon to come, one writer in *The Helper* could say '*Helpers and helped have often changed places through the oft changing crises which most of us are called upon to face as a result of war*' (BHC Guild Annual Reports).

Specialist Roles in the Poor Law

The RO's role in Edwardian years narrowed. The ILPV had to be a woman, boarding-out had to be supervised by a woman and any work relating to schools was lost when School Boards were abolished and County Councils took responsibility for schooling in 1902. The stigma associated with the Poor Law clung to the RO and was one reason why, when the Old Age Pension was introduced in 1911, the government decided that Poor Law officials should have nothing to do with it. And Poor Law attitudes to able paupers were still harsh. The Manchester Tame Street Test Workhouse for instance with its regime of stonebreaking, limited diet and barrack style dormitories was used between 1897 and 1907; a way of dissuading unemployed men from presenting themselves for relief (Kidd 1985).

But the cruelty of the Tame Street was more apparent because the sick, old and feeble-minded were being separated from able paupers. Bolton built an infirmary for the sick poor on land separate from the workhouse in 1895. Different staffing arrangements were made for the feeble-minded. And in 1900 the LGB Chaplin Circular advocated discriminating treatment for the aged poor who were to be '*adequately relieved and cared for*' (Mishra 1969: 161). At the same time, the requirement that people receiving out-relief had to travel to a pay station for payment was abandoned, being replaced by home payment, instituting regular visits by ROs to old people, cripples and those caring for the feeble-minded. This allowed, should the RO be so-minded, for a different kind of relationship to develop between the RO and the people receiving relief. By 1910 the LGB was stressing that relief should be adapted carefully to the needs of the particular case (Mishra 1969). The parallel between RO and COS visitor practice is striking here. We know that ROs from this time visited old people receiving relief weekly, to pay them and check up on them. Mary Stocks reports (1970) that her mother's work with the COS consisted of visiting old people for whom the COS provided a pension, to pay them and check up on them.

All this made organisation of the community aspects of the Poor Law more complicated and Unions began to respond by employing people to undertake duties other than the regular investigation of distress and payment of relief. In Bolton a General Relieving Officer was appointed in 1904, Henry Sumner, whose tasks included keeping records of the numbers of lunatics and numbers of children boarded-out, agreements with foster-parents, maintaining case histories, reporting fortnightly on the state of proceedings taken against people for neglecting children, and obtaining orders in bastardy, that is, ordering putative fathers of illegitimate children to fund their upkeep (BHC GBO/28/300).

The work relied a great deal on detailed recording and in 1904 the phrase 'Case Papers' is written in Bolton Union documentation in quotation marks, not yet part of the regular jargon of Poor Law administration. The majority of recording in these folders, related to finances, but not all; and comments about the assessment of need, previous applications for relief, reliability, behaviour and so on are found in these 'Case Papers'.

There is some dispute about where the case paper system started. Chorlton Union, near Manchester, certainly used them in the 1860s (Aveling 1909). Others suggest such a system was introduced in Shropshire in 1838 (Mishra 1969: 169). A case paper system was introduced by the COS in 1869, but the system which eventually spread across both Poor Law and voluntary charities was introduced by the chair of Paddington Guardians, a Mr Aveling, in January 1890 (Aveling 1909). He devised a set of proformas and entered into arrangements with local churches and the local COS district to use the same pattern of information for ease of communication. The idea spread but was opposed in places. Transferring information from the ledgers to individual case papers was laborious and rural Guardians argued with some force that their solitary RO would know regular applicants, so individual records were pointless. Supporters argued that more detailed information could be recorded on individual case papers and that this foiled fresh applications from rogues when experienced ROs left to be replaced by ignorant replacements. Eastbourne and Bethnal Green Unions claimed huge savings on the rates after introducing the system very early in the century, because false claims were choked off. So the argument was won and the LGB required all unions to introduce a system from 1911 (Aveling 1909).

The General Relieving Officer (GRO) idea was so successful that the LGB issued a circular in 1905 encouraging unions to use GROs. Bolton Union's response was to appoint two more GROs, one being an RO for Lunatics. This job involved assessing the condition of the alleged lunatic, consulting a medical practitioner if necessary and then escorting the lunatic to the workhouse. If after further medical investigation the lunatic still displayed florid symptoms, the RO escorted him or her to an asylum. The RO for Lunatics escorted people home as well. In Bolton at this time the RO for Lunatics, despite managing about 15 escorts a month, also had responsibilities for visiting apprentices and other young people sent into service from the workhouse or cottage homes (GBO/28/300).

And there were signs that the RO was acquiring a little more status. Superannuation for ROs became compulsory in 1897, resulting in a dramatic increase in the numbers of applicants for RO posts. In 1892 the *Poor Law Officer's Journal* began, lasting until 1929, transforming eventually into the *Health Service Journal*. There was a National Relieving Officers Association too, with branches across the country. The London version, the Metropolitan Relieving Officers Association (MROA), not only offered a regular programme of lectures for members but championed the idea of examinations for ROs. At the same time the COS in London was putting together a formal programme of training for charitable visitors. In 1894, Mrs Dunn Gardner, a District Officer of the COS in London, started systematic training of visitors. This developed into an annual scheme of lectures, presumably those Alice Hodson attended, which comprised lectures on labour and wages, local government, elementary education, the Poor Law, Factory Acts, thrift, accounts, public health and methods of relief. The COS Committee on Social Education, established in 1901, held a conference the following year at which it was decided to set up theoretical and practical training for visitors. Hodgson Craig, an RO in St Pancras, proposed a similar plan at a Poor Law conference the following year and in 1905 the Poor Law Committee of E.J. Urwick's COS sponsored School of Sociology proposed to offer an examination and certification for ROs. Although suspicious of COS principles an agreement was reached, with the MROA arranging for a selection of ROs to take part in the lectures offered by Urwick in 1906. In 1908 the first examination for ROs took place, resulting in 28 passes and ten failures. The first university-based training for social workers and social administrators had been set up in Liverpool in 1904, organised by the CRS and the Women's Victoria Settlement. ROs were offered training as well as voluntary workers, but numbers of both participating were small. Birmingham and Edinburgh followed, but by 1913 only 269 students had completed any university training (Macadam 1925, Mishra 1969).

Alice Kearsley

Early in 1912 Bolton Guardians decided to appoint a paid worker to manage the work involved visiting families and children which was not the direct responsibility of the Boarding-Out Committee (BHC/28/569).

In May the post of Lady Visitor, Assistant Relieving Officer was advertised to manage the '*system of After-Care of children placed out at service*'. The role was to look after the register and case papers of all children in public care placed in service after they left school at 13 and to follow up the small number adopted. The Lady Visitor had to arrange for an after care visitor for each child and to see quarterly reports from these visitors. In addition the Lady Visitor was to '*visit cases on the outdoor relief list, not to ... check on the ROs but to supplement their work in matters which may be properly within the scope of a woman officer*'. On such visits she was to '*by personal enquiry and observation*' pay close attention to:

- the appearance of children ... health, nourishment and ... cleanliness
- general condition of the house ... ventilation ... tidiness ... bedding
- for infants ... whether the diet contains a reasonable amount of milk
- supervision of children if mother goes out to work
- check whether out relief is expended with reasonable economy
- note any intemperance or immorality in the house
- in cases of sickness advise about obtaining proper medical attendance through the District MO (BHC/28/569).

This role definition is very similar to the visiting rules used by Miss Mason and Dr Turner. It also identifies the chief concerns of the time: TB (the mention of ventilation), the importance of milk for infants, the dangers of drink and the practice of bundling up bedding to be pawned weekly, thereby providing short-term funds at the expense of a set of bedding which spent most of its time in the pawn shop.

The advert attracted 74 applicants of whom six were shortlisted for interview: a housekeeper, an infirmary attendant, a private nurse, an assistant schoolmistress, an assistant to a housekeeper in a large house and Alice Kearsley.

Alice, 38 at the time of her application, was the daughter of a successful butcher, Edward Kearsley, who by 1901 owned three shops. Of his ten children two sons followed him into the family business, while another son was a joiner and another a solicitor's clerk. The family straddled the boundary between the working and lower middle classes. From the age of 50 Edward let his sons run the businesses, becoming in turn a Bolton Councillor then a Poor Law Guardian. Union records indicate that he was not a supporter of Mary Haslam's reformers, but was a traditionalist, more concerned with saving the rates than helping the poor (King 2006).

Alice herself started her working life as a dressmaker, living at home, but as her mother aged she probably took to running the household. It seems that it was only when her mother died in 1901 and her father in 1903 that her social work activities began. First she became involved in the work of the Girls Friendly Society (GFS). The GFS, with Anglican roots, offered a social framework for young women working away from home to prevent them falling into sin; drink or inappropriate sexual encounters. The GFS ran social clubs and GFS volunteers also visited girls, some of whom had been put out to service on behalf of Poor Law Unions. Alice may well have been one of those GFS visitors. Later Alice worked with the Waifs and Strays Society in an administrative capacity. She was almost certainly involved with the effort by Bolton Waifs and Strays to establish a home for 20 girls in Bolton, which opened in 1908 (BHC/28/569). Alice Kearsley's success in obtaining the Lady Visitor post may be linked to her father having been a Guardian, although she did have experience relevant to the job and at the time of interview her father had been dead nine years. She started on 22 July 1912 with a salary of £60, just over half what ROs were paid.

Alice Kearsley's new role confirmed a pattern of operation for many social workers until after the Second World War: the paid worker coordinating the work of a team of volunteers. Boarding-Out Committees operated like this and Mental After Care Associations had paid workers running friendly visiting schemes for people discharged from asylums. Associations for Mental Welfare, under the aegis of the 1913 Mental Deficiency Act, worked in the same way, as did Education Care Committees, both of which we shall consider later.

At the same time another Alice, Alice Foley, was engaged in visiting the sick. Coming from a family of eight children, her father was a fitfully working drunk. She was bright and determined and once working in a mill became active in her trade union, the Weaver's Association. The 1911 National Insurance Act introduced unemployment benefit and sickness benefits for a range of workers, with compulsory payments to the fund by workers and employers alike. Sickness benefit was to be paid out and supervised by Approved Societies and many trades unions applied for such approval. The Weaver's Association was approved and Alice Foley was appointed as sick visitor in 1912. She says:

> The job was not particularly exacting [her previous employment had been tending a machine for 11 hours a day], being confined mainly to a knowledge of the appropriate regulations and a tactful approach to their administration. But it did entail pushing a bicycle bearing a heavy cash bag and bundles of sickness claims over miles of bumpy cobbled street (Foley 1973: 76).

> The most disagreeable aspect of the job was 'keeping an eye' on suspected malingerers ... married women workers, during a period 'on't panel' had a tendency to indulge in household chores whilst registered as 'incapacitated'. But as this very natural behaviour was 'agin't'rules', a sick visitor was expected to be something of a snooper and had to report such cases. Here duty clashed a little with conscience (Foley 1973: 77).

Alice Foley did not regard herself as a social worker although she engaged in much the same work as COS visitors and relieving officers; visiting people's houses, checking up on claims of sickness, offering support and advice. The clear difference between her views and those of others mentioned earlier is that she took no pride in rooting out 'imposture', and was more exercised by the need to do well by the individual than to catch them out in a minor fraud.

These unspectacular duties brought their own measures of illumination. Pedalling idly, or purposefully, over miles of rough paving stones, frequently popping into tiny cottages ... I shared the blessedness and cussedness of close human contacts. Without much effort I became part of their simple joys, griefs, wranglings, pitiable gullibility and understandable insensitivity. It might dismay at times, but I was wholly at one with them in their heroic gropings through poverty and injustice to try and achieve a fairer hold on life with all its possibilities (Foley 1973: 77).

Social Work in Hospitals

The history of social workers in hospitals, which emerged during the early years of the century, has been well documented (Moberley Bell 1961, Walton 1975, Barraclough 1996). The orthodox view is that Mary Stewart, a COS organiser in St Pancras, was the first Lady Almoner, appointed to the Royal Free Hospital, London in 1895 on a trial basis for three months.

There had been discussion for some years about how out-patient departments in voluntary hospitals across London were being abused. Out-patient departments offered comprehensive consultation services, had pharmaceutical dispensaries, undertook operations and had a full complement of doctors and nurses. They also dealt with casualties. So out-patient departments were the hub of medical treatment in any given area. It is unsurprising then that they were thronged with humanity each day; the gravely ill, people suffering from chronic conditions, the mildly-afflicted, people in search of patent medicines, imposters after a hand-out and those wanting to come in from the cold. All voluntary hospitals struggled with managing this demand, both physically and financially; they did not want to be swamped by people who could not pay or whose presence was a nuisance, but in order to keep up the numbers of people paying into their provident association, and thus keep up their income, they did want to be considered the place to get treatment locally (Sackville 1989). They employed Collectors to seek new provident society members and collect subscriptions from current members, but all had difficulty managing the numbers coming to their outpatients departments. The Metropolitan Hospital in Dalston, London, in order to manage the crowds decided in 1889 to have fixed opening hours for the dispensary and not to accept any out-patients except for accidents and urgent cases between noon and 7.30 (St Barts Archive 1889). In 1893 an office was installed in the waiting room in which all prescriptions order books and records were kept, which meant all the various queries, advice and instructions could be given in one place. It was this year too that Thomas William Cramp, employed by the hospital as a Provident Inspector since 1890, was noted as having been working in the out-patient department with good results. The record is not clear what the work was, but as most mentions of the out-patient department were about the numbers and pressures, it is safe to assume Mr Cramp had been successful in bringing more order to bear. From

1895 he was employed as Outpatient Inspector. This role appears to have been very similar to Mary Stewart's at the Royal Free; imposing order amongst those waiting, checking that people had the means to pay or that they had a proper ticket for treatment and referring on elsewhere if not to charities or the Poor Law (Sackville 1989).

This social and financial triage was moderately successful in the Royal Free, although confusion amongst medical staff about the Lady Almoner's role dogged Mary Stewart, and funding for a continued almoner presence was only agreed after some wrangling. There was no such hesitation with Mr Cramp, whose employment at the Metropolitan was continuous until his death in 1923. From 1903 he was referred to as the Almoner and his work, as described in his annual reports, was the same as the small number of almoners being taken on in voluntary hospitals. Sackville reports that in 1905 Thomas Cramp saw over 9,000 of the 34,000 out patients presenting themselves (1989). Of these more than a third were directed to Provident Dispensaries, 297 to general practitioners, 220 to Friendly Societies, 228 to the Poor Law and 185 to the COS. He had over 4,000 case papers and identified 324 people who had abused the system. Among other things he arranged for 72 patients to go to convalescent homes, and prepared a pamphlet for local people about preventing consumption. He had a clerk and also directed the work of the hall porters and messenger boys and worked closely with the provident society collectors, introducing them to patients.

In 1903, in order to gain and offer support to each other the individual almoners who worked across London in voluntary hospitals set up an Almoner's Committee. Initially there were eight of them. Thomas Cramp was a member, sometimes chaired meetings and played an important part in the pre-war development of the role. The other almoners, Lady Almoners, were all middle class single women and despite growing unease at the association, generally operated in the COS mould. So as a working class man in this role Thomas Cramp was an oddity. The number of these middle class female almoners in voluntary hospitals increased only very slowly before the Great War, probably because other means were in place to manage out-patient departments; that of the male working-class man assigned to the job, ex policemen sometimes, or hospital employees like Mr Cramp with titles such as Inspector. This tradition, unresearched as far as I can tell, may have been widespread; Mr Cramp for instance asked for a testimonial from the Metropolitan in 1908 when he applied for the job of Outpatient Superintendent at the Royal London Hospital in Whitechapel.

So although Mary Stewart is credited as being the first almoner, in truth, what she did probably replicated what was already being done elsewhere by hospital administrations using male employees. She introduced COS notions in differentiating the eligible from ineligible and no doubt brought some refinement to what may have been sometimes rowdy proceedings, but the work she did offered a change of emphasis, not a new beginning. The real ground breaker in hospital social work was neither Miss Stewart nor Mr Cramp. It was Anne Cummins, another example of a comprehensive innovator in social work.

From a noted Scots family, she was well educated but since her father had died impecunious she had to work. She trained with the COS and aged 35 was taken on as London's St Thomas's Hospital's first Lady Almoner in 1905. From the beginning her ambition was wider than just being a sorting officer. First of all she made sure she put no foot wrong with the medical staff and built up relationships with social work and charitable organisations in Lambeth. Her two priorities were major themes of the day: teaching people about TB and support for nursing mothers. She convinced the authorities to start pre-natal visiting both to educate women and to investigate if their material conditions could be improved. Clubs for mothers combined friendship with education. These were notable achievements at the time, accomplished by someone who fully supported the COS principles that Alice Hodson and Harry Snell found so difficult to implement. Anne Cummins for instance opposed the introduction of subsidised meals for mothers in Lambeth in 1908 on the grounds that it would undo the efforts she and others had been making to raise the people from pauperisation (Moberly Bell 1961).

Then came a stroke of luck. A substantial gift to the hospital from a former patient led to the foundation of the Northcote Trust whose aims were to support social work with patients on the wards, develop pre-natal and maternity care and extend the work with TB patients. With staff and funding to carry out her vision, a full pre-admission and post-discharge advice and support service was possible. Anne Cummins is rightly regarded as the mother of almoners (Moberley Bell 1961, Barraclough 1996).

Chapter 3

1914–1930: The Great War and After: A New Breed

The Great War

On the August Bank Holiday two years after she started work Alice Kearsley sat down to write an application for a pay rise. There were no set salary scales so each RO had to do this and Alice was paid much less than her male counterparts.

The report shows Alice was responsible for visiting 300 young people once a quarter. First there were children over 13 placed in domestic service or live-in apprenticeships from the cottage homes. Then there were visits to families receiving out-relief where ROs had raised concerns about child welfare. Alice had to manage the work of the volunteers and also had to recruit more of them. Women already involved in the Guild or the GFS were given preference as volunteers and Alice commented in her report that Mrs Norbury and Miss Calderbank, both Catholic ladies, had been specially recruited to visit their co-religionists. But Alice reported that she could find no visitor for 25 of the 84 after care cases, so she had to visit herself. By this time she also had Infant Life Protection responsibilities: '*I keep the Register and case papers on the ... prevention of cruelty to children – visiting and making reports ... there are 101 cases on the Register*' (BHC GBO/28/569).

In addition she dealt with children found begging, children of tramps and any children the NSPCC inspectors removed from their parents. And she was entirely responsible for ensuring that reports on progress were presented to the Guardians regularly, acted upon and filed. The visits would have included direct observation of the children, sleeping arrangements and bedding and talking to the school or employer. Alice started work at nine and spent the morning in the office attending to paperwork. She did her visiting each afternoon, often staying out late into the evening. In conclusion she asked for her salary to be increased by £20 a year. The tone was professional, indicated a thorough grasp of the responsibilities and showed pride in her achievements.

Succinct and persuasive the report may have been, but it was doomed to failure. On the evening she completed it, 4 August 1914, Britain declared war on Germany. So the Guardians and everybody else had more to think about than Alice's pay. Mr Cooper in particular, secretary to the Guardians and member of the Guild's Central Committee, was concerned about the demands on relief consequent on the departure of so many men for the army. The Boer War had demonstrated how ineffective the army pay arrangements were and considerable financial distress was anticipated in army families. Nearly a thousand reservists were called up immediately and a flood of volunteers took the colours, single men mostly, but some family men. Guilds of Help across the country and other charitable visiting societies, decided to make their resources available to the war effort by offering to be the conduit for the wartime national relief funds. In the first year of war the local Guild helped 8,000 families with a vastly expanded army of volunteer Helpers, 1,200 in 1914 and throughout the war. As well as distributing funds from the Soldiers and Sailors Families Association and the Prince of Wales Fund, the Guild distributed 6,906 garments following a call for clothes for hard-pressed families and 11,000 toys to 10,000 children that first wartime Christmas (BHC 361.BOL).

While visiting charities were at the heart of such commendable efforts all over Britain, the circumstances created by the war weakened the need for them. The supply of financial relief from government became so lavish that raising small amounts of money to help individuals became unnecessary. More significantly, Guilds of Help in 1917 signed up as the local delivery agency of the War Pensions Committee. This included assessment of need for the bereaved and for families of injured men. This War Pension role took Guild Helpers into the territory previously only inhabited by sick visitors, School Attendance Officers (SAOs), Sanitary Inspectors and ROs. They became, to some extent, functionaries of the state whose role was as much to investigate claims and seek out fraud as it was to help and support the distressed.

Rogues

Although many charitable visitors, Guild volunteers and ROs joined the army and the call on mainstream Poor Law relief dropped off as employment rose during the war, day-to-day work went on in Poor Law Unions. Perhaps, in the difficult circumstance of wartime, standards slipped a little. There are two examples in Bolton from the war years of ROs defrauding both employer and applicants.

Robert Robbie was appointed RO for Lunatics in 1906 (BHC GBO/28/312). In the war years he escorted around 20 people each month to and from the workhouse and various lunatic asylums. The Union owned an ambulance, where more than one person could be escorted at a time, but Mr Robbie preferred taxi cabs, a hugely expensive means of transport. As his work required him to spend considerable sums of Union money on transport in circumstances where prior booking was often not possible, it is not surprising that ROs for Lunatics were required to post a bond of £50 lest they be tempted to abscond with Union funds, which they always carried. Mr Robbie's ruse was to submit inflated figures from the taxi driver to the Guardians while paying the taxi driver a lesser sum, possibly splitting the difference with the driver to guarantee his silence. After regular late submission of his expenses and continued use of taxis when he had been warned to use the workhouse ambulance, Mr Cooper asked Mr Evans the cross visitor (a sort of

Union internal auditor) to investigate Robbie's finances. The report revealed that Robbie's travel expenditure gave him a balance of £24 13s 8d owed to the Union. This was a staggering sum for someone earning around £180 a year and impossible to accrue without deliberate abuse. Somehow he found out about the report as it was submitted on a Friday and went on a bender in Liverpool. Alerted to his disappearance the following Tuesday by Robbie's wife, Mr Cooper made the wheels of the Union bureaucracy grind exceeding quick. He invited the Guardians to dismiss Robbie and they did the following day.

The case of Mr Knowles is typical of the temptations all ROs were faced with. He was an ordinary RO assessing financial need and paying out relief on his regular visits (BHC GBO/28/306). He just doled out a little less to applicants than the Guardians had agreed and pocketed the rest. He also delayed rises in relief which were due or kept people on the books after they had moved on. The crudest dodge was also the most transparent. Encouraged by a female Guild Helper, the Guardians agreed to have a pint of milk a day delivered to a penurious old lady, a simple and effective way of supporting her independence. Mr Knowles duly claimed money for the milk from the Union, but never paid the dairyman.

In 1915, tipped off by someone, George Evans investigated his practices, visiting a number of people to check Knowles's payments. Mr Evans's report includes 15 examples of underpayment. Mr Evans also found that Mr Knowles had been trying to smooth out the underpayments, once he got wind of the investigation:

> In each case I was informed [that Mr Knowles] was at their houses on Thursday night … at nearly ten o'clock [pm], and admitted that he had paid them short but would pay them something every week extra and begged of them if a man called to make enquiries to swear that he had paid them the full amount every week (BHC GBO/28/306).

The report was delivered once more on a Friday and again, somehow, the errant RO learned he had been rumbled. He made his decision. On the following Monday Mr Cooper received a letter from Mrs Knowles. The previous evening she had gone upstairs to see if George had finished in his bath and found that he had. He was lying there, in a brimming tub, drowned. He had left a suicide note, which mentioned '*a grave error in his official duties*' (BEN 1915: 4).

The Impact of the War

The war itself brought high levels of employment and a taste of prosperity for working families. With over four million men under arms, young women flocked to take their place in factories, on buses, everywhere. As munitions factory pay could top £2 a week, the previous staple employment of young women as domestic servants, paid at £10 to £15 a year, was revealed as the exploitation it was (Overy

2009). A flood of women into factories, where none had been employed before, stimulated industry to employ welfare officers, women themselves. They offered first aid, ran creches and made sure the welfare needs of women were accounted for. The pioneer in this initiative was Jesse Boot, the chemist and manufacturer. He employed Clara Heath as a part time welfare officer from 1891, who was provided with a bicycle so she could visit women employees who were ill or suffered hardship (Coles 2003). The real innovator in this work however was an American, Eleanor Kelly, who took over in 1911. Kelly was 27 and had trained as a social worker. Jesse's wife Florence enticed Kelly from a factory in Carlisle to work for Boot's in Nottingham which by then had 1,000 women workers. Kelly refurbished the staff canteen and set up a sick room which had a full-time nurse and doctor. She created record cards for all employees and visited sick female employees, seeking help for them from the Salvation Army or their church if they needed it. As her work and ambition grew she persuaded Jesse Boot to recruit two further trained social workers: Agatha Harrison and Miss Kerr (Coles 2003). Other firms took up the idea and by 1913 their numbers had grown sufficiently for the Welfare Workers' Association to be established. It started with 60 members. As the 1915 Munitions of War Act ensured that engineering works and factories filled with women workers, the number of welfare officers grew to about 1,300. In Bolton there were at least two firms who employed welfare officers during the Great War: Musgraves, an iron works and William Walkers, a tannery and leather works. Before the war Walkers had a first aid and ambulance department and a rest room with a nurse, a canteen and technical classes for workers. They also had a sports club and claimed to be ahead of the rest of the industrial world with the '*welfare idea*' (BHC ZWKG/8/1).

The war brought relative affluence and some freedom to young working men and women. Young people went dancing, went to the pictures or took charabanc holidays. More importantly, there was something of a shift in self regard for working-class women. By the end of the Great War the cotton workers' ubiquitous shawls had been replaced by coats and hats. Skirt lengths went up – working women could hardly be expected to undertake onerous activities in such confining clothing as had been obligatory before the war. The bra was introduced in the twenties as was the general wearing of make-up and, late in the thirties, the nylon stocking. This growth in concern for appearance and greater confidence was at least partly associated with the slow spread of the technology of birth control (the cap and the condom). Marie Stopes' *Married Love*, with its clear guidance about birth control, was published in 1918. Very few copies would have entered working-class homes, but it influenced opinion formers. From the mid 1920s Labour local authorities began to publicly support the use of birth control techniques and some independent birth control clinics were established. In addition improved infant health care, ensured by the 1918 Maternity and Child Welfare Act, was beginning to work away at the infant mortality rate, and so the pressure to have large numbers of children began to dissipate (Overy 2009). Stimulated by worries about wartime promiscuity, venereal diseases and a higher illegitimacy rate, the Act required local authorities to make provision for expectant and nursing mothers and children under five. One of the immediate consequences was an increase in the numbers of Health Visitors appointed.

A New Breed

But into the 1920s the major social concerns remained the same; housing and poverty. The latter though was now more often referred to as unemployment and, partly because of the high numbers unemployed through the 1920s and into the 1930s, was not so often seen as the self-inflicted wound that pre-war pauperism had been. Old Age Pensions were extended to cover all those over 65 and sickness and unemployment benefits were extended to cover almost all the working population. So the role of ROs became confined to the truly desperate and the role of visiting charities shrank. In addition the opportunities for middle-class women to establish careers in the professions, the Civil Service and in various welfare capacities constrained the supply of volunteers that traditional charities relied on (Walton 1975). So in the early 1920s the number of London COS Districts able to sustain themselves dropped from 40 to 28 in three years and the COS developed a reputation as being a provider of primarily practical help; such things as false teeth and periods of convalescence (Rooff 1972).

Nevertheless the development of social work responses to specific needs continued. One significant development of the inter-war years was the education care committee system. The 1906 Education Act made provision for free school meals for poor children. Care committees were set up by a number of education authorities, there usually being one committee for each school. The Birmingham Care Committee system set up in 1907 concentrated on supporting families after the newly compulsory medical examination was undertaken for poor children (Rimmer 1980). If the examination revealed poor eyesight, enlarged tonsils, ringworm or even TB, the care committee visitor saw parents and attempted to secure spectacles or operations, whatever was necessary. The London County Council (LCC) Care Committee system was developed by Theodora Morton and Miss Wragge on COS lines in 1908 (Wilmott 2004, Jennings 1930). As the Principal Organiser in the London scheme, Miss Morton appointed Care Organisers who themselves recruited and supervised volunteers. It was the volunteers who mostly visited families, their role including following up the findings of school medicals, helping with funding for convalescence, arranging holidays for groups of children and so on. Volunteers looked into absences from schools, often finding that a child was not attending for lack of a pair of boots. They also investigated the needs of delicate and maladjusted children, referred cases to the NSPCC or Sanitary Inspectors and many volunteers established long-term supportive relationships with families. Early volunteers included the then 17-year-old Mary Brinton (later Mary Stocks) and Clement Attlee (later to become Prime Minister). Mary Brinton had been brought up in an affluent Liberal family in Kensington, London, was involved in the struggle for women's suffrage from her mid teens and had at least two aunts and an uncle who were Poor Law Guardians. Through her family she knew Millicent Fawcett and Mrs Pankhurst, leaders of both wings of the women's suffrage campaign and also Octavia Hill, old by then but still lauded for her work in housing and imbued with the COS approach to philanthropy. Mary became Honorary Secretary of the Saffron Hill Elementary School Care Committee, her mother stipulating that she should run the administration and not visit families herself, as that, at her age, would be both inappropriate and impertinent. The system was initially controversial and Mary Stocks reports that Octavia Hill took a dim view of it, because it undermined the responsibility of working class parents. Even within the care committees there were arguments. In the case of spectacles for children whose parents could not afford them, which in Bolton the Guild of Help subsidised where necessary, was the subject or argument at Saffron Hill as one of the committee members, a cleric, vehemently opposed what he saw as interference in the parents' lives (Stocks 1970).

After the Great War the London Care Committees thrived, at one stage in the 1930s having 4,000 volunteers (Willmott 2004). Dismissed by some aspirant social workers as '*teeth, tonsils, eyes ... health work*' (Rimmer 1995: 178) care committees nevertheless attracted ambitious and able young women.

Although Theodora Morton demanded that her Care Organisers should have a social science diploma this was not always applied. One woman who crept into the work without one was Geraldine Aves (Willmott 1992). Her father, Ernest, spent ten years at Toynbee Hall settlement and while Geraldine was growing up he worked with Charles Booth on his famous survey of poverty and supported him in his work on the Royal Commission into the Poor Law. In 1917 Geraldine went up to Newnham College, Cambridge, but her father died and as the war ended she knew she had to make her own living, deciding on a career in public service. She had already visited Blackfriars settlement and knew about such things as youth clubs, collecting subscriptions for provident societies and sick visiting. For a while she floundered but after contacting the LCC Chief Education Officer Geraldine was put onto Theodora Morton who was persuaded, somewhat reluctantly, that her degree in economics might serve as well as a social science diploma to prepare her for work as an Assistant Organiser in the London Care Committee system.

Geraldine Aves went to work with Nancy Rackstraw in 1924 in the dispiriting surroundings of Islington, London. Rackstraw, who became a lifelong friend, set up a comprehensive training programme for her. This involved shadowing volunteers, getting to know the local schools, establishing a relationship with the local RO and working alongside people in the Islington COS district. Geraldine was horrified by the exhaustive enquiries required by the COS such simple work as applications for a pair of boots; the endless copying of correspondence, checks into every detail of the applicant's background and the weighty deliberations of the COS committee. But she took to the work. One of the attractions may have been that she was working alongside people she felt at ease with:

Miss Rackstraw is an Oxford Woman … one of the most capable people I have ever struck. Next in the hierarchy is … Miss MacAlister … also Oxford and most pleasant to work with. We share a room and so far have got on splendidly. The other organiser is a Miss Hillier who was my contemporary at Cambridge (Willmott 1992: 40).

All four women were at that time in their mid to late twenties and regarded themselves as a new breed. Geraldine Aves describes attending a conference with a '*redoubtable district organiser of a social work type now totally extinct, around her waist a black elastic band from which were suspended note book, waterproof, galoshes and other essentials*'. She also referred to a representative from the Institute of Almoners (Miss Kelly) as a '*true battleaxe*' (Willmott 1992: 41).

Geraldine Aves finished her probationary period and was appointed to a permanent post covering 18 schools in Finsbury, North London. Enthusiastic, and able she was soon regarded as a high flier. In 1930, after Miss Morton retired, Geraldine was appointed Principal Assistant Organiser.

For others however, not so young and enthusiastic, the round of visiting was less satisfying. After the war Alice Kearsley seems to have tired of her Lady Visitor work in Bolton, having more time off sick and receiving several notes from Mr Cooper about her time keeping. He also reminded her to pay attention to the bed clothing of children and feeding of infants. He wrote to Alice in 1921: '*All cases where there is an insufficiency of milk must be reported. Please arrange an early conference with the Health Visitors, ascertain the lines on which they work and adopt their methods where possible. Report fully to me on this matter after you have had the conference*' (BHC GBO/28/569).

Alice replied to his criticisms with sprightly notes, on two occasions mentioning she was late as she had been delayed in conversation with women Guardians, deftly putting Mr Cooper in his place. Then at the age of 46 she married. At first her marriage in 1920 to Robert Borland, an engineer from Scotland, was accepted by the Guardians, although she had to write to her employers asking permission to stay at work now she was a married woman. In many spheres of work the employment of married women was frowned upon, but also in the early 1920s the wartime opening of the ranks to women workers was being closed off again. This applied across industry and particularly to women teachers who were being ousted all across the country to allow men back to work. Sure enough a few weeks after her marriage, the Guardians terminated Alice's appointment on the basis of her marriage. Alice's response was that she had not taken a man's job. She was the 'Lady' Visitor after all and had been in post since 1912, so the dismissal was simple ingrained conservatism. Or maybe it was a ploy to get rid of her if she was not performing to Mr Cooper's expectations. Whatever the reason the decision was a mistake. Not only was Alice the only Lady Visitor, but through her work she knew many of the women Guardians, most of whom had been involved in the women's suffrage movement. After securing the franchise for women over 30 in 1918 many suffrage societies transformed themselves into organisations such as the Bolton Women's Citizen's Association (WCA). Alice turned to this new association on being dismissed. The WCA not only lobbied the Guardians about their decision, but referred the sorry tale to the press. Within the month Alice was reinstated to the obvious delight of the WCA and deep embarrassment of the Guardians. But Alice's triumph was short lived. In January 1921 she had a tumour removed from her breast and doesn't seem to have recovered well from the operation. She had several periods of sickness thereafter culminating in August 1922 when she resigned.

The Child Welfare Visitor

Alice Kearsley was replaced as Lady Visitor by a former national insurance sick visitor, Annie Higginson, but within a couple of years the Union decided to expand the child welfare operation considerably. A new post was established, Child Welfare Visitor (CWV), whose responsibilities included post-maternity support for all those receiving relief. Another innovation was that all mothers in receipt of relief needing in-patient care were to be referred to the Union Infirmary via the CWV. She would also have visiting responsibilities for those families receiving relief – 542 children in 1925 (BHC GBO/28/1290). The new function swept up the Infant Life Protection work as well as all Annie Higginson's work. The role advertised also included responsibility for rescue work, both supporting unmarried girls through pregnancy and the inevitable subsequent adoption of the infant. This post seems to have been established partly due to concerns about the numbers of illegitimate children and partly in anticipation of the 1926 Adoption Act, which created a legal framework for adoption for the first time.

The advertisement for the post attracted 36 applications (see Appendix 2). Of these, nine were Poor Law Visitors, six were other Poor Law workers such as mental nurses, four were nursing privately, four worked in voluntary agencies, six worked for local authorities and four worked as welfare supervisors in factories.

The application form included no precise questions about qualifications but almost all claimed one. The most frequently cited was the Central Midwifery Board (CMB) certificate, which could be obtained without a nursing qualification. Eight had general nursing training or were state registered nurses, two claimed St. John's Ambulance nursing training, while seven had the Royal Sanitary Inspectors certificate in Public Health Visiting. Two were in their twenties, 13 in their thirties, 14 in their forties and seven in their fifties. Thirteen lived in Bolton and nine more were from the North West, but the other 14 were from farther afield; Cornwall, Newcastle, Birmingham, London and the Isle of Man. Many had moved around for work. Eliza Fletcher, for instance, sister in charge of St Austell Infirmary, had worked in nursing and infant welfare in Burnley, Blackburn and Wisbech. A lot of this movement had been occasioned by the war, but a lot of the reported movement seems to have been for career purposes.

Mary Jane McCracken was a Moral Welfare worker with a voluntary group in Dewsbury; Margaret Kay was a serving maid but also secretary of the local Girl Guide Association and Bolton Rounders Association; Sarah Broome was a Welfare Supervisor at William Walker's tannery; Annie Godrich was a foster mother in charge of Birmingham Cottage Homes and had previously worked for the Salvation Army supporting unmarried mothers in East London; Agnes Hollingworth was a Health Visitor, Tuberculosis Nurse and Inspector of Midwives for Bury; Ellen Ann Jobling was in a job very similar to Annie Higginson's in Burnley, as was Alice Turton in Birmingham. Ada Simpson was a Boarding-Out Visitor in Newton Abbot, but doubled up in the removal of female lunatics. The area she covered was huge and her testimonial commented that the Guardians had provided her with a motor cycle to complete her rounds (BHC GBO/28/1290).

Hannah Dorothy Hughes had been the Probation Officer for women in Reading since 1916, whose services were dispensed with only because '*two women police had been appointed ... and a separate probation officer for women is no longer needed*'. The Home Office had encouraged police forces to employ women police after the war and many forces did so from 1919. The Metropolitan Police took on 50 immediately and Bolton took on four (BHC ABJ/23), all women in their early 30s. Their role included tracing missing girls, managing custody and escorts of women prisoners, the protection of children playing in streets, work with young girls '*stranded in dangerous surroundings*', and increasingly work with neglected children or where cruelty was suspected. They also became intimately involved later in work with children subject to removal from parents under the Fit Person Orders after the 1933 Children and Young Persons Act (Jackson 2003). So, striking as the decision in Reading that Women Police Officers should take over the role of the women Probation Officer was, it may not have been untypical for the time.

But the most intriguing applicant for the CWV post was Patience Baggallay, daughter of a successful architect from Loughton in Essex. She had worked in the YWCA in Cairo during the Great War (employment and club work) and then in the War Pension Committee in London. At the time of her application she was training at the Josephine Butler Memorial Home in Liverpool, the pioneering training centre for moral welfare workers. Patience Baggallay was middle-class and had been awarded the M.B.E. for her war work. She was not the sort of woman traditionally associated with work for the Poor Law Union, but nevertheless she applied for the job, and was shortlisted.

Young, Single and Looking for Work

This post was seen as something of a plum with a good salary of £240 a year. This sort of post was new and there was no established constituency of potential applicants nor was it seen as an example of a distinct occupation. There was a requirement that applicants should have a nursing qualification, but such a qualification did not match this role – an observation confirmed by the fact that several women without nursing qualifications were confident enough to apply. But the range of applicants suggests a thriving nexus of child health, welfare and social work jobs across the country and a developing willingness both nationally and locally to make arrangements for the children of poor families that was more comprehensive than before the Great War.

The one thing applicants for the CWV post in Bolton shared was their single status, with only three being married (and one of them, Katherine Primold, stated she had not seen her husband for 12 years). All Geraldine Aves' colleagues were single. All the women police appointed in Bolton between the wars were single. The shortage of men, the traditional perception of this being women's work, and the opening up of such opportunities for women are all partial explanations for the ubiquity of women in such roles, but so was the lack of any firm expectation about particular qualifications for these roles. This meant that women could dip their toes into welfare work before committing themselves.

Eileen Younghusband was dipping her toes in following Alice Hodson's path when, as a young woman, she went to live in a settlement in 1922 (Jones 1984). This move could be interpreted as a studied snub to the idea of the life her mother had for her. Eileen's father was the celebrated explorer of the Gobi desert, Sir Francis Younghusband, who had won Tibet for the British Empire in 1904. Eileen's mother, whose money supported a lot of her husband's activity, was a conventional Victorian who wanted nothing more than that Eileen should be presented at court and after a successful season marry well. But Eileen found the social conventions her mother aspired to dull and frustrating, for by then she had begun to find herself. First of all she was enthralled by the sermons of Dick Sheppard at St Martin's in the Fields, becoming convinced of the need for disarmament and an avid supporter of the League of Nations. Eventually, at the age of 22, spurred on by a friend to find a purpose, she approached Edith Ramsey, organiser of Stepney Care Committee, and was taken on as volunteer. It seems from Kathleen Jones's biography that the young Eileen was as horrified by the poverty as Alice Hodson had been 20 years before and noticed similar things completely new to her:

> The fish and chips and jellied eels eaten out of a newspaper … the staple diet of white bread margarine and cheap jam, the weak tea and condensed milk … the crowded pubs that no respectable woman would enter (Jones 1984: 19).

She was fired by the life of Stepney, in contrast to her previous round of deadening social events. She took the next step and joined the Princess Settlement in Stepney – persuading her parents that it was suitable for a young lady as she would have her own room and a maid to bring her tea in the morning. At this Anglican establishment Eileen ran play groups and the library and established a discussion group for young women who talked about their families, boyfriends, violence from husbands and so on. Discussions about the nature of poverty with her colleagues and her determination to find a cure for it convinced her that she needed formal training.

Lucy Faithfull's motivation to become a social worker was more clear-cut. She had always wanted to work with children because of the fractured and peripatetic nature of her own childhood after her father died. There was no neglect, but relative penury in an otherwise affluent family meant she, her mother and brother, unable to afford a house, were constantly on the move between relatives' homes. In 1928, on leaving school and being invited by an aunt and uncle to go to Paris, she joined a settlement there where she worked in a nursery school. Her appetite whetted, she returned to undertake the Diploma in Social Policy and Social Work at Birmingham University and lived during that period in the Women's Settlement. She stayed on as a member of staff after her diploma and in the mid 1930s she was running clubs and collecting for the provident society on a Monday. Lucy said she always visited Brearly Street, '*one of the worst streets. We always went alone and we always carried a bag of money and never at any time was any one of us attacked. Yet ... the police used to go about in threes!*' (Niechcial 2010: 16). Her mother moved to London in 1935 and Lucy followed her, undertaking six months family casework training with the COS. She then took the post of Assistant Child Care Organiser with the London Care Committee, covering 26 schools in Bermondsey and Southwark. Looking back Lucy felt that the well off married women who made up the bulk of her volunteers provided an effective service. '*Social structure of England was different then, the East Enders were not resentful of the West Enders and the West Enders had a tremendous sense of service*' (Niechcial 2010: 22). Not everyone shared this view. Barbara Wooton, a socialist teaching at Westfield College, London between the wars, always sceptical of social work, thought that some of the young women of means she was teaching, who arrived in their elegant clothes, wanted to engage in a little charitable slumming and nothing more (Walton 1975: 110).

Class and Status

By 1925 ROs were encouraged to sit the Poor Law Examination Board exam, which the young Bolton RO Fred Crossley passed in that year, along with another 191 other ROs nationally (BHC GBO/28/1117). This post-employment training consisted of having to learn the law and regulations and not much more (Dumsday and Moss 1935). But the CWV post requiring as it did a nursing qualification was the first of any Poor Law visiting post in Bolton which had any entry requirement. And this is one of the major changes compared to the pre-war world. By 1925 health and welfare occupations were beginning to coalesce and differentiate themselves from each other. Nurses had to be trained in order to take up posts in public service, as did District Nurses, and there were nationally recognised qualifications for Health Visitors (from 1895) and Midwives (from 1903). At the time, the task of each aspirant occupation, if it was to claim anything like professional status was, in broad terms, to:

- mark out territory for itself – what did it do that no one else did?
- identify a body of knowledge and ethics
- establish a national qualification and standards
- establish the authority of a national board which could guard entry and maintain standards (Greenwood 1957).

District nurses had received a huge boost towards this sort of status with the decision of Queen Victoria to support, from her 1887 Golden Jubilee fund, a National Institute of District Nursing, the Queen's Institute (Stocks 1960). With determined leadership, national standards, a comprehensive pattern of local inspection and the carrot for local nursing agencies of the Queen's Institute badge, this organisation swept all before it and by the 1920s there were 2,000 Queen's Institute District Nurses in London alone. But before a strong occupational profile for district nursing could be achieved the decision had to be made about what class the workers they should be drawn from. Should they be ladies or women of a lower order? Traditionalists, influenced by the brooding presence of Florence Nightingale until her death in 1910, were convinced that gentlewomen could exercise more influence over people than could nurses drawn from lower down the social scale. As it happens, the first inspection of nurses in the young Bolton District Nursing Association (in 1890) is recorded, and Miss Paget was impressed, noting wounds being dressed in proper surgical style, nurses mucking in and making butties and washing the faces for the children of a neighbourless woman. Not only did she think that all the Bolton nurses were eligible for enrolment as Queen's Nurses, she looked favourably on Bolton being accepted as a training school for probationers. And in the end the Institute accepted that lower class women could learn what was necessary and do the job as if they were gentlewomen. Just as well, because the demand for nurses and the full time nature of what was required soon outstripped any possible supply of the superior sort of woman for the work (Stocks 1960).

There were similar debates in 1907 within Whitehall about the sort of person magistrates should be encouraged to appoint as probation officers once the Probation of Offenders Act came in. One side urged that employment of university educated gentlemen should be encouraged. The final decision was in fact made by scores of local courts which appointed the men they were accustomed to, the missionaries most often from Church of England Temperance Society, who had been offering their time to mission to offenders for years. Some of these men were educated, but many were not, their only characteristic feature being their commitment to the cause of saving souls from drink (Bochel 1976).

Perhaps the moves to professional occupational status for some groups of paid workers affected the status of volunteers. Voluntary visitors, by definition, could afford not to work and COS volunteers were, as Harry Snell experienced to his cost, valued more than paid enquiry agents. But in the 1920s changes in land values, taxation and domestic servants' wage rates meant that more of the previously wealthy were obliged to work. Geraldine Aves, Eileen Younghusband and Lucy Faithfull are examples of young women from affluent backgrounds whose families could fund social science certificate training at universities, who as they wanted to lead independent lives, chose to work. Before the Great War, there were very limited opportunities and like Alice Hodson, they would instead have volunteered. But the care committee system gave them the opportunity to work in an environment where their colleagues were also their social peers; where they could feel socially at ease, do useful work and earn a living. But some women went further, or tried to: Patience Baggalley for instance in her CWV application. There is other evidence of educated affluent women in public service employment, one such being Kathleen Bartlett who became an RO in Brighton in 1934 (Rimmer 1995: 78). The background of the women taken on by the Metropolitan Police between the wars indicates some were affluent. Thirteen had been school mistresses or governesses, 25 nurses and midwives and so on, but a small number were university-educated (Jackson 2003).

Almoners and Psychiatric Social Workers (PSWs)

By the mid 1920s almoners were the only group of social workers who had developed a distinct professional profile. They were all from affluent backgrounds, had staked out their territory, entrance requirements and training. They were paid workers, but maintained an entirely educated and middle to upper class workforce. And they were all women. The working-class tradition of men doing almoners work died out with Thomas Cramp just after the Great War.

In 1922 the Hospital Almoner's Committee became the Institute of Hospital Almoners, which established initial training and acted as a General Council, controlling entry to the occupation. In the 1920s and 1930s the training consisted of four months work with the COS, three terms with the LSE, then eleven months under an almoner in a hospital and a month outside hospital in a rescue home, infant welfare centre or TB clinic. Trainees needed a university education to even apply and although part one of the course could be taken in any of several university social work courses, supervision by an almoner for the final part of the training could only be sought in London, restricting the occupation to the affluent, educated and mobile. Elizabeth Macadam counted 74 almoners across the country in 1925 (Macadam 1925). Arguably the tight control of entry and type of candidate was only possible because of the relatively low demand for almoners.

Apart from almoning, there was no firm consensus about what training for social workers should consist of. One hindrance to a defined syllabus was the range of occupations which huddled under the then broad umbrella of social work. Macadam identified the following jobs as social work: Factory inspectors, Inspectors of Boarded-Out Children, Health Visitors and Sanitary Inspectors, organisers of Child Care Committees, Managers and rent collectors under Local

Housing Authorities, Women Police, Probation Officers, Relieving Officers, Welfare workers in factories, organisers of Councils of Social Welfare, Charity Organisations, Almoners, Child Welfare Agencies, Social activities of churches and settlement workers (Macadam 1925).

And Macadam accepted that, unlike other occupations, social work in Britain had not acquired its own technique or distinct body of knowledge. Elizabeth Macadam was one of the leading lights in the development of social work training at Liverpool University and in the 1920s was the secretary of the Joint University Council on Social Work Training. She felt uneasy about the way training was structured and lamented the lofty attitude of universities to vocational training. Eileen Younghusband's experience at the LSE demonstrates the problem nicely. The subject matter on which students received lectures was wide and the cast of LSE lecturers was positively stellar. Eileen and her colleagues received the attentions of T.H, Marshall, R.H. Tawney, Malinowski, Harold Laski and Beatrice Webb among others. But lecturers only lectured and did not engage with the students in debate. Low status tutors were employed to try and link what was being taught with what the students were reading and experiencing elsewhere. So in some aspects of her learning Eileen was on her own:

> There was a day when Eileen sat down ... with McDougall's Principles of Psychology, in the confidence that when she had finished it, she would understand human behaviour. She was disappointed. Theories of instinct, perception and conation were not related to human behaviour as she observed it. She learned more from her friends from Stepney and Bermondsey (Jones 1984: 29).

With this sort of experience some were keen to improve on the learning on offer. Many of the affluent social workers in the 1920s were accustomed to travel, so it is unsurprising that many went abroad to further their studies. After the publication of Mary Richmond's *Social Diagnosis* (1917) – a crisp exposition of orderly assessment of need – many went to North America. Elizabeth Macadam visited the emerging centres of social work training in Chicago and New York in the mid 1920s and saw significant differences in their approach to what was being done in the UK. She was impressed by the teaching of psychology and sociology, much beyond vocational training. She also appreciated the use of more discussion in class than was the norm in British universities. But the emphasis in all the schools she visited was on practical training in the classroom, rather than learning from experience on placements, which unnerved her.

Related to this was the second and overwhelming difference – the concentration in American social work schools on '*case analysis and diagnosis*', (Macadam 1925). This was not the casework practiced by COS and Guild of Help workers; careful investigation, weighing of facts and a focussed plan of action, but instead emphasised the production of case histories of families back two and three generations and the interpersonal relationships between family members. Macadam was wary of '*a class of 50 students with type written records of a life history of, say, an unmarried mother discussing minutely the diagnosis and treatment of an unfortunate example of "social maladjustment"'* (Macadam 1925: 181). And she noted both a *'lack of a due sense of values'* in the teaching, a distancing from the humanity of the people under discussion and a tendency to overcomplicate things in which *'teachers and class appear to ... wrestle with a task that would present no difficulty to the worker with common sense, supplemented by well planned experience'* (Macadam 1925: 180).

Although Macadam coined the phrase *The New Philanthropy* for what she saw as the emerging integration between universal supports for the poor both in public service and the voluntary sector, she did not clearly propose a body of knowledge for British social work. She haltingly restated what the Wickwars called the traditional British definition of social work as referral and follow up, by what they referred to as an outdoor worker, which emphasised the brokerage role of social workers, knowledge of community resources and ability to relate across agencies, allied to a clear understanding that the recipients are human beings just like the social worker (Wickwar and Wickwar 1936). Macadam went to America seeking something more energetic and demanding that she could bring back to Liverpool. But the body of knowledge she found in America did not appeal to her. She reacted against the concentration on individual maladjustments and *'the exaggerated emphasis given to the medical and psychiatric approach to social problems'* (Macadam 1925: 181).

Perhaps Macadam was too old and set in her ways. The approach she had seen in America was the coming thing, attractive to many of Geraldine Aves's generation of social workers.

There were a number of developments which influenced this new thinking. The numbers of men who were maddened by their experiences of war had driven the authorities to take their plight seriously and in 1917 men with shell shock, neurasthenics as they were called, were declared eligible for war pensions (Barham 2004). Then there was the furore caused by post-war placement of discharged soldier neurasthenics in Poor Law asylums. This practice led to a fierce campaign by the Ex Services Welfare Society who asserted that these men were *'not ordinary lunatics'* and should have special treatment (Read 2007). In all this the public focus was not on psychological treatment but financial support and public standing. But it coincided with the establishment of the Maudsley Hospital in 1907, Bowdon House in Harrow in 1911 which offered treatment for nervous disorders and the Tavistock Clinic in 1920. All these establishments offered what help they could to those suffering from shellshock (Barham 2004).

And there were a few psychiatrists, like Millais Culpin and the young Donald Winnicott, men who had been exposed to Freud's tantalising ideas of the unconscious mind and the re-emergence of childhood trauma under stress, who became convinced that treatments based on talking and listening to these men might offer a lifeline. Interest in the relationship between the human mind and physical diseases and symptoms had developed strongly in the last decade of the previous century, stimulated by the work of Jean-Martin Charcot, the neurologist at the Saltpetiere Hospital in Paris who used hypnotism on hysterical symptoms. This stimulated many, including Freud, to experiment with mental cases. Freud's works were first available in English from 1909, although limited to a small audience, and his early English adherent, Ernest Jones, set up a psychoanalysis society in 1911. A broader slice of the medical profession and the wider public were introduced to Freud's ideas from around 1920 onwards when more of his work was published in digestible form.

His was by no means the only influence underpinning the post-war development of psychological and psychoanalytical approaches to helping people adjust to adverse circumstances. Cyril Burt's early work with LCC was in categorising the feeble-minded under the 1913 Mental Deficiency Act. His initial work on intelligence testing confirmed the inheritance of intelligence and his surveys of levels of intelligence confirmed and fed the popularity of taxonomical approaches to identifying types of maladjustment. His publications, particularly *The Young Delinquent* (1925) was immensely influential, which confirmed the inheritance of intelligence, but made it clear that environmental factors influenced behaviour considerably. Susan Isaacs made a contribution too. After training as a teacher and following a period as a researcher in Cambridge, she became head of Malting House School in Cambridge, an experimental school which fostered the individual development of children. Isaacs also trained and practised as a psychoanalyst and established an advanced course in child development for teachers of young children at the University of London. Such influences all contributed to the drive to establish the first child guidance clinics in the late 1920s (Overy 2009).

This new thinking offered vast opportunities for helping people, promised new skills, and offered new standing. While Burt and his psychologist colleagues with their categorisation and delineation had a strong following, psychoanalytical ideas were seen by many of the younger generation to be the really modern idea (Overy 2009: 145). From the mid 1920s a stream of teachers, doctors and social workers visited US child guidance clinics, psychotherapy units and social work courses, some on scholarships and some on observational visits. Early social work tourists such as Olive Crosse, Nancy Fairbairn and Noel (Kathleen) Hunnybun won fellowships from the Commonwealth Fund of America (CFA) and were, in effect, trained in psychiatric social work in America. Others, a score or so, were funded by the CFA on observational visits (Rockefeller Archive Centre). In 1928 Edith Eckhard, tutor at the LSE social science department, made the trip, like her colleagues funded by the CFA. Unlike Elizabeth Macadam, Edith Eckhard was bowled over by what she observed both in practice and at social work schools and urged William Beveridge to set up an experimental mental hygiene course at the LSE in anticipation of the establishment of child guidance clinics in London. Beveridge secured funding from the CFA to support scholarships and employ specialist staff and the mental health course started in 1929. This was, until 1942, the only such course in the UK (Stewart 2006).

Alexander's analysis of the content and focus of US social work courses between the wars contradicts the view that US social work was overtaken at that time by a '*psychiatric deluge*' (Woodroofe 1962, Alexander 1972). However the people asked by the CFA to advise on the mental health course, Barry Smith and Mildred Scoville, were both trained social workers and were imbued with the social psychiatric notions that Elizabeth Macadam had reacted against, but by which the young firebrands of social work in the twenties were so excited. So in return for CFA funding, Smith and Scoville outlined the content they wanted on the course. Once established, it included teaching on Freud, Jung and Adler, psychiatry and its bearing on social relations and symptoms of disorder specific to children such as thumb-sucking, nail-biting, bed-wetting and so on. This was completely new territory for social work training in Britain and Noel Timms suggests that the new tutors, on returning to the UK from US training, struggled to adapt teaching to the British context.

The LSE mental health course required that students should have a social science or social work qualification on entry, were offered up-to-minute training, and the majority went to work in child guidance clinics, or in voluntary hospitals for those with mental health problems working close by psychiatrists and psychologists. The numbers qualifying on the course as psychiatric social workers were low – only 179 in total by 1939 (Timms 1964), but from the beginning the course produced an elite cadre of social workers, entry to whose ranks was carefully guarded and who claimed a distinct body of knowledge. The lure of this exciting development was considerable and many in social work at the time were attracted to it. Lucy Faithful applied for the Mental Health course and both Eileen Younghusband and Geraldine Aves considered it. For all three however the war intervened and in the event none took that particular path.

Chapter 4
1919–1939: Public Assistance: New Ideas, Old Attitudes?

Ada and Annie and Alice Again

The successful candidate for Bolton's CWV in 1925 was Ada Wainer (BHC GBO/28/1290). Brought up in Nottingham her father was a jobbing builder and before the Great War she worked as a housekeeper. As with so many others the war offered her greater opportunities and she trained in the war years in *Sisterhood Social Work*, i.e. rescue work or moral welfare. She then took her CMB in London and subsequently ran a crèche in Hammersmith, London in 1916. After that she was employed to look after the three children of a widowed vicar in Manchester and then in 1921 was appointed Woman Visitor for Oldham Union – a similar job to Alice Kearsley's, except that she had additional moral welfare responsibilities.

Part of Miss Wainer's role in Bolton was to oversee the work of Lady Visitor, Annie Higginson. From her appointment Annie had tried to set her own path in a way that Alice Kearsley never had. She asked Mr Cooper, for instance, if she could do her visits in the morning, between 9.15 and 1pm, and write her notes in the afternoon, rather than the other way round. Mr Cooper sent her a terse note back saying he wished her to operate to the pattern he had laid out. Annie Higginson also took a fair amount of time off sick, on two occasions at least having to have her work covered for a week at a time by a locum, Alice Kearsley being brought back to fill in. When Miss Wainer arrived in 1925 Annie had been in her job three years.

The work involved the two visitors tramping across Bolton and into Manchester following up after care cases. Sometimes, if the young people moved around a lot, the visitors were led a dance trying to keep up with them. They also still investigated and chased up fathers ordered to pay for illegitimate children under bastardy orders, investigated claims for orphans' pensions and managed the various aspects of the adoption of illegitimate children. The two women worked with at least 800 children – visiting, checking, reporting. I can find no direct reference to the continued use of volunteer visitors, but as it still operated in other parts of the country and had been a long tradition in Bolton, it would seem safe to assume volunteer visitors were still used, although perhaps smaller numbers of them. Miss Wainer also worked in tandem with both the NSPCC and probation officers.

It is evident that the two women, in the case of families receiving out-relief (even such small sums as 5s a week), were expected to inspect homes, check expenditure, cleanliness and morality as well as how the children were being cared for. But the emphasis seems to have been on getting visits done and recorded, rather than offering any practical support. Two examples illustrate this.

Annie Higginson's caseload included Anne Marie Long, in receipt of relief because her husband was in hospital slowly sinking with an unnamed illness, probably TB. She noted that Mrs Long was '*inclined to depression*', but had dyed pieces of lace curtain to brighten up the house, made clothes for the two children, and had well-mended and clean bedding. She appeared, in Annie Higginson's words, to be '*thrifty*'. The final comment of the record was that Mrs Long was '*anxious to get to a dryer house*', but there is no record of either Miss Higginson or Miss Wainer attempting to help Mrs Long get to a dryer house. Miss Higginson comments after the next scheduled visit seven months later that '*home clean, children well cared for*' and includes an account of Mrs Long's need for false teeth to replace her own teeth which had been removed when her husband was well. She had been saving up the £3 required by the dentist for a set of dentures, but was a pound short. Miss Higginson asked in the record '*could anything be done in this case to obtain same?*' Her answer was '*there is no hope until the son obtains the age of 14 years and his earnings would allow of the extra expenditure*'. Had this been a Guild of Help or COS visitor before the Great War, funding for the teeth would have been earnestly sought. These notes indicate that the Welfare Department's attitude to visits to the relief cases was primarily one of checking there was no abuse of funds and that the children were not being neglected (BHC GBO/28/1290).

Annie Higginson also visited Emily Long. On one visit she noted that the '*widow with two boys 8 & 6 ... smelled strong of spirits. Downstairs was very clean but the stairs and the back bedroom was very dirty*' with the bed unmade, clothes piled on it in a heap and the chamber pot unemptied – clear evidence of slovenliness because, as we know, Annie Higginson invariably visited in the afternoon. The note of the next visit reports that Mrs Long was giving her children a '*bread and butter dinner*', but declined to allow Annie upstairs, as she was '*washing the bed-ticks*' (covers). When Annie persisted in her request to go upstairs Mrs Long said she would rather give up the 5s a week than '*have people coming troubling her*'. She asked Mrs Long four times to be allowed to inspect the bedrooms, but Mrs Long was firm. Annie warned her that the committee might therefore stop the payment. '*To my mind their* (sic) *appeared a more serious reason for refusing inspection of bedrooms – this was reported to the RO*'. She undoubtedly thought a lodger or husband was upstairs, or that the bedding was at the pawnbrokers.

These two women with the same name were visited the same day and Annie Higginson had mixed them up, recording the details of one visit against the record of the other. As a consequence she had to go to both again. This may have been evidence of Annie Higginson's lack of rigour in her work, but also indicates that she and Miss Wainer had to visit so many homes they did not really know the people concerned. No relationship existed with them. So these relief cases and aftercare visits were done to the calendar – ten or a dozen a day – a rote approach to dealing with people. And these visits took up even more time when you consider that each of the continuation sheets, when completed by Annie Higginson, was signed (or rather stamped with a signature stamp) by Miss Wainer as confirmation that the visit had been done and the write-up accepted.

Annie Higginson's slapdash approach irritated Miss Wainer, that most feared type of all organisational characters: the 'new broom'. She was confident, demanding, determined to get her own way and, perhaps, lacking a little in the diplomacy required of a supervisor in her relations with staff. Annie was demanding in her own way but more emotional and was prone to cutting corners. The two women shared an office. They did not get on.

When she arrived Miss Wainer found the visiting schedule hopelessly behind, the office dirty and recording systems primitive. She postponed the start of the work with unmarried mothers until the aftercare visiting backlog had been cleared. This took three months. Annie accepted the visits were behind, but what could you expect with so many cases to look after? She denied that the office was dirty. Soon Miss Wainer was writing notes to Mr Cooper saying that Annie Higginson refused to take instruction and insisted on doing things her own way. She also claimed that, when confronted, Annie Higginson had flown into a rage and stormed out of the office. Within the year Miss Wainer produced a dossier of six records which demonstrated that Annie had been recording events on the wrong record, mis-recording information and recording visits she had not made. Annie in reply gave plausible explanations for each case and stated that Miss Wainer was overbearing and deliberately set out to trip her up. Mr Cooper convened a meeting of a specially-established Child Welfare subcommittee of Guardians who interviewed both women. The result of this unprecedented action must have been deeply unsatisfactory for both of them. Annie was told she had to apologise, shape up or be dismissed. Miss Wainer was told she was tactless and should be more sympathetic. Mr Cooper, however, took practical action to resolve the conflict. He split them up, giving Annie a separate office and her own typewriter. There was comparative calm for a number of months but then Miss Wainer began making the same accusations that Annie's practice was poor, her attitude uncooperative and her temper worse. Annie countered by claiming that Miss Wainer had taken her typewriter away for mending and had refused to return it, thus making sure that Annie's recording was behind.

In the end Mr Cooper did the only thing he could. He made Annie Higginson an offer she couldn't refuse. He extracted a resignation letter from her in return for the promise of a good reference. The subsequent reference appears in the record, in answer to a request for one from an insurance company in Bolton where Annie had secured a job as a sick visitor. The reference is supportive and gives no hint of any problems with the employee at all. Mr Cooper had not been Secretary to the Poor Law Guardians for 26 years for nothing.

But by then Mr Cooper's time was coming to an end, along with the Bolton Union he had run for so long. The 1929 Local Government Act did not abolish the Poor Law but it did get rid of the Poor Law Guardians, transferring their responsibilities to the Local Authority within a new department – the Public

Assistance Committee (PAC). Plans for the new service were put in place including the establishment of a post of hospital almoner at Townleys. Bolton was one of several PACs to create such a post – the first in public as opposed to voluntary hospitals. By chance we know who was appointed as almoner. It was Alice Kearsley – aged 56 by then, the appointment being one of Mr Cooper's last acts as secretary to the old union before he retired. We can surmise that, despite his previous doubts about and disagreements with Alice, he plumped for a safe pair of hands rather than risking another 'new broom' or inexperienced 'fly-by-night'.

Relieving Officers and the Depression

As we have seen, the dole for unemployment, sickness benefit and old age pensions reduced the work of ROs in the 1920s. But the unemployed only received money for a limited period before it stopped. Through the 1920s unemployment increased and then exploded in 1930. In some places the levels of unemployment were grotesque – over 30 per cent on occasion in Manchester; up to 40 per cent in Bolton and touching 20 per cent nationally. The National Government, committed to sound money principles, reduced public expenditure and cut unemployment pay by 10 per cent. In August 1931 Transitional Benefit was introduced, a benefit for the unemployed based on need and not on contributions made. It became available once the six months' unemployment pay had run its course. Applications for Transitional Benefit were judged using a test of means which required all goods, spare clothes, heirlooms and even lino to be sold before benefit was offered. PACs were asked to assess applicants' eligibility for Transitional Benefit and ROs did the assessments. This Transitional Benefit immediately became a political battleground with some Local Authorities following these crushing principles to the letter, others openly defying them – West Ham and Chester-le-Street for instance. There is evidence that some ROs were sympathetic. One unnamed RO from St Helens said *'a lot of houses were beautifully kept. The people were proud of their cottage property. None of my brother officers would urge them to sell anything. I used to say, "keep your little home together", and they did'* (Forman 1979: 165). Ministry Inspectors made it plain these practices were not to be tolerated. The York Public Assistance Committee on 14 April 1932 was admonished by a Ministry of Health Inspector, Mr Hughes-Gibb, who suggested that applicants for Transitional Benefit should be dealt with in the same way that able-bodied applicants for public assistance were dealt with, because he was of the opinion that the committee were being too generous with the unemployed (York City Council 1932).

Yet the majority of work done by ROs was still with the old, chronically sick and the crippled. Four accounts from ROs who worked in the twenties and thirties shed light on their attitudes and how they operated. The RO from St Helens said:

> It was a job I thoroughly enjoyed. A relieving officer had to take people who
> … were considered a danger to the public, to Rainhill Asylum. That wasn't

funny, believe me: I've had some free fights. People with nervous breakdowns, schizophrenia, religious mania … they used to visit me afterwards quite alright (Forman 1979: 164).

He enjoyed the regular payment visits, saying:

> … that's the thing they looked forward to, the visiting. We became friends. When I went round, they treated me as judge, jury and someone to talk to and ask for advice. I'd keep off legal or medical advice, although people used to bring their sick children to me. You solved everyone's problem, wayward daughters, wayward sons, people who owed four weeks rent and feared the landlord would turn them out (Forman 1979: 164).

Walter Watkinson's account of his work as an RO in Holderness, East Yorkshire, is uniformly positive about the job. He worked as an RO between 1908 and 1948 and, writing in 1955, was not impressed with what had replaced the RO role. He had seen his weekly visits to old people and '*those laid low by sickness*' replaced by a system he felt '*too logical and rigid to work well in this country*'. His fear was that '*the service that has displaced the Poor Law will look upon [people] as cases which come under some rule or regulation*' and suggested that:

> people are not just units requiring so much cash each day to maintain them in health and happiness (Watkinson: 1955: 37).

> They need something else. A person to confide in, who knows at least part of their family history. I cannot help but think that the weekly visits of the RO meant quite a lot to [people] (Watkinson 1955: 1).

Working in a country area Mr Watkinson claimed '*everyone knew the RO and where to find him. He was always available to turn to in trouble or difficulty*'. He also says that '*even six years after retirement I still receive letters from people asking for me to call*' (Watkinson 1955: 1).

Over and above the visiting to check applications for relief and payment visits, he:

- made wills and acted as executor
- advised on family quarrels
- tried to bring peace to broken homes
- supplied much that was needed: money, spectacles, teeth.

Mr Watkinson operated within a skein of voluntary support, with him backing up the relative, the neighbour and the parson, who he suggested visited all the poor. And of course Mr Watkinson had to remove people to the Institution. Even this he expressed in positive terms, as the older people concerned could no longer '*do for themselves*' and were often living with son or daughter with a young family and '*all were at breaking point*' (Watkinson 1955: 18).

Mr Watkinson had mixed views about boarding-out infant children in private homes. He said he had known both good foster parents and bad, suggesting it was not unknown for a little girl to be taken into a private home with a view to her becoming a domestic servant. Mr Watkinson seemed particularly irritated by foster parents who used him as a '*bogeyman to frighten the youngster*' (Watkinson 1955: 21), with many foster parents thinking the RO's job was to make sure the child was behaving properly rather than looking out for its wellbeing. He also felt that many foster parents did not let the children forget the fact that they were boarders. Mr Watkinson himself thought children needed companionship, routines, security and adults living with them who knew how they ticked. Most of all they needed to feel they belonged. He thought good institutions by and large were better able to do that than foster homes, although he much preferred certain voluntary homes to others. He tells a harrowing tale to illustrate this point. The daughter of a Church of England couple lost her father. Her mother remarried a Catholic man who demanded she and her daughter convert. Subsequently the mother died and the girl, uncared for in the step-father's home, ran wild. She was sent to an aunt in Holderness who, unable to cope with her, wanted to place her in an Anglican home but the local vicar refused because the girl was a Catholic. The aunt turned to Mr Watkinson for help and she was placed in a non-denominational voluntary home. He says that four years later she had become a mature, radiant young woman.

But Mr Watkinson was at sea when it came to girls who had fallen pregnant. Even though he was involved in finding mother and baby homes for some of them he did not know what advice to give them. On the other hand he was confident that families of mental defectives, of which he thought there were probably one or two in each village, showed them huge love and affection. He tells of visiting and supporting people looking after mental defectives well into their old age.

Walter Watkinson was, it seems, the only RO on his patch and he covered the full range of work, unlike in towns where there were specialists. He may well appear fleetingly in Winifred Holtby's novel *South Riding* (1936). The action takes place in a barely disguised Holderness and the author shadowed her alderman mother in her research and attended PAC meetings. In *South Riding's* PAC meeting, the RO presenting cases is described as '*a thin, decent red headed man*' (Holtby 1936: 294).

Twenty-five miles from Mr Watkinson, in Howden in 1930, Ken Powls was taken on as an RO's Assistant at the age of 16 – a job he thinks he got because his brother-in-law was an RO (Powls 2010). After six months his brother-in-law fell ill and at 17 Ken was asked to take over the full duties. These consisted of paying out-relief to old people and the sick in the surrounding villages, much like Mr Watkinson. He also occasionally transported women in the advanced stages of labour to the workhouse infirmary in taxis and on one occasion Ken had to carry out an order of the Medical Officer of Health to forcibly remove a man who had taken to his bed in unsanitary conditions. The man did not struggle but had to be carried down a winding staircase. Ken dropped him, the man breaking his leg. In those days Ken was expected to carry out all these activities on his own.

Like the RO in St Helens and Mr Watkinson, Ken was involved in the assessment of assets of those men whose unemployment benefit had run out. They had to produce a case history to present to what Ken called the Guardian's Committee. Although he accepted this to be demeaning for the families concerned, his sympathies lay more with those casual farm labourers and domestic servants, both still excluded from unemployment benefits. Finally Ken was asked to find work and accommodation for the boys in public care who had reached school leaving age. He felt unsuited to this work because he hated begging favours and admits that often he just put boys out to farms. He pulled out all the stops for one boy though, who asked if he could be apprenticed to Mr Thompson of Coxwold, the furniture maker known as the Mouseman. Thompson asked for a hefty premium for apprentices, and took on few. Ken however negotiated with Thompson and the PAC, both having to give way quite a bit. Another odd placement was arranged with the Duchess of Devonshire who agreed to take on a boy who expressed a wish to become a butler. He started in the kitchen at Beningborough Hall near York, but soon blotted his copybook by telephoning a Rolls Royce dealer asking for a car to be sent round for a test drive to the very plausible-sounding address. He was later sent packing after attacking the butler.

Cyril Bustin

The territory covered by Assistant RO Cyril Bustin, Bermondsey and other poor areas of London, could not be more different from rural Yorkshire but the work done was similar. His account *From Silver Watch to Lovely Black Eye* would defy publication because of the idiosyncratic typing and the style of expression, and yet the story told has a clarity and candour like few others (Bustin 1981).

Cyril Bustin was an evangelical Christian. His mother, Annie Ryall, and her husband William Bustin ran the Bermondsey Gospel Mission from 1891 to 1946 and Cyril followed in their footsteps thereafter. But from 1927 he worked as an Assistant RO. He did a lot of work with lunatics (from 1930 referred to as mental cases) and most of the rest of his work was visiting old people and the chronically sick who often lived in wretched conditions. Mr Bustin regularly makes mention of his reluctance to enter infested houses which again were common. Of course the dangers of infection were real, Mr Bustin reporting that he and colleagues had regular checks for TB right up until 1960. On one occasion, his whole family came down with dysentery, caught from cow dung floating in a bottle of milk – the cow being in the back yard of the retail dairy in Bermondsey. This wariness about infection was common to all social workers in the 1920s and 1930s, one of the London Care Committee volunteers commenting: '*We used to take paper lavatory seats – you could buy a packet at the chemist – and we'd take Keating's Powder because we were always afraid of getting fleas*' (Willmott, 2004: 102).

The constant theme that comes from Mr Bustin's account is the terrible despair he encounters – people lacking all spirit and capacity or maddened by disease and poverty. Nevertheless he offers comfort and, as often as will be accepted, offers spiritual support too – Jesus Christ being his constant companion. One of the women he had to support had lupus. She lived on the fourth floor of a tenement and could hardly get out. On his weekly visits Mr Bustin often heard her in conversation before he entered, but on entry found her alone in her single room. He arranged for a doctor to visit as she deteriorated. That visit gave him the opportunity to investigate the only furniture in the room beside the bed – three chests. The phantom conversation was explained by the existence – in one of the chests – of the desiccated skeletal remains of the woman's illegitimate child with whom she talked to comfort herself. But most of his work was with mental cases. There was a call one day from a ship in the Thames, when the captain reported that a foreign sailor had gone mad. Mr Bustin had to commandeer a rowing boat and, on seeing the state of the deranged sailor, cunningly pointed out that the ship was closer to the north bank of the Thames than the south, therefore technically not in Bermondsey. The captain weighed anchor and manoeuvred the ship across to the south side of the river so Mr Bustin had to take action, manhandling the poor man to the shore. But some removals he questioned:

> ... a doctor's certificate was not to be accepted of itself but for the relieving officer to make the decision ... that such a person SHALL make a personal visit before ordering the ambulance for removal. The day it occurred a young man came rushing in with a medical certificate stating the person to whom it referred was mental. Going to the telephone lifting the receiver [to call the ambulance] I remembered the word 'SHALL' replacing the receiver did the right thing with the following result. Walking ... to a large house in nearby street I learned it was his sister who had locked herself in the toilet threatening suicide. On arrival the place referred to was empty I was then taken to upstairs bedroom and resting quietly in bed was the sister (Bustin 1982: 13).

There were signs of things having been thrown around and Mr Bustin proceeded to talk to the young woman, having asked the young man to go outside. He found that the brother

> had recently been discharged from the army and found his sister had had illegitimate child was without employment and unable to get the dole owing to lack of stamps and he did not see why she should be eating food provided by him and wanted her out of the house. Asking if she would like to go away for a few days (my having in mind the doctors opinion) the doctor recommends it, what doctor? I haven't seen one (Bustin 1982: 13).

Mr Bustin returned to his office and rang the doctor to ask why he had signed a certificate without having seen the woman, commenting that had he seen her and would not have agreed to her removal. The doctor, deeply embarrassed, visited straightaway, said he had been too busy to get out to see her and signed thoughtlessly. The doctor offered to pay for the missing stamps so the young woman could get some money, and accepted the idea of Mr Bustin's (who refused to tear up the original medical certificate, for fear of being caught out himself) to write out another certificate countermanding the first one, as if he had made a second visit and found the situation changed.

Mr Bustin thought many removals were unnecessary as:

> men were being taken as insane when … it was no more than mental depression being the result of failing to find work I watched men walking along the street muttering to themselves my strong objection being that once removed if only for a short time it brought a taint on the family in so far that a member of the family in future years applied for a job and given a form to fill in it could well ask the question 'has there been any mental illness in the family?' and lose the job (Bustin 1982: 12).

He felt so strongly about this he sought out the local MP and proposed that men getting so distressed could be offered a weekly stay at an occupational centre, but still paid their dole. Nothing came of it.

There is a humour and pathos in Cyril Bustin's idiosyncratic account, real passion to help the people in his charge and fierce love of the Lord. But what is most striking is the eye-watering level of squalor, the slightness of the formal response offered by the PAC and the level of responsibility carried by this assistant, the lowest of the low.

One Almoner, Two Probation Officers and a District Visitor

Close by to one of Cyril Bustin's pre-war stamping grounds, Paddington, lies St Mary's Hospital where Dorothy Manchee worked as a hospital almoner. Her account is told in the form of a novel – the tale of Ann Clavering, an almoner on the point of retirement (1946). The pattern of the days she describes is unpredictable, with doctors dropping in every now and then to ask for help and a constant stream of patients seeking advice about all sorts of things. Dorothy Manchee's approach in the novel is to convey the emotional content of the work rather than outline exactly how almoners spent their time, so discussions with colleagues, students and doctors and her own reflections loom large in the narrative.

> Being an Almoner … is rather like being a universal aunt. Everyone in the hospital and many outside come with their troubles and problems for us to help solve. We find homes for babies and jobs for cripples; extra food for the hungry and extra money for the needy; glasses for those who can't see and wheel chairs

for those who can't walk. The man in the street usually thinks we collect money
for the hospital and that's about the only job we don't do (Manchee 1946: 8).

That job was done by a special payments office. There was a lot of practical
work involved. Convalescent stays were arranged, confinement beds booked, the
bereaved counselled and encouraged, and the about-to-be-bereaved prepared.
Some post-discharge care was arranged and dentures, sticks and other invalid
equipment procured. And some of the work appears to have been simple kindness.
In the 1930s hospital stays could run into months – even admissions for births led
to stays of around a fortnight. So:

> Sometimes … Almoners planned a visitor for a lonely patient who was long in
> hospital, by asking some kind friend to call in out-door clothes with a gift and
> time to chat … The incredulous joy that shines in those lacklustre eyes fully
> recompense anyone with the time and thought to do this kindly deed (Manchee
> 1946: 26).

But the work is carried on in a calm spirit and the days wind down predictably.

> Ann Clavering looked round her office to make sure that records were completed
> and papers relating to the morrow were sorted and ready. Filing cabinets … were
> all locked and at last she could turn to the final task of the day – that of refreshing
> the flower bowls and vases so that they might look their best (Manchee 1946:
> 78).

Another specialist branch of social work with a strengthening profile was
probation. The 1925 Criminal Justice Act obliged magistrates' courts to appoint
probation officers, replacing the permissive 1907 Act. But even into the 1930s
many officers were still part timers, offering their missionary services across the
community, not just in court. Mr Burton, Bolton's probation officer missionary
for 34 years retired in 1930, but Jo Harris, the Lowestoft probation officer we met
in Chapter Two carried on until 1934, in much the same vein as before the Great
War. He seems to have been an orderly worker believing that case sheets should
be faithfully kept, not *'verbose or exaggerated, just fact and observation which
diagnoses the case clearly'* (Harris 1937: 31). And he claimed startling success.
Of the 2000 offenders he had on probation in his career, 96 per cent made good.
Mr Harris was also a supporter of keeping statistics to demonstrate the work done.
But he professed a great hatred of *'officialism'*, which he felt should only belong
to forms, records and rules.

> Outside these it should have no place … For this reason I always used my home
> instead of an office, and I always barred official note-paper; and in my opinion
> to drive right up to the door of the home of the offender gives the visit an official

stamp at once … it is quite true to say that what Friendship and Brotherhood cannot bring about, officialism certainly never will (Harris 1937: 31).

This attitude was shared by Mary Ellison, a London probation officer in the 1930s who, like Jo Harris and Mr Burton in Bolton, did not use an office. She tried working in an office once she said, but '*is there anything more cheerless than the sight of a locked office door*'. So she saw people in her home. '*One gets very near to the homeless by opening one's home to them*' (Ellison 1934: xvi).

If her home was often her workplace, Mary Ellison also spent at least two days a week in the police court. As well as picking up people on Probation Orders and interviewing in the cells she was often asked to get involved in matrimonial cases (affiliation and separation payments were both made and collected in court so it was a matrimonial crossroads) and used by magistrates and court staff to look after children and comfort the relatives of those sent down. Equally as often parents would knock at her door seeking help with wayward daughters.

Following the practice of the time her criminal caseload was entirely female and included prostitutes, female tramps and first offenders. One of these was a young Scot, Jane, prosecuted for stealing. Mary Ellison was asked to speak to her in the cells. There being no work in Scotland Jane had found a position as a maid in London. She was prosecuted for taking money and a silk scarf from her employer. Jane explained that her employer had promised her the silk scarf and paid her only fitfully. Mrs Ellison persuaded the magistrates to discharge Jane to her care and introduced her to Daddy Dobbs, who owned a boarding house where he put up young single girls. Mrs Ellison is at pains to explain there was nothing fishy about Daddy, '*he was an elder for some severe chapel*' (Ellison 1934: 10). Mary Ellison and Daddy Dobbs treated Jane to lunch in a restaurant once she had been discharged to Mary Ellison's care. Mary found her a new position and jointly with Dobbs paid her train fare home for Christmas. Mary also rang the employer who was stolen from and tore her off a strip. Jane returned after Christmas to work in London, paid off her debts and was given permission by the magistrates to complete her probation when she wanted to return to Scotland to marry, on condition she wrote to Mary Ellison on a weekly basis.

Mary Ellison's analysis of crime was that bad material circumstances created the conditions for moral lapses. She felt that poverty did not cause prostitution but was more likely attributable to a combination of laziness, mental or moral defect and a broken heart. Whatever the cause she expressed considerable sympathy for those driven to drink or crime. The one class of people she was less sympathetic to were the parents of mental defectives who mistreated them, especially middle class parents who she felt were often cruel.

Mary Ellison does not mention the numbers of people she worked with, but Harold Kersey had a caseload of 70 in Essex in 1939 and 148 matrimonial cases in a year. George Threlfall remembers supervising 60 offenders in one year in Wigan in 1937 and later dealing with 199 matrimonial cases in Old Street Court, London in 1939. He recalls that there were so many men to supervise that he could not talk to men individually. Instead he set up three card tables in the reporting room, on each of which was a pile of forms which the men on probation were expected to complete with basic information about work and earnings.

> He then gave the form to one of the POs who shook him warmly by the hand and said 'How are things going?' On being assured all was well he was told come and see me in a week's time. We had a semi official issue of cigarettes which we handed to the men – and that was the end of reporting (Rimmer 1995: 181).

The motivation for becoming probation officers seems still to have been primarily religious and, until after the war, the working day in some offices started with prayers and the CETS tradition was still strong. Norman Grant, a Congregationalist, complained that even as late as the 1940s non-Anglican probation officers were rare (Rimmer 1995: 179). Kenneth Brill reports that his own motivation in 1936 as not being happy as a council chartered surveyor.

Anglican district visitors (DVs) were still active too; enough operating during the inter-war years to justify the Society for the Promotion of Christian Knowledge (SPCK) publishing a practical guide for visitors in 1935. The author, Helen Cobbold, claimed 30 years' experience as a visitor, working in Stoke for a while, then Worcestershire and latterly in Kentish Town, London (Cobbold 1935). She described the DV as a kind of telephone between the clergy and the people. She seems to have been a practical woman and thought that ordinary common sense was the DV's greatest asset. Her guide gives a clear idea of what the DV should carry: a small despatch case and not a shopping bag, a sharp pencil with India rubber, a fountain pen, blotting paper and notebook, and '*If there is provident club work the appropriate books and cards must be taken; if sick visiting is in view a book of prayers and devotional readings. There may be also grocery or coal tickets, circulars and magazines to deliver, so the case must not be too small*' (Cobbold 1935: 16).

As the DV comes as '*friend to all, not a giver of charity*', the DV '*must not give doles*' Cobbold proclaims (1935:19). She is also clear about records. She used a loose-leaf folder with two pages per year for each family visited and advises that records kept should be sparse: '*never write anything that can cause trouble if the book should fall into the wrong hands*' (Cobbold 1935:19). So her recording of visits was limited to the date and some bland comment, such as '*husband likes gardening, children all confirmed, or wife regular communicant*'. The chief concern of the visitor, each of whose visits she estimated lasting seven minutes, was checking on and encouraging adherence to a religious life. But although she says '*DV work consists of rather humdrum routine*', she reports considerable experience of '*abnormal cases*', by which she means venereal disease, incest, drink and rescue work (Cobbold 1935: 73).

Regarding the latter she refers to categories: '*first cases*' for first pregnancies; '*second cases*' for second pregnancies and so on. She points out that young women on the third of fourth pregnancy will have been feeble-minded or abnormal and should be induced to enter an institution as a permanent inmate (presumably under the auspices of the 1913 Mental Deficiency Act). She points out though that there are also '*hardened*' cases – girls who might sin regularly but do not get pregnant. One of the few cases she mentions seems to have occurred just after the Great War. A married woman whose husband was away, had a baby by a wealthy man. He paid her £25 to have the whole affair hushed up and Helen Cobbold prevailed upon the woman to have the child adopted, to complete a reconciliation with her husband when he returned and to repent her sin. She saw this as a brave success having persuaded the woman to give up her child as its very presence would alienate the husband who himself would never be allowed to forget the child's origins.

Despite the differences in circumstance, aspiration, training and class of the people referred to above there are also striking similarities in the accounts. The primary aim of all of them, clearly expressed in each case, was to help people. The practicalities of the work were very similar and Helen Cobbold's painstaking account of the equipment necessary surely applied to all of them. There is also no reason to believe that the recording of contacts by any of them was much more complete than Helen Cobbold reports.

In each account the informal, personal or opportunistic nature of much of the support given is highlighted and reliance on friends and family members for help is often mentioned. Perhaps most striking is the deep sense of satisfaction felt when some of the people who had been helped kept in touch, offered thanks and praise or, even in Mr Watkinson's case, apologised for a lie long forgotten.

Children Again

The 1937 annual report of the NSPCC in Bolton reads much as it did 30 years before. There was one inspector rather than two, but the work pattern: the initial visit, a warning and the low number of prosecutions was much as it had always been. But support for children had developed since the end of the Great War and the people providing services had changed too. From 1930 Child Life Protection work (the monitoring of private fostering arrangements), became the responsibility of Health Visitors in local authority Public Health departments. The 1933 Children and Young Person's Act, which came about largely as a result of the recommendations of an interdepartmental Young Offender's Committee, included the registration of offenders against children under Schedule One and the establishment of Schools Approved for the Care of Children, replacing Reformatories and Industrial schools. Also, in any hearing regarding children, courts were obliged to '*have regard to the welfare of the child or young person ...*', remove children from undesirable surroundings, '*and for securing that proper provision is made for his education and training*' (Children and Young Person's Act 1933).

Much of this nurturing tone was a consequence of the more child-centred developments in education and psychology referred to earlier. Education committees already had responsibility for mentally defective and crippled children so it made sense, under the legislation, that it was the local education authorities which were required to prepare reports on children brought before the courts and to take responsibility for any subsequent placements with a Fit Person ordered by the court. This legislation had profound consequences for SAOs who, across the land, took on the responsibilities of court work and whose titles changed in many places, including Bolton, to School Attendance and Welfare Officers (SAWO). SAOs had from the beginning been male, many drawn from the same military/ police background as NSPCC inspectors for the same reasons, and they were male up to and through the Second War. But this role gendering was mitigated by the legislators and the 1933 Act required that any child between the age of 14 and 17 detained or waiting in a police station should be in the charge of a woman. The response to the legislation was different in different places. In some areas the NSPCC undertook prosecutions for neglect and prepared papers for 'care and protection' proceedings; in others it was the local authority, but in others it was women police officers (Jackson 2003). In 1937 for instance in London, women police officers instigated 62 proceedings for the care and protection of children and by 1941 that figure had risen to 231. In addition the Metropolitan Police kept indexes of missing girls and other children who had come to the attention of the police for other reasons. In Bolton four women police officers were employed in 1919, one of whom was Ethel Jeeps, who must have been successful in the role as she was made up to sergeant two years later (BHC ABJ 23). Records of the activities of these women are thin, but there are occasional mentions in the local press in the 1930s. A considerable proportion of the work seems to have been much as described above – related to children subject to court proceedings. One such case in 1937 had Ethel receiving an abandoned child who was '*scantily clad with sceptic sores on both his heels*'. She first of all made exhaustive enquiries in search of his mother and then spent an hour disinfesting and washing him, still not being content with the results by the end. The way she describes this suggests she must have committed the best part of a day to this task and was obviously a crucial part of the team working on investigating child neglect (BEN 1937: 3).

Into the Community

At this time police officers were still obliged to live in section houses as were some groups of district nurses; and institutional care for people in need was still at the heart of both state and voluntary responses. We have seen probation successfully persuading magistrates not to imprison first offenders; and between the wars there were two other examples of social workers and voluntary visitors shifting determinedly into the community; moral welfare workers and workers with mental defectives.

One of the oddities of Victorian welfare development was the success of the Church of England Penitentiary movement. Mariquita Tennant's first house set up in 1848 in Clewer near Windsor, for local women caught up in prostitution, became associated with the reviving notion amongst High Anglicans of a religious life. Young Anglican women congregated in convents for the first time since the reformation, and many of these offered refuge for fallen women, penitents, thus the penitentiary movement was born.

Penitentiaries offered asylum to women who were pregnant, women who had been seduced or raped, or were victims of incest. If their circumstances were publicised they had no chance of getting a respectable job and many fell into prostitution. A typical penitentiary offered training in a higher domestic trade, cookery or embroidery, encouraged women to accept the religious teaching on offer and acquiesce in attitudes of modesty and subservience which would help them fit into society. The penitentiaries claimed not to turn anyone away. Of course many women went in for the warmth and respite from a tough life in winter and often there was a stream of people leaving as the weather warmed up in spring. Nevertheless real support was offered and by 1903 over 7,000 young women were being helped in 238 Anglican penitentiaries (Mumm 1996).

The assumption of the penitentiary movement was that only gentlewomen could wield the moral influence necessary to reform fallen women. So middle-class women with a vocation worked with these primarily working class women with the same confusions and consequences suffered by Alice Hodson on her COS beat. One sister admitted that the penitents could be '*disagreeable, uninteresting, evil tempered, low and repulsive*' (Mumm 1996: 533). But for many women the penitentiaries provided the means of escape. There was no bar on leaving, and while manual labour, especially laundering, was a requirement in most, proper training was offered and on completion of their stay penitents were offered a new outfit, positive references and help in finding a position (Mahood 1990).

It was from this tradition that moral welfare work took flight into the community. Concerned about prostitution in Liverpool, the Anglican Bishop, Frank Chavasse, asked Jessie Higson to organise rescue work in the city. Higson had worked in a settlement and had experience running a club for adolescent girls, so took charge of St Monica's refuge and set up training for workers in rescuing prostitutes. The training took three forms: devotional, theoretical and practical. She and her colleague Miss Parker dressed in grey cloaks and bonnets, toured the streets at night looking for young girls who might be saved, putting on midnight hot-pot suppers in an attempt to make friends with them. This approach was immensely controversial and while they were supported by the Union, Walton prison and local taxi drivers, who collected money for them, some local churches refused them entry.

The increase in VD and illegitimate pregnancies in the Great War caused huge concern and the Church of England, in response, appointed a national organiser for moral welfare, Jesse Higson. The primary action she took was to open a residential training school for moral welfare workers, Josephine Butler House. This was where the applicant for the CWV job in Bolton, Patience Baggalley, was training in 1925. At the same time Higson encouraged the appointment of diocesan committees for moral welfare. Moral Welfare Associations sprang up across the country taking on educational and club work with girls, advising pregnant girls and setting up maternity homes. Newark's had been established in 1912, and nearby Retford's in 1914, then Whitby's in 1919, Cornwall's in 1922, Blackburn's in 1926 and so on (Higson 1955). These followed a pattern, being funded by donations as well as the Poor Law Union. Lancaster and Morecambe's Moral Welfare Committee was typical. Set up in 1933 its purpose was to raise funds to support the rescue home known as the House of Help. Committee discussions had a recurring theme; had the girls made good or were they disappointing or worse. The Superintendent, Miss Baines, constantly refuted suggestions that the '*many of the girls helped were incorrigible and made use of the house unjustifiably*'. In 1939 for instance she pointed out that only 22 of the 106 girls admitted were '*readmittances*', and most of those were for illnesses or convalescence. As time went on the committee accepted more outdoor cases (support for young women who did not come into the House of Help), and with the onset of war Miss Baines began to encourage the committee to appoint an outdoor worker (Lancashire Record Office DDX/1952).

The influence of the Josephine Butler training home was considerable. Graduates became secretaries to the Moral Welfare Associations and in the 1930s moral welfare outworkers, one becoming the first social worker in the VD clinic in Guys Hospital, London. I have not been able to find what job Patience Baggalley took immediately after her training, but in 1928 she was appointed to the prestigious position of National Diocesan Organiser for Moral Welfare, working at the heart of the Church of England. She streamlined the relationship between the National Board and Diocesan Boards, against some local opposition and with the support of the Archbishop of Canterbury, she launched the Church of England Board for Moral Welfare Work at a garden party held at Lambeth Palace in 1932 (Higson 1955).

Work with Mental Defectives

Support in the community for the feeble-minded had been proposed in 1908 by the Royal Commission on the Care and Control of the Feeble-Minded. The subsequent Mental Deficiency Act (1913) attempted to categorise people and ensure that those who could not be controlled were kept in hospitals. In part this was a response to the concern about the degeneration of the race proposed by eugenicists, but it also required local authorities to make arrangements for the support of mental defectives at home. The key vehicle for such support was the Central Association for Mental Welfare (CAMW), established in 1913 and pioneered by Dame Evelyn Fox (Overy 2009). Although there was local variation one pattern was that a Local Association appointed an enquiry officer who recruited volunteer visitors and coordinated their visiting schedule – another example of public service relying on voluntary effort to fulfil statutory duties. One example of how support developed was a COS mental deficiency sub-committee of the Cambridge COS branch. This dissociated itself from the COS and in 1920 the Cambridgeshire Voluntary

Association for the Care of the Mentally Defective was set up. By 1925 the Association had two Enquiry Officers and their work included organising parties, days out, Wolf Cub and Brownie packs and an after care service for ex patients of the Fulborn Hospital. When the Mental Deficiency Act of 1927 came into force, the County Council asked the Association to draw up a scheme for an Occupation Centre for defectives, which it did, and a centre opened in October 1929 (Mind, CamMind 2011).

In Accrington, 12 miles north of Bolton, a branch of the Central Lancashire Association for Mental Welfare was active. A single surviving record about a ten-year-old girl, Amy P, shows the work of the visitors. Amy, born in 1927, was admitted to an occupation centre in 1936. Every six months her home was visited by a volunteer called Mary Hanson. The visitor completed a proforma about each visit, commenting on the defective's language, physical control, personal habits, social attitudes and other attainments. Amy at first was regarded as '*talking incessantly but nonsensically ... very mercurial, never still and lacks control*'. No comment was required about the home situation or her parents. The following entry states that Amy was a '*likable child, with possibilities, already gaining control*'. She had made a doll's scarf and a small mat, '*likes manual work and has learned to wash up*'. This focus was to judge Amy's fitness for work, she being noted as '*the most able*' of the children at the centre. She continued to do well and left the centre in 1941, at the normal school leaving age 14, '*to work in a chip shop as a washer up and potato peeler*' (Shorrock 2010).

A Slow but Discernable Change

Before we consider the changes wrought by Second World War it is worth marking a couple of other emerging themes. Clement Attlee had demanded in 1920 that the social worker rid himself of the idea of his superiority (Attlee 1920: 129) and this appeared to be happening. Timms noted in his 1961 review of COS case records between 1877 and 1937, '*a ... discernable change after 1920 ... an increasing helpfulness to applicants and a growing flexibility of method*' (Timms 1961: 10). While supporting Rooff's observation that COS activity with the poor contracted towards the procurement of surgical appliances, clothing and bedding, he concludes that by 1937 the records indicate '*caseworkers become less God-like*' (Timms 1961: 10). Sybil Clement Brown in a review of COS records in a ten-year period between the wars reached a similar conclusion (Walton 1975). Others also suggested that in the late 1930s judgements of a person by social workers were less likely to be from a morally superior perspective (Burt 2008).

At the same time as the elite groups, almoners, PSWs and probation officers, had identified firm boundaries for their occupations, there was a growing recognition that they were also part of a broader group: social workers. At the end of 1935, and after considerable discussion, a set of occupational groups came together to form the British Federation of Social Workers (BFSW). Workers represented included the associations of care committee organisers, moral welfare workers, health visitors, PSWs, ROs, probation officers and tuberculosis visitors among others (Burt 2008). So a broad idea of social work and social workers was coalescing just as a new war loomed.

Chapter 5

1939–1948: The Impact of the Second World War

Preparations and Evacuations

The preparations made for the conflict with Nazi Germany belie the 'make do and mend' myth about British preparedness (Edgerton 2011). Britain was the first combatant nation to be put on a total war footing and some of the social aspects of planning for the war were profound and long lasting. In 1939 all hospitals, voluntary and PAC, were subject to central control for the first time. Unemployment, sick pay and PAC relief arrangements were amalgamated in the Assistance Board, a test bed for the post-war National Assistance Board. District Nursing arrangements were centrally funded and directed and mental health services were unified under national direction (Titmuss 1950).

All this was necessary as the war caused unprecedented disruption to society and family life. Nearly five million men and women joined the armed forces; another four million worked in war industry; millions more joined the Local Defence Volunteers, Women's Voluntary Service (WVS), Air Raid Precautions or the Observer Corps. Tens of thousands of displaced persons from across Europe arrived in the first year of the war, then millions of Commonwealth and American servicemen. Schools moved, were closed or seriously depleted of teachers. Thousands of sick or disabled people were summarily discharged from hospitals or institutions and thousands of buildings were commandeered by local authorities or the armed forces (Titmuss 1950). A key feature of the disruption was the evacuation of millions of children from cities thought likely targets of bombers (Brown 2000). There were three great waves of evacuation nationally; September 1939 as the war began; the summer and autumn of 1940, when invasion was threatened and cities bombed; and the summer of 1944 when London and the south east was bombarded by V1 missiles. But arrivals and returns were constant and managing the transport, billeting and payments, let alone any emotional problems, was a serious and continuous undertaking. In rural areas few children could be accommodated and PAC workers, such as RO Watkinson in Holderness, had an important role in settling evacuees. He says the evacuees, mostly from Leeds, were almost without exception ill-mannered, dirty, verminous and badly behaved. But he also reports that his previous suspicions of foster parents were heartily confirmed by the number of people taking evacuees who were more interested in money and domestic service than the children (Watkinson 1955).

But in urban reception areas, towns with no war industry but plenty of accommodation, the evacuation administration was more complex. One reception area was Cambridge, where a comprehensive view of the role of volunteers and social workers was recorded in the Cambridge Evacuation Survey of 1939/1940 (Isaacs 1941). Each of the 13 political wards in the town had a Ward Billeting Officer, all of them head teachers. Each of these was allocated a Senior Voluntary Worker (SVW) by the Women's Voluntary Service (WVS) centre leader. They were to '*promote the general welfare of the evacuees and to help the householder in what must inevitably be a difficult situation*' (Isaacs 1940: 32). These were selected because of their experience in social work and were to be responsible for finding a Friendly Visitor for each evacuee or family. There were between 12 and 36 Friendly Visitors in each ward. Some of these had care committee work or other visiting experience, but in some areas visitors were taken from where they could be found. Ted Perry's mother, from Worthing in Sussex, was recruited like this:

> My mother was a lone parent with four children, my dad having died. When [we were evacuated to Mansfield], parents were granted two train tickets a year to visit their children. When Mum went to Worthing Town Hall to collect hers, they offered her a job working as a Welfare Officer in Mansfield ... being desperate for the money, she accepted the job ... In Mansfield Mum worked from the Billeting Office [which was] staffed by two full time administrators, Mrs Neale and Mrs Halfnight. Her role was to visit the host families to all the Worthing evacuees and check for any problems ... [and] ensure that medical needs were attended to. When relationships between host and child broke down, she would have to sort out a new placement (Perry 2011).

The system in Cambridge was fully tested when over 6,000 evacuees arrived in the first wave in September 1939, though so many returned that by November only 3,650 remained. Without clerical help the SVWs were besieged by complaints both from and about evacuee families, key concerns being loneliness, mismatched placements, class conflicts and, just like in the Great War, endless queries about money. Visiting schedules broke down and some families were forgotten while others were visited by more than one FV. Five London Care Committee Organisers, all trained social workers, were brought in to help but had to refer to the locally knowledgeable SVW all the time, so merely duplicated the work.

Early on it was recognised that emergency accommodation was needed for children whose circumstances or behaviour defeated the billeting officers, and in February 1940 in Cambridge the Ministry of Health sanctioned the use of the youth hostel as an emergency hostel for 25 children.

The same difficulties; the returns, the worries about children's health and behaviour were replicated all over the United Kingdom. As a result Geraldine Aves, by then a senior figure in the London Care Committee system, was seconded to the Ministry of Health as Chief Welfare Officer with responsibility for liaising between local evacuation welfare arrangements and the centre. She appointed

Regional Welfare Officers (RWOs) to support the work. By the end of the war she had 27 RWOs, one of whom was Lucy Faithfull who was sent to the East Midlands where she witnessed Britain's Two Nations colliding. Working class children, new to the countryside, asked innocently about the horses with handlebars, and middle-class women bemoaned the evacuee children damaging furniture in private houses. Lucy reports on children from Manchester:

> … they were enchanting but their habits were appalling … doing their jobbies on the floor of sitting rooms … The Dowager Duchess of Devonshire mustered … her friends from the country houses, the billeting officers got the foster parents and the town hall was full. The Duchess, in the chair … said 'Miss Faithfull, we want the Government to know that we think these children should be kept in camps'. I said … 'I want to ask you one question: if we put all the children … together and it was bombed and all the children were killed, would you really feel happy?' There was a silence and finally one woman got up and said, 'I can't possibly face such a situation. I'll take children' (Niechcial 2010: 32).

Although the work involved liaison, spreading knowledge of good standards and recruiting welfare staff, there were plenty of individual needs to be dealt with too. When she moved to the West Country Lucy was introduced to an old lady who was filthy and claimed never to have had a bath. She had been billeted in a prestigious hotel, which wanted her custom about as much as she wanted to suffer the indignity of a bath. Careful negotiation by Lucy led to the old lady acceding to an all over wash and the hotel accepted her. Removing her wig, she washed that too and hung it out to dry on the balcony. Predictably this was born off by an intrigued seagull, and the old lady's screams were only quelled by Lucy lending the lady her own hat and then paying for a new wig.

Bolton was an evacuee reception area, it being anticipated correctly that textile mills would not attract much Luftwaffe attention. Records indicate that 9,000 evacuees and refugees came to Bolton between 1939 and 1945, but there is no mention of social workers until late in the war. In July 1944 during the V1 attacks on London 3,526 new arrivals were received in Bolton, the majority of them unaccompanied children. A welfare officer was sought immediately to work with the children, but it was October before Mrs L.O. Green, under the Education Department, took up post (BHC AB/36/1/[1]).

The Response to the Bombing

On Saturday 6 September 1940 the East End of London was bombed for nearly 12 hours. This was followed by an eight month bombing campaign targeting London and nearly all of Britain's industrial centres. Careful preparation for death and injury had been made; a million cardboard coffins were ordered and nearly half the beds in London's hospitals cleared. But little thought had been given to the plight of shocked, scared, penniless people bombed out of their homes. The original rest centres were mostly schools and were thinly manned by PAC employees, had minimal bathing facilities to clean up dust-covered survivors, too few toilets for the hundreds of people forced to sleep there and inadequate kitchens. No insurance arrangements had been made for bomb damage, no alternative housing arranged and no supplies of furniture or clothing stockpiled (Titmuss 1950). And the PAC staff in the rest centres failed the people miserably. This was for a number of reasons. First of all ROs were expected to operate rest centres in addition to their normal work. Moreover the whole tradition of the PACs had been to operate a careful decision making process with parsimony as one of the main ends. As Titmuss comments: '*The treatment of local government, in the interwar period ... the curbing of progressive ideas and the pruning of local expenditure left a legacy which could not be quickly dispelled ...*' (Titmuss 1950: 252). At first PAC staff followed normal practice, which led in the early days of the Blitz to people turning up at rest centres terrified, disoriented and bedraggled being asked for all their details in case reimbursement from another borough had to be sought for helping them. And of course no one had told the ROs that they were allowed to use their initiative or imagination, so they didn't. Rita Tuffin, training at the time as an almoner, worked for the PAC in Paddington and remembers seeing people '*herded into the Relief Hall, queuing for their allowances after appearing before a committee to plead their needs, and suffering visits from the RO who had power to inspect the larder before reporting whether money or feed tickets were necessary*' (Rimmer 1995: 179).

In the middle of September, the situation chaotic, John Anderson, the Home Secretary, offered complete reimbursement for feeding, clothing, housing and resettling the homeless. Freed from financial worries LCC overrode local PAC arrangements, recruited hundreds of volunteers and placed young people in charge of rest centres (many of them teachers), set up a proper shift system and invited Citizen's Advice Bureau (CAB) volunteers in to give advice and WVS workers to sort out furniture and clothing needs.

In October Herbert Morrison, Minister of Home Security, appointed a Special Commissioner for the Homeless in London. Henry Willink acted swiftly, bringing in the WVS to manage clothing and furniture stores, the Assistance Board to advise about pensions and local authorities to supply accommodation. He divided London into four administrative areas, destroying at a stroke any boundary disputes and he appointed four welfare inspectors, one for each administrative area. Their task was to patrol the rest centres reporting back any emerging problems and to coordinate help and support and rehousing.

The Voluntary Response

The COS, WVS, care committee volunteers, settlement workers and many others swung into action behind Willink. In October 1941 it is estimated that 200,000 women were working for at least part of their time, for free, in rest centres (Titmuss 1950). And tiny voluntary organisations, which might employ one welfare worker, aligned their activities with the war effort too. Vere Hodgson, a social worker with Winifred Moyes' Christian Spiritualist Greater World Association in Notting Hill Gate, London, distributed supplies coming from North America. She took applications for whatever was available from local people, deciding who should receive what and then parceling up and delivering whatever the items there were. She supported a local constituency of regulars, poor people who lived within a couple of hundred yards of her centre (Hodgson 1971).

More significant contributions were made by two new, nationwide, government funded, voluntary organisations, one of which was the CAB. A national information service was proposed by the National Council for Social Service in 1938 to counter the anticipated social disruption in cities in wartime. Preparations were made and at the advent of war 200 bureaux opened. They dealt with problems arising from the bureaucracy of wartime; loss of ration books, homelessness, missing relatives, problems for people evacuated and latterly chased information about missing service personnel and prisoners of war. But again the majority of people coming to them faced money problems. Many of the first CABx were run by people of standing in the community, bank managers, for example. This high status was diluted over the next couple of years, as the number of CABx increased to 1,000 by 1942 and some CABx were run by trained social workers, Eileen Younghusband being one of them.

But of all the voluntary groups which contributed to the war effort none was more to the fore than the WVS. Home Secretary, Sir Samuel Hoare, broadcast an appeal for volunteers to help with civil defence in March 1938. As many volunteers were women he decided to set up a women-only branch of Air Raid Precautions. He asked Stella, dowager Marchioness of Reading, to lead a new organisation. With experience helping unemployed people she briskly organised a network of local groups, entirely government funded. First of all volunteers were trained in first aid, fire watching and fire fighting. But as the war approached and the scale of the proposed evacuation became clear, when the order was given on 1 September 120,000 WVS volunteers were alerted to help and were used in a variety of ways – escorting evacuees, surveying towns for potential billets, meeting evacuees and providing food and clothing for them.

The WVS was engaged in providing tea and food for troop trains, offering clothes and food for those bombed out and settling into new homes, providing lunchtime pies for farm workers and supporting and befriending isolated Land Girls. Through the war a million women brought their brave enthusiasm to the WVS. Bolton WVS alone attracted 2,000 women volunteers, and had the good fortune to obtain as a base a large former convalescent home, Watermillock – two miles north of Bolton. The centre, under the leadership of Mrs Clara Kay soon had a clothing store, rest centres for munitions workers, a club for Land Army girls – often isolated and out of place on surrounding farms. But the work that most of the Bolton volunteers were engaged in during the war was the rolling evacuation crisis (Cox 2003).

If the CABx and WVS were examples of enormous state funded welfare organisations which relied on volunteers to function, the Pacifist Service Units (PSUs) – later Family Service Units (FSUs) – were tiny, marginal initiatives, which required little funding, whose philosophy and practice had huge influence on post-war social workers. Only 42 people worked full time in the PSUs between 1942 and 1945 in Liverpool, Manchester and then Stepney, although there were also part time volunteers (Stephens 1945). PSUs were set up as opportunities for conscientious objectors to contribute to society without engaging directly in war work. They were based in blitzed areas and contributed what they could: cleared up the mess, helped in rest centres, carted goods around, rehoused people. Gwen Hall from Wrexham had heard about the PSU in Liverpool and volunteered to help at weekends (Hall 2004). In 1941 the PSU in Liverpool consisted of four young men, all pacifists, who worked there full time for half a crown a week and their board. During the day PSU volunteers helped people shift their belongings in handcarts from bombed out homes. The evening included cocoa and first aid rounds to shelters, where the volunteers got to know many needy people. Gwen describes working with a lady who was deaf and nearly blind, who lived in one room at the top of an old tenement, with a single shared cold tap and a shared toilet. She had to cart coal up two flights of stairs to an open fire, which provided heat and the only means of cooking. The council wanted to demolish the building and Gwen, having established a means of communicating with the lady, offered to help her move and find some clothing for her from the clothing store (Hall 2004). During the following week a PSU worker visited the housing department and a room was found in a new house, the removal effected and bedding and furniture found for the room. This simple but often emotionally charged work was at the heart, in the first couple of years, of what the PSUs did.

The need was still there after the bombing scaled down from May 1941, so PSUs continued. During this period it became clear that some families were difficult to rehouse; people often with limited parenting skills and large numbers of ill-fed, grubby, unruly children. These families were frequently known to Health Visitors, ROs, the police and many had significant debts. The term 'Problem Families' began to be used to describe them, being first used in the influential review of urban life amongst the poor *Our Towns* in 1944 (Women's Group on Public Welfare). In an imaginative move the PSU in Liverpool made an arrangement with the housing authorities, whereby their workers would offer support to such families after rehousing. The PSU in Liverpool started out tentatively, as Tom Stephens explains:

> Conscious of their inexperience, they began by offering the humblest services and attempting to find a sound basis for their relationship to the families they met. Cleaning, decorating, removing, repairing and disinfesting were the first forms of service, and on this basis the rest was built. Friendship was made the

foundation of the work: a friendship without condescension or professional aloofness; not forced or superficial, but a relationship of mutual trust and respect as between equals (Stephens 1945: 46).

The PSUs did not approach families themselves but had families referred to them by local welfare agencies and their offer of help could be turned down. Having said that they tried not to give up on people. They became known for getting their hands dirty and willingness to do that was a key selling point to the families concerned. In a sense this sort of approach was inevitable because however strange this might have sounded to pre-war social workers in the chaos of the Blitz few welfare workers had much choice but to get stuck in. But other innovations may not have been triggered by immediate circumstances. The PSU workers made a point of being available 24 hours a day, encouraged families to call them by their Christian names, and invited the families to meals at the PSU living quarters. While working closely with other agencies, offering in many cases for the first time a coordinating role between four or five workers visiting these families, PSUs claimed not to take state-sanctioned action other than to protect children. Stephens says that the workers tried not to become sentimental, but argued that erring on the side of humanity was the wiser course. But he added *'when a mass of practical experience and some theoretical training had been acquired, a professional attitude and high standard of efficiency took their place beside the human motive of friendship'* (Stephens 1945: 46).

The book *Problem Families* (1945) gives a number of examples of work done with families living in appalling conditions where there was no furniture, no bedding and ill-fed and infested children; where beating and abuse were commonplace. The PSU workers cleaned places up, got debts paid off, acquired furniture, took children to school, arbitrated between mum and dad – visited four and five times a week. Some families started to cope with life, children were better clothed and went to school more often. But others carried on much as they were.

Unlike those young Edwardians who joined settlements in which experienced support was on hand (and servants), PSU workers were literally making it up as they went along. Of necessity they developed a pattern for their work very quickly. All the volunteers lived in a large house in the district where they worked, owned or requisitioned by the local authority. In Liverpool there were up to ten workers, in Manchester eight. Later in FSUs there was a housekeeper but each volunteer nevertheless contributed to the domestic work in the house. Each group had a unit leader and a secretary. The leader would usually make the first visit to a family and then allocate the work to a volunteer. Each volunteer had a conference with the leader every week and participated in the weekly unit casework meeting, where new cases were reviewed and policies discussed. The unit leader liaised with other agencies and organised lectures for the volunteers on things like public assistance, moral welfare, probation and so on. And the volunteers from all three units got together two or three times a year to discuss their work.

PSU workers came from a range of backgrounds, some sharing a religious commitment, but by no means all. They were all young though: the age range of the whole contingent of the PSUs between 1942 and 1945 was between 23 and 34 – leaders as well. If it was a young idea, it was also largely a male idea. Of the 42 volunteers who contributed to the three units between 1942 and 1945 only ten were women, and men were the leaders. But the volunteers had something very significant in common with the families they worked with – they were outside society's mainstream. Of the 42 workers nine were prosecuted during the war for refusing direction for work by the Ministry of Labour and five served prison sentences. These were people following their own consciences, pioneers trying to make something better out of the chaos and destruction of the old blitzed and squalid world. And by 1945 on the slim evidence of work with only 62 families the PSUs caught the imagination of social reformers such as Seebohm Rowntree and housing reformer Irene Barclay. The PSU work faltered with the end of the war, but gained funding in 1948 to relaunch under the new title of Family Service Unit (Eisenstadt 1998).

Always Look Bravely at the Dead

As the war went on and illegitimacy and VD infections increased the Ministry of Health actively urged hospitals to employ almoners. A contact tracing service was established for women thought to be spreading infection. Contact tracing was conducted by almoners and although the spread of such specialist almoners was slow at first, most areas had appointed one eventually, including the almoner for VD appointed in Bolton in 1944 (BHC ABCF/17/39).

But it was the bombing that gave almoners in cities most work. They were involved in supporting those arriving at hospitals shaken but otherwise uninjured, finding places to stay for the walking wounded who had been bombed out, finding clothes and domestic equipment for those being discharged to nothing, arranging transport, searching for relatives, comforting the injured, the bereaved, their relatives and staff.

Dorothy Manchee mentions a particularly grizzly task which almoners were asked to undertake:

> Always look bravely at the dead, however badly they are hurt … we can so often save a parent or … wife from a distressing round of mortuaries in the effort to trace missing relatives. If we can put on police forms, things like distinguishing marks, descriptions of jewellery or clothes, it often gives someone a key to identity at once (Manchee 1942).

But traditional work continued too. Kathleen Bartlett reports her work was '*checking the financial position of patients; raising money for appliances and transport; and placing deserted and neglected children*'. Rita Tuffin did the same but remembers this being '*the introduction to social work as the information could be used as the basis for assessing need*' (Rimmer 1995: 180). Barbara Totton, who started as an almoner at 21 just as the war ended, reports that a significant part of her work was assessing the patient's financial situation and telling them how much they would have to pay. On occasion she says, a consultant, concerned about the voluntary hospital's income, would summon her and say '*I know this family, and you haven't charged them anything like enough. What the consultant said went*'. Fortunately, says Barbara, about the first hospital she worked in, the head almoner had married a consultant, which gave her some sway (Totton 2011).

Nora Cooper was also young when she trained. Born in 1925 and brought up on a farm near Uttoxeter she can remember, as a 16-year-old in 1941, a careers talk about work as an almoner. In 1943 she started the two-year social studies course at Leeds University. On that course Nora remembers a placement in the newly established CAB in Derby, where the great majority of advice sought was about rent arrears. Her second placement was at Chelsea and Fulham COS doing '*charitable work*'. Here in the summer of 1945 Nora worked in almost the same geography as the Hammersmith and Fulham COS mentioned in Chapter One. In the intervening fifty years change seems to have been limited.

There was a qualified social worker though, Janet Torr, who coordinated the work of volunteer investigators. One was a Red Cross worker, one a war widow with children, but Janet also used students when she could. The secretary was a Miss Bailey, '*very cool and elegant, like someone from a Barbara Pym novel*' but, Nora says, she was very tough with high standards. There was a large committee chaired by Viscountess Linlithgow. Nora's role was to take a request for help which typically was about rent arrears or an application for convalescence. Her task was to interview the applicant and find out their circumstances – their finances and whether they were married or not for instance. Previous records had to be checked and a written report presented to the committee which met every week, and a great many of the committee members turned up. Nora says she would present maybe three cases a week and also have to report on continuing work. Once the help was agreed she had to secure the money which funded whatever support had been agreed and this, according to Nora, was not easy. Nora comments also that there seemed to be no question of involving public agencies.

The work was interesting she thought, but it is clear that the ethos of the COS was that applicants '*had to be deserving*'. The COS also wanted repayment for any loans, being very tough about that, and although this part of the work gave her a feel for budgeting, Nora says she sometimes felt like a detective while with the COS.

After Leeds Nora, 22 in 1947, managed to win a place on the Institute of Almoner's training course. Her first placement did not go smoothly. She was at Birmingham Accident and Emergency Department and her supervisor was Ida Lambourne who had particular expectations. Nora reports that on one occasion she referred a man to the Disabled Rehabilitation Officer (DRO), whose role was to seek training or work for people with limited chances of gaining employment.

But this was a gaffe, because the man was regarded as a tramp, and therefore not worth taking up the time of the DRO for.

Her second placement was at St Thomas's Hospital, London where, forty years before, Anne Cummins had started her pioneering work. Nora loved it. The almoners were friendly and supportive – Audrey Read, the Head Almoner, going so far as to buy her a typewriter. Not only did she like her colleagues but she felt that they were powerful and well respected within the hospital, in which almoners and doctors tended to be the same class. One of the colleagues who Nora liked was Pheobe Cresswell, '*a socialite who lived in Chelsea. I don't know if she had been presented at court but she was that sort*'. Nora found the teaching helpful too, which focussed on the importance of family relationships, attachments in upbringing, the impact of the worker's presentation and clear recording. Nora reports being relieved at being introduced to such ideas; that there was a way of finding out what was going on, that there were tools for the job. '*I was not one of those with common sense, so casework principles were useful*'.

When she completed her course she wanted to stay in London but because she had been ill, the Institute had doubts about her being robust enough for a busy outpatient department which was her likely destination. She was still very young, surrounded by older students and was not quite the same class as many of her peers, so the pressures on her must have been considerable. She got through because several good things came together. The experience at St Thomas's helped and she was befriended by another almoner, Cicely Saunders. They were part of a group sharing a flat in Bayswater and started to attend services at St Peter's in Vere Street. Cicely had a conversion experience and for Nora it was obviously a time of spiritual reawakening. The support she found and the friendship with Cicely was '*marvellous, life changing. The Lord looked after me*' (Cooper 2009).

Myra Curtis and Dennis O'Neill

In Bolton social workers adapted to wartime conditions just like everyone else. Aileen Dunbar remembers a tale her father, a local detective, told. He used to go round various pubs in the evening, picking up information. Sometimes she says he was accompanied by Marmaduke Fraser, the local NSPCC Inspector. Marmaduke it was said could, just by entering, clear a pub of female customers. These women had money for the first time in their lives and their husbands were away. Consequently those who had left children on their own and who may have been with men other than their husbands got out of the pub as quickly as they could. Aileen remembers her father's description of Marmaduke as being a highlander, a very large, raw boned man. Perhaps his impact in the pub was aided by local people knowing of his twenty years experience as a police officer in Bolton before joining the NSPCC.

If evening nursery provision for children was limited in Bolton, an immense amount of work had been done to increase provision during working hours. A special committee of the local authority had been set up and supported by national funding and following the national pattern, the numbers of nursery places had been increased from 40 to around 350 during the war years, with eight nurseries operating in 1945 compared to one in 1939 (BHC ABCF/17/37). Across the country the establishment of hundreds of nurseries and hostels created a gigantic laboratory for investigating children's behaviour. The Cambridge evacuation survey for instance and Burlingham and Freud's work (1942) confirmed that a large number of evacuated children were underweight, ill-educated and close to neglect and that separation from parents had a significant impact. But the everyday experiences of billeting officers, social workers and hostel workers contributed as much to an understanding of child development as formal studies. Clare Britton, a PSW who qualified in 1938 and wanted to get onto the front line after training rather than work in a hospital or clinic, was responsible for visiting and supporting a number of hostels for difficult to place children in Oxfordshire. At one for children with behavioural problems a psychiatrist, Donald Winnicott, visited every Friday. The staff did not know what to make of him. They said he observed the children, but did not tell them what to do. Cleverly, Clare advised that they should never ask him, but just do what they thought was right, and see what his reaction was. Put on the spot Winnicott had to start engaging properly with the staff and began a close working relationship with Clare, which culminated in their marriage in 1951 (Kanter 2004).

Their collaboration contributed to the thinking about the importance of early attachments between children and mothers, ideas most closely associated with the psychiatrist John Bowlby. But the upheavals of war stimulated a more specific concern. Analyses of poverty such as *Our Towns* (Women's Group on Public Welfare 1943) and the PSU's *Problem Families* (Stephens 1944) stimulated a public debate which focussed on the bland and unconcerned treatment of children in public care – particularly those brought up in institutions. As part of the reconstruction effort a committee of enquiry was established into children in public care, led by Myra Curtis, an Oxford academic (Parker 1983, Curtis Report 1946).

Public interest in this issue was limited largely to the broadsheet press. The death of Dennis O'Neill in January 1945, however, was a national sensation. At first there was only local news coverage. But subsequently events contributing to the story appeared in the press every few weeks; the inquest in February, an adjourned trial in March, then a completed trial later the same month at which the foster father Mr Gough was convicted of the boy's manslaughter. The announcement of the Monckton enquiry followed and six weeks later, at the end of May, the report was published. This turned the whole affair into a rolling scandal. This was the first time public child care issues had achieved such a high profile since the trial and hanging of Mrs Dyer in 1897.

The Monckton enquiry, at 20 pages long, is precise and readable (Monckton 1945). The O'Neills were a large family living in Newport, Wales and there had been concerns about neglect of the children for years, Richard Jones, the NSPCC

Inspector, having made 200 visits to them over 17 years. In 1939, the children were removed under a Fit Person Order and although some were taken to live with relatives, three of the boys were boarded-out. Adverts were put in newspapers seeking Catholic families and Mr Edmonds, an SAO, placed them with a lady in Herefordshire. She fell ill so they were moved on, then moved on again. In July 1944 arrangements were made for the three of them, Dennis, 12, and his younger brothers Terence and Freddie, to be placed in Shropshire. The day before they were due to be moved by another SAO, Mr Easterby, a man with little experience of boarding-out, he received a letter from the foster mother saying she had taken two girls from Shropshire so could no longer take the O'Neills. He took them anyway and tried to persuade her to take them. She relented and took Freddie, the youngest, and gave Mr Easterby the names of two local farmers who might take the other two. He went to Bank Farm unannounced, prevailed upon Mrs Gough to take the two boys and, without any background checks and without inspecting sleeping arrangements, he left them there. By chance, Mrs Gough had already been accepted to foster two other children, having been assessed by Shropshire's single paid boarding-out visitor. The responsibility for visiting these children was delegated to a farmer's wife, a member of the local Clun committee of voluntary visitors; a similar arrangement to that led by Alice Barlow in Bolton 50 years before. When, in August, Shropshire County Council somehow found that Newport had placed the boys at Bank Farm, the boarding-out visitor returned to review the situation along with the head of the Cottage Homes and Head of the PAC Institution. They were not impressed with the cleanliness or attitude of the Goughs but even they failed to inspect the sleeping arrangements. Shropshire removed the other two children, but only because the number of children at the farm surpassed the number allowed. Then, as Shropshire thought Newport were dealing with the boys and the 19-year-old clerk in Newport, Miss Edwards (now dealing with the case) had appendicitis in the early Autumn, then went on leave; and because the original letter to Shropshire from Newport had been lost, no one in either authority paid any attention to the boys until December. Just before Christmas Miss Edwards visited Shropshire County Hall and Bank Farm. She advised that Dennis be referred to child guidance and proposed an early move, mostly on the grounds of the boys being Catholics, thus needing Catholic carers. She did not look at the sleeping arrangements. She was concerned about Dennis, but not enough to propose immediate action. Dennis died from exposure and beatings three weeks after Miss Edwards's visit.

It is the mundane nature of the delays, bureaucratic wrangles and misconstructions which are striking here and the instant and opportunistic nature of some decisions. It is true the war had stripped both Newport Council and Shropshire County Council of experienced workers and the pressure to place evacuees had diluted any concern for the suitability of placements. It must also be noted that the date of the actual placement, 28 June 1944, coincided with the height of the V1 panic when tens of thousands of children were leaving London, many of them being placed with similar insouciance. The concern for placements of the appropriate religious sect also shines out, as does the slap-dash approach of all of the people involved to simple things like checking bedding and talking to the children on their own, practices which had been commonplace for decades.

Boarding-Out Visitors in Bolton

All the while the work of boarding-out visitors went on across England. Ada Wainer was still visiting children in Bolton, but seems to have retired in September 1945, 20 years after starting. Her colleague visitors were all women, three of them: Miss Striffler, C. Ross and Mavis Smith. All also seem to have been employed in a teaching role for the older children in care.

Two surviving records show what Mavis Smith thought about the children's needs and the foster parents she was working with. One of her girls was Molly B, 14, previously living in the Cottage Homes but now about to start work. Mavis Smith's report of January 1947 reports that Molly was thrilled about moving out to Mr and Mrs C's where she would live with them and Mr C's mother. Mavis was alive to the need for the couple to be careful lest Molly be spoiled, and had noted in class that with her new placement and new outfit her head had swelled. But Mavis foresaw only that danger, which she thought a childish conceit. She also noted carefully that the home fitted the requirements of section 21 of the new Boarding-Out Rules, whose introduction was associated with the Curtis Committee proposals (BHC ABSS/1/768).

The placement collapsed almost immediately and at the end of February Mavis Smith records a visit to Mr and Mrs C in which they complained that Molly did not enter into family life and did not value the family home. The nub of the breakdown, Mavis noted, was that she refused to call Mr and Mrs C Father and Mother. Also Mr C's mother was jealous of the child and Molly had been disappointing in not being as big a help round the house as anticipated. This placement and breakdown, and the analysis of the reasons for the breakdown, illustrates the fresh start approach to child placement as well as Mr Watkinson's perception of boarding-out as attracting people who wanted servants. It also implies poor preparation for the placement by Mavis Smith, or at least an over optimistic perception of the family's attitude and a naive understanding of Molly's needs. But of course we only know this because Mavis Smith records several of her own her views – the report showing that the recording of work was more comprehensive than in the past. The record also shows her care for and willingness to take considerable responsibility for Molly's welfare.

Another report, this one directly to the Social Welfare Committee, relates to a 15-year-old girl who had moved on from the Cottage Homes, this time to a small hostel. Mavis reports spending considerable time with her in August when she had discovered that the food at the hostel was awful and there was no hot water. No attempt to engage or nurture her was made by the staff at the hostel and she was left with no money. Mavis was enraged at this treatment and put it all on paper, clearly wishing the committee never to use the hostel again. Her own care for the girl stands out brightly. First of all it is clear that she and other staff had taken several girls camping in August, during which time the poor treatment at the hostel emerged. Mavis took the girl to her own home and seems to have looked after her there for a week rather than send her back to the hostel. The easy way in which she mentions this indicates that she did not think the Social Welfare Committee would think ill of her for admitting to such an action. Mavis's analysis of the child's needs is simple, as she puts it '*the great lack in this child's life is <u>Mother love</u>*'. Simple as this observation is it chimes in with the more sophisticated thinking referred to above about the need all children have for appropriate attachments and the consequences of thwarting that need (BHC ABSS/1/768).

The level of anger expressed in the report may be a result of Mavis Smith's powerlessness. She was stuck in an awkward bureaucratic cul-de-sac because as the girl was in public care she could not apply for a Fit Person Order to remove her. But she needed the Committee's approval to change the placement, thus the special report.

Curtis and the 1948 Children Act

Although Mavis Smith's commitment to her work and to the children was strong, boarding-out visitors in general, both paid and their voluntary counterparts, had received stark comment in the Curtis Report. Curtis confirmed that the arrangements for visiting children boarded-out which relied on volunteers were by no means limited to Shropshire. In one rural county the committee found that the voluntary visitors:

> ... were largely women and usually held some recognised position, such as magistrate, doctor, councillor or councillor's wife; they were usually aged between 50 and 60 (Curtis 1946: para 348).

The system relied upon local knowledge, social eminence and experience, but Curtis was unimpressed by the effectiveness of the visitors:

> They were apt to pat the children on the head and think they were quite happy. Other officials mentioned unreliability about visiting, and slowness about paying emergency visits if the foster home was isolated. We ourselves noticed ... the poor standard of reports, the infrequency of visits and the difficulty of officials in mentioning such defects to the visitor who might be a person of some importance in the locality ... the inadequacy of some visiting was brought home to us [by] a visitor who always visited on horseback and was unable to remain for more than a few minutes 'because the horse would not stand' (Curtis 1946: para 348).

In addition the committee found that few of the paid workers had received specialist training and that the work was carried out by a wide range of people from nurses to health visitors, and included someone who had attended a police training course and, in places, clerks from the Education Department. And while they found many workers '*displayed great interest and industry ... they were often lacking in imagination and resourcefulness*' (Curtis 1946: para 351).

Curtis and her committee took 18 months about their task, taking evidence from over 200 people including Donald Winnicott, John Bowlby and Susan Isaacs, and received written submissions from hundreds of organisations. The report was published in September 1946 and recommended:

- The amalgamation of functions relating to children in public care under one local authority department, a Children's Department (CD).
- The creation of a Children's Officer (CO) to head up each CD whose characteristics were described thus:

> The Children's Officer shall be highly qualified academically, if possible a graduate who has also a social science diploma. She should not be under thirty ... should have marked administrative capacity ... and should have some experience with children ... Her essential qualification however should be on the personal side. She should be genial and friendly ... have a strong interest in the welfare of children ... faith and enthusiasm [and] very high standards of physical and moral welfare, but should be flexible enough in temperament to avoid sterile institutional correctness (Curtis 1946: para 446).

- The CD's work of assessing foster parents, assessing children's needs and visiting children boarded-out was to be undertaken by 'one or more' salaried boarding-out visitors, with caseloads of between 100 and 150.

It was also suggested that children were to be most effectively brought up in family homes, fostering being the preferred option, after adoption, for raising children. New regulations for boarding-out enshrined good practice and a number of alternatives to advertising for foster parents were canvassed to increase the numbers of placements and the number of families applying.

These changes, carried through to the 1948 Children Act, are justly celebrated but it is worth noting the limitations of the changes made. First of all the 1948 Children Act was a small piece of legislation compared to the 1946 NHS Act and the 1944 Education Act and did not attract much funding, save a small central government grant to set the CDs up. The focus of the Act was limited – concentrating on how that minority of children looked after by the state should be brought up. It did not cover child protection, the province of the NSPCC, or disabled children. And the requirement for local authorities to establish CDs separate from other departments presented a grave difficulty: the CDs were to be tiny. To establish economies of scale many authorities discussed having a joint CD; Blackpool and

Preston, York and Beverley, Bury and Bolton among them (Brill 1991). Some local authorities fought shy of or could not attract the highly educated candidates envisaged by Curtis for the post of CO, and as with the appointment of probation officers in 1908 local authorities in large numbers carried on with the people they knew, staff from their education authorities. Mr J.B. Burns who became the CO with Bolton held a similar post with the Education Department before transferring across. After a competitive interview with two other candidates Mavis Smith was appointed Child Care Officer (CCO) in Bolton, the only one. Having previously been a SAWO in the Education Department Mr Herbert Wells was appointed as trainee boarding-out visitor. For some with a background in education the transfer was not as smooth. Harry Mapstone had been a SAWO before the war and took a leading role in the evacuation from East Ham. Appointed CO there in 1948, the Home Office refused the appointment on the grounds that he was not qualified. East Ham advertised again, appointed him again and this time he was accepted on the proviso that he did a course at Birkbeck College (Corrick 2011).

The continuity between the workers in the old PACs and the new post-1948 local authority Welfare, Mental Welfare and Public Health Departments is even more marked. Samuel Kinley became the first Chief Welfare Officer in Bolton in 1948 having been Chief Officer of the PAC since 1930 and whose father (and his grandfather before him) had been superintendent of Mrs Greg's workshop for the blind before the Great War (BHC GBO/28/799). His department inherited responsibility for old people, mental cases and mental defectives in the old PAC institution as well as homeless families, so had many more staff than the CD. But the new department was not associated with an exciting bundle of ideas or any central government funding. The new Welfare Departments were staffed overwhelmingly by people who had been ROs, as were those working in the new local authority Public Health Departments or Mental Welfare Departments.

One of the other changes wrought by the Attlee welfare legislation was the change of emphasis required of voluntary effort. With the introduction of the NHS, into which all voluntary hospitals were incorporated, their huge charitable support network was bypassed. The new CDs were not to rely on voluntary visitors as their predecessors had done – a huge change. Similarly charitable efforts such as the Central Association for Mental Welfare, which we noted in operation in Accrington before the war, became redundant as local authority Welfare Officers took over the visiting role. On the other hand new Welfare Departments continued to use volunteers to visit older people and as many as 300 of the estimated 750 post-war probation officers were part-timers, some still using their free time continuing the traditional work of missioning (Rimmer 1995). The more comprehensive financial support provided by the NAB and NHS funding for false teeth, spectacles and convalescence support obliged the COS to change its name to the Family Welfare Association (FWA) and offer a more focussed social work service. The changed landscape was to see new charities emerge but two, which had contributed so much to the support of old and vulnerable people during the war, the WVS and the Older People's Welfare Committees (OPWC), had to re-evaluate as well. The first OPWC was set up by Eleanor Rathbone at the beginning of the war, as a sub-committee of the Liverpool Personal Service Society, in response to the impact of the war on older people. The idea spread, secured government blessing and a National Old People's Welfare Committee was set up which took on a coordinating role for the activities of local committees (Means and Smith 1998). Many of the staples of support for older people in post-war generations first appeared in the war years. Darby and Joan clubs were first set up in Streatham, London, in 1942. Invalid Kitchens had been operating since the Great War but meals on wheels was devised by the WVS during the bombing. In 1947 the WVS started a regular peace time service in Welwyn Garden City and Hemel Hempstead and the idea spread. Home Helps were first offered to nursing mothers just after the Great War but the offer spread to older and disabled people in the early 1940s and had an established place in the new Welfare Departments in places like Oxfordshire, Manchester and Bolton by 1950 (Means and Smith 1998).

Chapter 6
1948–1971: Social Workers: Public Servants

The Post-War World

Full employment, the social security net and improved health care gave society a settled feel throughout the 1950s and into the 1960s. Penicillin quashed the threat of fatal infections which fell from public consciousness and cancer became the major health fear. Streptomycin finally conquered TB and the Salk vaccine curbed the threat of polio. Use of contraception, the cap and the condom, was widespread and infant mortality continued to fall.

The overwhelming social concern during this period was housing. Despite substantial building programmes waiting lists for council homes were huge and demand for owner occupation outstripped supply, so many young couples had to live with parents before setting up their own homes. But by the end of the 1960s the outside toilet was a thing of the past, few children shared a bed with more than one sibling and televisions were standard in most houses. This growing comfort in working-class homes contributed to the steady fall in pub attendance throughout the period, and drunkenness fell away in the public mind as a key social evil (Kynaston 2007, 2009, Sandbrook 2005). But slum conditions were not banished completely. Housden's account of NSPCC work (1955), Worth's about her work as a midwife in the East End of London (2007) and Rees's about homelessness (1965) attest that many poor people still lived lives of want and squalour.

Workers in Children's Departments

In 1960 John Stroud published *The Shorn Lamb,* a novel based on his experiences as a Child Care Officer (CCO). Stroud's protagonist, Charles Maule, trained in the lee of the 1948 Children Act and was determined to set children free from forbidding institutions:

> Our impression at the University was that the country … was dotted with castle like institutions in which hundreds of children dressed in blue serge were drilled to the sound of whistles. We were going to tear down these mouldering bastions … boarding-out in foster homes, of course, that was the answer, I mean, this I knew (Stroud 1960: 8).

He starts work and of course discovers that boarding-out had been in practice for years. This mix of young enthusiasm and continuity with the past was the experience of many starting work just after the war. Mary Mason became Assistant Children's Officer in 1952 in Dewsbury and reports that there was a comprehensive boarding-out approach, inherited, like the CO Mrs Clark, from pre-1948 arrangements. Mary Mason had been brought up in Didsbury, Manchester, in a non-conformist family. After Manchester High School for Girls she went on to Girton College, Cambridge. But in 1942 she was directed to work on sickness benefit for the Ministry of Health in Stockport, visiting claimants and dealing with all sorts of problems. She completed her final year at Girton in 1946 and then did teacher training, which she did not take to. She then secured the post in Dewsbury ... the second member of staff. The CO was the other – even the typist belonged to the Welfare Department. Mary Mason had always wanted to do useful work and in Dewsbury she found what she wanted. '*It was a wonderful job*' she says and admired Mrs Clark. She was a '*nice homely woman*' with years of experience and a considerable network of foster parents, so much so that in those early years Dewsbury, Mary Mason claims, had the '*third highest boarding-out rate in the country*' (Mason 2009).

Her work included finding foster homes and assessing prospective foster and adoptive parents, receiving children into care, attending juvenile court and latterly beginning to undertake preventive work with families. She confirms that the philosophy followed in placing children in the early 1950s was '*clean break*': the assumption that it was best for children to remove them irrevocably from any contact with their parents and '*giving a child a home for life*'. The high rate of boarding-out was partially due to the regular use of grandparents, aunts and other relatives as foster parents, duly assessed and registered – thus maintaining family continuity for children, despite the '*clean break*' philosophy. The children included orphans, children referred by the courts and a small number of '*residual evacuees*' whose parents had died or washed their hands of their evacuated offspring. It was estimated there were over 4,000 '*residuals*' in 1946 so most CDs would have had some. Neither cruelty nor neglect featured in Miss Mason's work, but there were many parents who applied for short term care for children during confinements, convalescence, or other difficult periods. This short term service was by no means unusual – in Manchester later in the 1950s there were two homes especially set aside for such purposes (Mason 2009). Brill suggests that workers and families accepted such usage as part of the new Welfare State dispensation. People could now get false teeth and spectacles free. There was the Family Allowance, free school milk and free health checks. It is a short step from accepting this innovative state largesse to assuming that the state would also look after your children if you asked. Some CDs – Croydon for instance – made no bones in the early days about receiving children into short term care with the slimmest of investigations into any alternative possible arrangements (Brill 1991).

The work in CDs initially was split on gender lines. In Bolton for instance, Herbert Wells (a SAWO before the war) worked exclusively with adolescent boys. In Stroud's novel Charles Maule worked with boys about to leave school. His caseload was entirely of 14-, 15- and 16-year-old boys. He had to find employment and digs and help boys manage the uneasy transfer from having everything done for them to having to take responsibility for their own lives, as well as trying to achieve some sort of rapprochement between the boys and what families they had. The arrangements he made frequently broke down so Maule was engaged in a permanent roundabout, chasing accommodation and jobs for his boys again and again.

You'd Have to Have Some Fun or You'd Go Nuts

This gendered management of the work survived into the late 1960s when Keith Hiscock, then a young CCO in Westminster, reports having a caseload biased towards teenage lads. Keith was at University College London in 1963, involved in the University Methodist Society. He and others took up a challenge to run a Christmas Party for 50 local children. The party, despite careful planning, was marked by constant rough and tumble, food throwing and the theft of anything movable. Keith had never met kids like it, decided to find out what it was all about, undertook a social science diploma in Sheffield and then in 1966 trained as a social worker at Liverpool University. In Westminster CD when he started work he had the usual run of frustration, including placing a girl in an Approved School who immediately '*went over the wall*' and the boy who liked his Nautical Training School so much that when he was discharged he stole a car in order to be sent back. Keith remembers that he could never interest child guidance clinics in offering their services to his clients because he could rarely guarantee that the child would have a stable base or even the same address. But he was always determined to make connections between the CD and related services and struck up a good relationship with the psychology service in the Inner London Education Authority (ILEA), particularly with a psychiatrist, Fitz, who acted as consultant on placements, advised about families and did assessments relating to special education (Hiscock 2011).

Keith was always fascinated by what made young people tick, as was Stroud's Charles Maule who makes heroic efforts to understand what motivates his various charges. He reaches neat conclusions then is confounded by a bout of odd behaviour. In fact Stroud's central conceit – Maule's naïve adherence to psychoanalytical explanations in the face of incomprehension from everybody else – provides much of the humour in the novel. Here he is talking to a Probation Officer, Mr Bland:

> 'Why do you think he chucked the brick? … I was wondering … if … he did it because he was revenging himself on the fantasy image of his father while sublimating his own incest guilt?'
>
> Mr Bland gave me a … stare.

'No', he said briefly (Stroud 1961: 112).

Stroud's implicit dismissal of the probation officer as *Mr Bland* may well have summed up the view CCO's like Stroud had of probation officers; staid and traditional. But just after the war the 1948 Criminal Justice Act swept away traditional sentences such as corporal punishment and some probation officers were innovating. Silverwood Lamb, for instance, was asked to supervise eight girls aged between ten and eleven from the same street. They had broken into their school and taken costumes from the acting box so they could put on a sketch for their fathers and elder brothers returning from the war. Miss Lamb decided, as the girls were all first offenders, to supervise them as a group. They met weekly and made dolls, giving them the opportunity to talk about all manner of things in a relaxed way. Miss Lamb asked any girl who seemed to need particular attention to help her clear up afterwards. Clever, human and effective as this approach seemed to her, Miss Lamb reports that the Principal Probation Officer and the Home Office criticised her for not carrying out her duties in the customary way (Rimmer 1995).

And perhaps caseloads were too heavy to rely on untried approaches. When Joyce Rimmer started work in Birmingham she was handed a caseload of 150, while the average for men was 70 and for women was 46. The establishment was 30 male POs and 12 women who worked in one of four geographical divisions. But when she was appointed in 1956 the other women in her division had left. A male colleague made it worse, she says, by telling her he would not have a woman PO's job as women offenders, he said, *'are more devious ...'*. What he did not dwell on was that Joyce, as a woman, was paid less than her male colleagues. Joyce has her diaries from those years, which on many days in 1957 has 13 or 14 visits marked to be undertaken. Her caseload included mothers caught shoplifting and adolescent girls, a lot of whom were pregnant. Joyce had to tell them they would have to give up their baby for adoption and support them through that process. There were also lots of stand-down interviews in court, a woman PO having to spend proportionately more time in court because the expectation was, until 1967, that women would be dealt with by women POs. Officers were also engaged in *Kindred Social Work,* which included work with '... *illegitimate children, adoption, befriending lonely people, financial and material aid and consent to marry'* (Rimmer 2011, 1995: 183).

Despite the considerable pressures on officers, Joyce reports a lighter side, saying that '*you had to have some fun or you'd go nuts'*. She had bolt holes, the FSU office and Birmingham Settlement, where some of the POs lived. She called in when she had been shouted at and '*called names you did not quite understand'*.

As the age of criminal responsibility was eight, a lot of her clients were children. Joyce is still proud of the work she did with an eight-year-old boy. '*"I am nothing", that's what he said. I never heard such a tragic statement from a child'*. Ignored by his parents, he regularly rang 999 for a fire engine, enjoying the bright glory of the fire tender's arrival. She worked with the parents, but encouraged the boy to ring her instead of 999, which within a short period of time he began to do.

She talks of being determined to help children express themselves and on home visits tried to get communication going between all members of the family in a sort of family therapy or play therapy. '*Families were families by name only ... Nobody sat down and talked together ... there weren't any chairs – and only an orange box for a table*'.

The trickiest area for her was the matrimonial court work all POs had to do. Often if a summons was issued for cruelty against a husband, the case would be adjourned for a month for Joyce to talk to the couple. As an unmarried woman in her twenties she did not quite know what to do, but says that after listening to them more often than not they got back together. '*In overcrowded back to back houses there was never any chance for couples to talk privately so we just gave them space, time, boundaries and information*' (Rimmer 2011). Ten years later when Peter Hewitt started in probation at the age of 23, he too struggled with what was still a marked feature of the work: '*I shudder to think what such a young man could have brought to matrimonial agonies*' (Hewitt 2011).

Getting Around

At first Joyce could not drive. As her work was restricted to inner city areas and her caseload was women and children home visiting was the norm so she walked everywhere, much like the Probation Officer in Ealing Film's *I Believe in You* (1952). The initial training offered to a Mental Welfare Officer in Manchester, as reported to Rolph, was advice to get a pair of stout shoes and an umbrella (Rolph 2003). Brain Fox, an officer in a Welfare Department, used his bike, as many social workers must have done (Fox 2010). More sophisticated arrangements were made in Kent, where from the beginning all 23 CCOs had access to cars (Brill 1991) and in Devon there were '*county cars*' which Phyllida Parsloe, a young probation officer, used. She remembers every single one of them being a black Ford Anglia (Parsloe 1972). Olive Stevenson, a CCO in the same county, remembers that those cars had no heaters, which must have been some trial in winter (Stevenson 2005). Later, in 1960, trainee PSW, Val Burnham, was told she needed a car and was given time off to take driving lessons (Burnham, V. 2011). CCOs often needed access to cars. Ruth Evans had to visit children placed hundreds of miles away (Evans 1977). Mary Mason had to escort a 15-year-old from Manchester to Southampton to join a maritime training ship and most CCOs had to trek off across country to pick up a runaway on occasion. Keith Hiscock's experience in Westminster was that around two thirds of the 750 or so children in care were placed outside the borough. He had children placed in Wales, Margate, Dorset and Slough and short-term foster placements were in Hastings. By the 1960s Bolton CCOs were allowed use of a car for any transport beyond the town's boundaries. The car, a Ford Cortina Mk 1, came with a driver, Tommy Derbyshire, who according to Ron Standring, always wore a peaked cap, which must have made for a rare sight when bemused children accompanied by a harassed CCO arrived at foster homes (Standring 2010).

But long trips were not as common as local travel and public transport was the norm. Many, like Maurice Ffelan, had to be '*expert in bus timetables*' (Ffelan 2010). This was certainly the case for Mary Mason. In the mid-fifties she worked in Manchester CD, a big department with 14 CCOs. Mary covered Chorlton and Didsbury, suburbs four or so miles south of the town hall. On one occasion she had to pick up four children about three miles from her office. She took the bus from the town hall to get there, then onto the GP in Whalley Range to get the children confirmed as free from infection – another bus ride. Then she had to pack them off to a foster home in Cheetham Hill – five more miles and two more buses. This sort of job took all day, ameliorated only a little by the rolls of bus tickets supplied by the council to CCOs.

At the beginning of her time in Manchester one of the places Mary Mason had to get the bus to was Styal, ten miles south of Manchester, where the old Poor Law Cottage Homes were. In the early 1950s, 400 Manchester children lived there in a vast complex of cottages. Manchester CO Ian Brown was determined to unpick this institutional relic and transfer children from Styal into a new type of accommodation, the Family Group Home (FGH). Brown's vision was to recreate a normal working-class upbringing for children in care so FGHs were all on council estates and were at first without telephones. His plan was to establish 50 of them across Manchester, each run by a paid housemother, whose husband it was anticipated would carry on with his normal job. Each of the homes had up to eight children (Holman 2001). Lauded in the 1950s as a human scale solution to the problem of bringing up children where fostering or adoption was not possible, Mary Mason reports some cynicism amongst the CCOs. She observes that parents who were content to allow their children to stay in Styal promptly removed them at the thought of losing their child's affections to more intimate relationships in the FGH. She compares the accuracy of the phrase Family Group Home with the old slur about the Holy Roman Empire, which was neither Holy, nor Roman, nor an Empire. She observes drily: '*The Home Office thought they were wonderful. They weren't.*'

Look Mr Fox, You Can't See a Bloody Thing!

As Mary Mason was on the bus between Chorlton and Didsbury she would have passed Southern Cemetery four miles from the city centre. A few of the many funeral services held there attracted only a single mourner. Often this was Welfare Officer (WO), Brian Fox. Brian had responsibility for homeless men, another Poor Law legacy, and attended deathbeds in lodging houses. As such men often died isolated and destitute Brian would arrange and attend their funerals. This happened once or twice a month. He also had to take inventories of belongings and arrange for them to be sold. On one occasion an auditor became suspicious that deceased people's assets were only realising a few pounds so he tagged along with Brian to check that everything was above board. At the unpleasant room they visited, the auditor asked on the doorstep whether '*we have to go in*', and was unwilling to touch anything when inside. He did not follow Brian round again. Brian observed that he most often picked up fleas in empty houses as '*the fleas were hungrier there*' and used the facilities at a local isolation hospital for a bath and to get his clothes disinfested.

Brian began work in 1943 as a clerk in the Health Department in Manchester, a '*cushy number*' for a 16-year-old (Fox 2010). After national service he returned in 1948 and started with the brand new Welfare Department (WD) as an Assistant Records Clerk. From 1952 he was an Assistant Welfare Officer and WO from 1955. The first task he was involved in was the categorisation of people who had been in the Withington Institution, south Manchester's workhouse. A decision had to be made about whether the people there were so infirm they should become the responsibility of the NHS, or were merely '*in need of care and attention*' and thus eligible for support by the WD under Part III of the 1948 National Assistance Act. The accommodation was divided up and the WD inherited six of the 10 blocks of the old Institution. They were three storeys high with 30 or 40 beds in each ward, men and women segregated. Between each iron-frame bed was a locker, but there was no storage for clothes so each night the residents' clothes were removed and replaced in the morning. Each man had a grey herringbone suit and each woman was issued with a limited selection of coloured frocks. As destitution rather than disability determined entrance to Part III, residents often went out during the day and Brian says you would see them around town, instantly recognisable by their clothing.

Brian also has a clear memory of the WOs, all of whom had transferred from the pre-1948 PAC. In a survey of social work activity in Rochdale undertaken in the late 1950s researchers reported all ex ROs as having '*Poor Law attitudes*', saying things like '*you've got to be on top of these people*', and '*you must keep your distance*' (Rodgers and Dixon 1960). When I asked Brian Fox whether the old ROs in Manchester displayed a common set of beliefs and methods, he laughed. '*No*', he said, '*they were chalk and cheese and each had their own approach*'. Among them were:

- Norman Thomas: '*very officious*', concerned always '*to get your facts straight*'. On the doorstep he went into a routine asking name, age and so on, noting all this down before going indoors.
- Dorothy Prendegast only worked in the nicest areas and always wanted to work with the nicest people. Brian described her as '*very far back*'.
- Frank Nuttall worked Openshaw. Brian remembers him as a '*natural social worker*'. Just as Brian went away on his training '*Frank wrote an essay which he gave to me, about the characteristics and principles of social work. The ideas expressed were spot on.*'

Referrals came in on tiny sheets and each worker took referrals according to their likes and the numbers arriving. Brian would visit people on his bike and says he only ever had his authority card asked for once, although was occasionally mistaken for the rent man. Usually the starting point of the referral was a stated desire for the old person to go into a home. In the early 1950s the WD tried to humanise the Institution by making smaller units out of the wards, but this was unsatisfactory. Then Frank Nuttall was sent round scouting for large houses for the council to buy and refurbish as residential homes. Once a number had been purchased the Institution was closed. When he first met people Brian says sometimes their view of what residential care might be like was a little rosy and he had to explain that the chances of getting a single room, even in the grand new homes, were slim. Sometimes he says people were very apprehensive at a visit from '*an official from the town hall*', and some were uneasy because the idea of needing help was not their own, but somebody else's. So he had to gain the old person's confidence, ascertain their needs and discover where any pressure was coming from. He reports one occasion he was with an old lady when her doctor called. The doctor tried to persuade her how living in a home would be better for her and although she argued against it, in the end she agreed. The doctor left, implying on his departure that he had done Brian a great favour. Alone again with the lady Brian, sensing her tactic, asked her whether she really wanted to go into a home. She replied that, no, she did not, '*and that's the last time that bugger'll get into this house*'. If the person did not want to go into a home there were a number of supports available to help people. Manchester had home helps and an extensive meals service. There were also hundreds of volunteers willing to visit isolated old people.

Brian himself made the decision about putting someone's name on the waiting list for a home, for demand outstripped supply and the waiting list was considerable. Brian suggests that the list was inflated with people who really only wanted to have someone visit regularly, a bit of company. So when a vacancy arose the person who eventually took it up was not necessarily the next person on the list, but the person in greatest need willing to go. On the odd occasion when a person could not cope but refused to go into a home only patience and persuasion was possible, because removing someone against their will (under section 47 of the National Assistance Act) was extremely unpleasant and in Brian's view once they were cleaned up and in a home they did not last long.

When a person was placed, the WO would visit after about three weeks and sometimes subsequently. One lady from Hulme, at the time a tight labyrinth of terraced housing, was placed in Hazel Croft, Manchester's new home in Alderley Edge, a very affluent village in Cheshire. The view from this lady's window took in the Cheshire plain and stretched across to the Clwydian mountains. But she was not happy and took him to her room, pointing out of the window, '*look at that Mr Fox, you can't see a bloody thing!*'

Brian also ran a regular trip to Southport for disabled people, taking groups of wheelchair users for a two week holiday. Although he was ribbed by his colleagues about being paid for a day out at the seaside he said it was an exhausting 13-hour day, both escorting people out and then a fortnight later bringing them back. By that time the WD was situated in Manchester Town Hall, where electricity and gas show rooms were located. Brian remembers idly looking out of the window one day watching cookers being unloaded from a lorry on an electric tail lift. '*Bloody hell*', he thought, '*that's what we need*'. So arrangements were made to have a van adapted with a tail lift to help transporting people who could not themselves get into it. Brian mentions two other innovations he is proud of:

- There were between 300 and 400 volunteers used by the WD to visit older people. He encouraged the council to host an annual event to thank them for their work. These were still volunteers in the complete sense in that they were paid nothing for expenses or travel. Brian's idea was frowned on at first but then put into practice.
- Brian also noticed that many older people on the residential care list were being looked after by relatives, many of whom were at the end of their tether. Again he suggested, at first vainly, that a couple of beds in one of the new residential homes should be set aside for use as 'respite', in circumstances where the relative caring for the older person needed a rest for a week or so. This too came to pass.

In Bolton when Samuel Kinley retired as Chief Welfare Officer in 1951, he was succeeded by Kenneth Davies. Davies had started work as a clerk in the PAC in Bolton in 1930 and spent time as a '*social services officer*' in Bootle WD after 1948. When he left Bolton in 1964 after 13 years as Chief to take up a similar post in Tower Hamlets, London he was interviewed by the Bolton Evening News. He is quoted as recounting a tale about entering an old lady's home, when he was a social services officer, just as she was in the act of trying to gas herself, the common method then being to put money, in pennies, into the gas metre and lie with your head in the open gas oven. She was taken to hospital and on discharge went to see Mr Davies to thank him for his help. As she left she asked if he had change of a threepenny bit. He duly gave her three pennies and she went home and gassed herself (BEN 1964: 4). However apocryphal this tale, and I have heard it before, its inclusion suggests that Mr Davies was either caught very much off his guard during this interview or public sympathy for the likely despair of isolated older people was undeveloped in 1964.

WDs also had responsibility for homeless families. In Surrey families were housed in Milford, in former Poor Law accommodation with rudimentary facilities. Women and children were taken in, with a rule that after five months they had to move on and the children taken into care if no other accommodation was found. Bronwen Rees was a WO working with these families and in her autobiographical novel she includes a sterling account of a meeting of the Medical Officer of Health's (MOH) Prevention of Break-up of Families Coordination Conference (Rees 1965) which met regularly to consider how to coordinate work with problem families. Present at that particular meeting were Public Health Visitors, as she calls them, the housing welfare officer, the probation officer, SAO, someone from the NAB and the MOH himself. Rees makes merry with the punitive attitudes of all other members of the committee who want to punish a family of 13 children in considerable debt by committing them to the homeless families unit, in the face of steadfast and eminently sensible alternatives put by her and her older colleague Ted. She rates Ted who she describes as '*really loved by the old people, councillors and social workers ... been working thirty-three years with the blind, halt, maimed, layabouts, or anyone who needs him and isn't trying to pull a fast one*' (Rees 1965: 94). But of course there are others she comes across who represent the dark side of the old Poor Law mentality, like the warden of the Homes. '*I don't interfere with 'em*' he says, '*they got into the mess, let them get out of it. I don't hold with being soft to evicted families*' (Rees 1965: 155).

Marie McNay was another young woman working in a WD. She was taken on in 1965 at the age of 23 as a trainee social worker in Wandsworth, with a view to secondment to qualifying training. The legislative requirement underpinning work with older people and people with physical disabilities had not changed since 1948, save for more focussed expectation to use services such as home helps, but there was a growing emphasis on employing trained social workers. The Principal Social Worker in Wandsworth in the mid 1960s offered trainees weekly seminars and each one also had individual supervision. Marie herself was supervised by a Home Teacher for the Blind, who taught craft and other occupational training. Marie took on some of this work as well as dealing with applications for residential care, homeless families and people with physical disabilities. She thought the work was wonderful, liked the freedom of visiting and felt trusted. She was also encouraged to think about how to improve support for younger people with physical disabilities. She developed, with other trainees, a club for people under 30. She wrote a constitution but was determined that members should run the club themselves, which they did, blossoming in the process. Forty-five years later she still feels immensely proud of that achievement (McNay 2011).

She Works Well and Gives No Trouble

Amy of Accrington who we met in Chapter Four was still being visited in the late 1940s and a slim set of records survives from August 1949. At the age of 22 she was still referred to as a mental defective, still lived with her parents but no longer worked in the chip shop, having moved to a cotton mill. The supervision was no longer done by the Central Association for Mental Welfare, which had by then been incorporated into the National Association for Mental Health (NAMH) – but by an unnamed social worker from the new Mental Welfare department. The report is sparse, one of a series no doubt of three or six monthly visits, reminiscent of Annie Higginson's terse commentaries: '... *a very dirty, untidy and poorly furnished home ... the property is very dilapidated and the mother finds great difficulty in keeping the house dry'*. And later: *'Defective is well behaved and amenable. She works well and gives no trouble'* (Shorrock 2010). And that's it – a note of a rote visit to check that she does not need to be institutionalised.

In 1948 Ken Powls transferred from the PAC to the new Mental Welfare department in East Yorkshire and learned from an extra mural course that it was good practice to talk to people showing florid and dangerous behaviours before they were removed. Ken's long-standing practice in apprehending a mental case was to burst in and overpower the person using a blanket and rope as restraint. He said people struggled too much for him ever to use a straight jacket. Armed with his new knowledge the next time a man was reported as being out of control, Ken secured an ambulance and a police presence but went into the house on his own first to discuss the situation with him. *'But before I could sit down ... he had picked up a poker and slashed it across my neck. By this time they had all rushed in, and I reverted to my former practice'* (Powls 2010: 62).

In the decade or so after the war a series of developments offered some promise in work with mental illness. The use of Electro Convulsive Therapy (ECT) spread, which was thought to calm sufferers' behaviour. And new medications, such as chlorpromazine and benzodiazepines, promised to manage sufferer's symptoms. But for Ken Powls much of the work he engaged in was the same as it had been before the war. He had to be available 24 hours a day, with no additional recompense for call outs. When needed there was no place to hide. *'I was once reminded of how precisely the police knew my whereabouts ... one Sunday evening I was in church ... when there was a tap on my shoulder: it was the local police constable who said a doctor at Ferriby wanted to speak with me'* (Powls 2010: 59). This rota system for emergency duty was a ubiquitous feature for all local authority social workers at the time. David Custance reports that in his early days, living without a telephone, he was often summoned to emergencies at night by the arrival of a police car (Custance 2010). And for Ken informal methods continued: *'When attending a female patient, I had to pay ... the local midwife, ten shillings to help me restrain the patient, but once I was unable to contact this woman and had, once again, to use my wife as an unpaid assistant'* (Powls 2010: 59).

There were some Psychiatric Social Workers in Mental Welfare Departments but a lot worked in child guidance or mental hospitals. A compendium of comments from ex PSWs (Liman 2001) confirms that the pre-war camaraderie was still strong in the 1950s. One of the respondent's comments about the experience of setting up a 'prevention and after care service' in London was that *'we felt like young Turks ... in awe of our mentors ... who had provided the first platform for what we thought was a new generation'*. All commented that their work situation allowed them to get to know the people they worked with and *'use ... long term relationships'*. All 22 respondents felt their work was valued and progressive (Liman 2001). Rolph et al. surveyed 29 retired Mental Welfare Officers who worked during this period and found that some traditional MWOs saw their role as being to remove people from the community, being the *'fifth wheel of the ambulance'*. Others were more committed to helping squeeze what limited resources there were to keep people at home. Many also undertook work with old people or even youngsters, much as Ken Powls reported before the war and Robert Robbie was doing as RO for Lunatics during the Great War (Rolph et al. 2003).

Rolph also reports the development of elements of care in the community and closer working with parents groups towards the end of the period which matches Val Burnham's experience (2011). Val's interest in social work was sparked in the sixth form when an FSU worker visited the school and spoke about the work she did. In 1960 Val applied to take a social policy degree at Manchester University. The course lived up to her expectations and while there three students were encouraged by a research fellow, Kathleen Jones, to contribute to one of her projects by spending three months working as psychiatric nurses in different settings. Val's arrival at the large psychiatric hospital in an isolated area was stark: '*I was warmly received by staff, while at the same time a young patient arrived and I saw the institutional admission. I was welcomed as the patient was processed and subdued. The whole experience was absolutely disheartening*' (Burnham, V. 2011).

But she developed a commitment to mental health work and in 1960 started as a trainee PSW in North Manchester. Both her supervisor and his female colleague were former ROs. Val has fond memories: '*She was in her sixties and was a brilliant social worker, seriously believing in the importance of each individual as an individual. She ... was very keen to get in touch as early as possible with families where there were learning disabled babies*'.

Once Val had been appointed a Duly Authorised Officer (DAO), she experienced an immediate divide. The work with learning disabled people was positive, but the mental health work '*was all about removing people. There was no contact with psychiatric clinics or GPs*'. She was also clear about her status. '*In removals the doctor's word went*'. One of her early experiences concerned a physicist;

> ... a brilliant man. He was staying with his mother at an Anglican Conference Centre and was stigmatised because of his mental health problems. On the occasion of his detention, the doctor had sedated him when I arrived and he was already in the van. He was seen as an embarrassment and I was asked to concur with the admission. I felt it was terribly wrong, but I signed (Burnham, V. 2011).

She says that was the last time she was browbeaten in such a way. She recalls another occasion when she was with a youngish GP. The two of them sat up all night with a very disturbed woman. '*In the end we agreed that she could probably cope and ... benefit from treatment as an outpatient. That was remarkable*'.

Although she says her supervisor tried to keep up with people over a long period, it was difficult, and Val has no memory of working with people on discharge. Later she moved to Accrington and was able to operate much more constructively, attached to a psychiatrist who wanted to set up a support service. He would take her on domiciliary visits and tell her what he wanted her to find out. He asked her to do the interviewing, she thinks, because he was a poor communicator and also because he found her amenable to his constructive ideas. At the clinic Val took a social history, the psychiatrist saw the patient and then he and she would discuss the case. '*He was in charge but he certainly listened to me*'. Val does not think the Council's Health Department knew much of what was going on with this work. '*As long as the monthly returns were filled in no one bothered us. It felt like guerrilla infiltration*'.

Another constructive aspect of her role was the groupwork she did. Along with volunteers she started *a 'little social club'*. She refers to it as unpretentious, where people talked and played games, but it improved people's relationships, people's ability to conduct their lives and their confidence. She also feels that her work with families of people with learning disabilities was supportive. She herself worked with a group of parents setting up a club for young people.

> They were a progressive group … and it was a lovely club, but they did insist on calling it the Peter Pan club. It carried on for a long time. In fact when I was teaching at Manchester University later I taught the grown up son from one of the families, whose interest in social policy had been nurtured by his experience of that club (Burnham, V. 2011).

Jersey Suits Are Very Useful. Children Might Be Sick On You

Others joined up as young as Brian Fox. The 18-year-old Maurice Ffelan wanted to help people when he left school and after considering other options he applied for and was accepted in October 1962 as a trainee CCO in Preston County Borough CD. This job was '*an office junior with a small caseload*'. The department had four CCOs and no more than ten staff in all in the early 1960s. Maurice filed everything about the cases and visited homes with all the CCOs, answered the office window regularly and did escorts (of children to and from placements). He valued this ad-hoc training but having been brought up in the country he was shocked at the poverty and the brutishness of some of the families. But he accepted the job for what it was and was happy to muck in and clean up houses, help people move and so on. Preston at that time had a Family Casework Unit, modelled on the FSU, where Sylvia Cox, herself ex FSU, was dedicated to real hands on preventive work. Maurice reports that one of the more fastidious CCOs looked on the family casework people with horror. But he says most of the CCOs were down to earth, particularly Margery Decker, the CO. She had trained in Oxford just after the war, having worked previously in a settlement. He describes her as avant garde, benign and encouraging. Perhaps these attributes contributed to the dislike of her shown by the other Chief Officers, which Maurice put down to her being a woman and not a Freemason.

If Maurice fell into the work by chance, Isobel Groves, from North Yorkshire, decided early on what she wanted to do. Isobel's solicitor father acted occasionally for the NSPCC and Isobel can remember being showed photographs of children's injuries. Her social conscience was galvanised by teaching at school about the work of the World Citizenship Group, a United Nations organisation which addressed social problems around the world. Isobel began social work training in 1961 and by the age of 23 was a CCO in Bradford. Although Isobel reports that most of the other workers were '*mill owners' or solicitors' daughters*' one at least had survived from Poor Law days, Miss Blagborough. She had been a boarding-out visitor during the war and advised Isobel on the wisdom of wearing '*washable clothes. Jersey suits are very useful. Children might be sick on you*'. Miss Blagborough also taught Isobel observation skills. They had done a joint visit to a woman living on her own and after she had asked Isobel what she had seen, Miss Blagborough pointed out that there was a man's shaving brush on the sink, which Isobel had not noticed. Isobel worked with several older women like Miss Blagborough and was impressed: '*These women worked their socks off, night and day. They were old school, didn't moan, but expected you to be available at all times*' (Groves 2010).

Almoners

One of the 921 trained almoners in the UK in 1949 (Rodgers and Dixon 1960) was Nora Cooper, whose first job was at the Royal Hospital, Wolverhampton, which she took up in 1948. The Head Almoner was Mary Fox, a '*woman of intellect*' who had a languages degree from Oxford, and for whom Nora had great respect. Nora felt she blossomed in that role and could interview well, record proficiently and put into practice strategies that worked. There were three of them: Mary Fox did paediatrics, Nora did surgical and Dorothy Corbett did medical. The most demanding part of the work, Nora felt, was arranging discharges for people who were terminally ill, where there was no family support. And there was drudgery. Monday was surgical appliance day. Newly free under the NHS there was always a crowd of people gathered for appliances. Although it tied her up all day Nora said she tamely accepted filling in the forms for leg irons, insoles for shoes and so on.

Nora felt it was important that she visited people's homes, which she did when she could during afternoons when out-patient clinics were not operating. But it was regarded she thinks as '*not quite on*'. Looking back at her first job, Nora feels that although she was confident and was '*very busy, too busy*' she was '*very immature*'. In her defence she feels there were few proper systems in place as the NHS was so new, and understands now that Mary Fox did not offer supervision, although she did arrange group discussions and weekly tutorials at Birmingham University. Then in 1950 Nora got married and moved to Kenya. She returned in 1959 and again worked in Wolverhampton Royal in the same role, under Mary Fox. So she was given what is afforded to so few of us, an opportunity to review an earlier experience from the same standpoint. This time she felt she got on well with Mary Fox and stayed in touch with her for the rest of her life. Nora also felt much more confident in making visits outside the hospital, '*it seemed more possible to do it*'.

Bolton Children's Department

In 1950 Marmaduke Fraser, the NSPCC Inspector in Bolton, was still ploughing his furrow visiting 239 homes that year. But things were changing in the CD. Bill Freeman, CO in Bolton between 1951 and 1955 closed Hollins Cottage Homes, established smaller homes, expanded boarding-out and set up a coordinating committee across all welfare agencies (BEN 1955). The coordinating committee had dealt with 25 problem families in 1954 and thought it was essential that a family caseworker operated in Bolton. The Children's Committee took up the idea and Miss E Morgan was appointed woman visitor to the Bolton NSPCC branch soon after (BEN 1954).

The CD was also taking on more staff, a younger generation, including Marian Penny. Born near Bury, Marian talks of a deep yearning for an education after failing the 11 plus. She worked as an auditor in the late 1940s, but took a WEA course in which John Bowlby's brief commentary *44 Juvenile Delinquents* fired Marian's enthusiasm (Bowlby 1944). She then did a social science diploma at Hull, followed by a stint in Blackpool CD. She was impressed by Philip Varey, the CO there, but her only peer was an older lady, a legendary figure whose approach to teenage girls was to give them a '*good dressing down*'. Marian frankly describes her as '*a battleaxe*'. Marian took on the breadth of work straightaway, but unable to seek advice from her colleague Marian found this a lonely baptism. She recalls one child she had placed with foster parents who went missing. Marian followed the route of many a runaway along the front and through the Pleasure Beach, failed to find him and could not sleep. When he was found the foster mother said she would not take him back, even though there had been a close bond between them, the foster mother being concerned about the impact on her own daughter. Marian can still remember the boy's screams as he was taken to a children's home. A decision was then made that there should be no further contact between the boy and foster mother. '*I was unhappy about this and felt it could have been managed less brutally*' (Penny 2010).

After completing qualification training Marian followed Philip Varey to Bolton, where he had moved as CO in 1955. The team she joined in 1958 had five members including Herbert Wells, the pre-war SAWO, still there, working with adolescent boys, a great character according to Marian. She could not speak more highly of Mr Varey for his leadership and willingness to help. He allocated all the work and offered individual support if there were difficulties. On one occasion a teenage girl placed with foster parents complained that the husband had 'interfered with her'. Philip Varey offered to go out and visit the couple concerned. At first the man denied it, then after careful questioning he said he was sorry for what he had done and that it would not happen again. The girl was close to the foster mother and wanted to stay with her so she went back to the placement, prosecution not being considered. All went well for a couple of years but Marian heard some time later that he had done it again.

Marian was not unusual in recalling '*failures*'. Breakdowns did not happen much but '*if things broke down you wondered if you should have been able to foresee it*'. Could she for instance have foreseen that Peter, placed with a couple who had a child of their own, would become so jealous of him that he tried to push him under a bus? (Penny 2010).

Marian reports also that CCOs worked with the NSPCC inspector and his assistant and in close collaboration with the police and remembers regular coordinating committee meetings about problem families. Once a family was identified for action '*a glut of workers descended on them*'. Such coordinating committees where problem families were identified and significant resources committed were a ubiquitous feature of the period. Although some social workers I interviewed were positive about this approach it has been suggested there were strong elements of social control and lingering hints of eugenicist thinking in the idea (Welshman 1996). One recollection supports such a view. Ted Perry, as a new probation officer in the late 1960s in Sunderland, was on his local coordinating committee. He recalls monthly meetings in a hotel with the usual collection of agencies where the committee had a nice lunch. A number of families were discussed and strategies agreed, but Ted cannot recall any thought being given to telling the families themselves (Perry 2010).

As a result of this increasing focus on prevention, and under the influence of the FSU approach, a Family Casework Unit was set up in Bolton in 1960, which reported directly to the Children's Officer. Maurice Ffelan says this was not quite as hands on as the Preventive Unit in Preston, but had staff willing to go to great lengths to keep families together. Ron Standring remembers that the unit only had around ten cases at any one time and included a Health Visitor among others and two staff who would move into a family's home on a short term basis to help make sure the children were cared for, teach domestic skills and prevent admissions to care. Ron had started as a CCO in 1966 (Standring 2010) and while he undertook the general run of work he mostly did Approved School after care. He comments that some lads thrived in Approved Schools with discipline, gym, football and so on, but had nothing similar once discharged and promptly went back again. He cannot remember formal supervision from his team leader, Peggy Holt, but she was always supportive. He religiously completed his '*write ups*' immediately after each visit and very much appreciated that they could get on with things, his working day being uncluttered by many meetings. Looking back Ron feels he used a few simple rules, such as never meeting aggression with aggression, and although he thinks he was over anxious waiting for bad things to happen, he is proud he stayed calm and in control when things did go wrong. He also thinks now that '*the hours we put in then were stupid*'.

The Welfare Department in Bolton did much the same work as Brian Fox described in Manchester. In the mid 1960s, having spent some time in the commercial insurance sector, Richard Pool started work there as a clerk. His first job involved pulling together all the pensions for the people in residential homes. '*I used to go round to all [of them] and the residents would be required to queue up to be handed and sign for their 17s 6d pocket money (with an additional 2s 6d if they helped in the kitchen) each week. I used to go home and weep at the degradation of it*'. Later, in 1970 as a Welfare Assistant he recalls having 110 clients, each of whom were visited once a month. He was expected to do eight visits a day. Once he had completed his rounds for the month he was told to look in the electoral roll, get old people's addresses and visit them to advise what services were on offer. He polished off 50 such visits a day. His visiting regime was as rigidly controlled as Annie Higginson's had been in the 1920s. The workers had to be out of the office by 9.15 and could not return until 12.45. A similar rule operated in the afternoon. This sort of regimentation was by no means unusual. At that time Clifford Hilditch, Chief Welfare Officer in Manchester, expected his WOs to do 20 visits a day. And until the mid 1960s WOs in Cheshire had to report every other day to County Hall in Chester, booking in at 8.40am and not being allowed to leave until 4.45pm (Hewitt 2011).

One Friday Richard was in Breightmet, a big council estate in Bolton. He knocked at the door of one lady and there was no reply. Peeking through the letter box he could see the lady lying prone at the end of the hall. Pulling the key up on the string from behind the letter box he let himself in. The lady was in a faint, so he made her as comfortable as he could and got a neighbour to fetch the doctor. The doctor confirmed that there was not much wrong with her and left her to Richard's care. He made her enough meals to see her through the weekend … rousted out neighbours and did a bit of shopping for the lady. This took the best part of the day but Richard felt that he had spent his time well in helping someone in a very tangible way. On his return to the office late that afternoon, Richard completed his weekly 'visits completed' return and handed them in to the appropriate senior officer. Within minutes he was summoned by that senior officer. Richard's views about him are crystal clear. '*Nobody liked him. We thought he was a bully*'. So what happened next came as no surprise to Richard.

> He had a small square of carpet in front of his desk and on that day he literally carpeted me for only doing one visit … I was given no chance to explain. His only concern was how he could report to the Welfare Committee that one of his Welfare Assistants had only done one visit that day … I had got a place on a qualification course and I was starting in a few weeks. Someone had advised me not to apply for secondment as Bolton was so awful at that time I had got my own place and was not tied to the Welfare Department. So what did I have to lose? I told him exactly what I thought of him and turned on my heel and left (Pool 2010).

Voluntary Sector

The work of the FSUs, as we have seen, greatly influenced CDs, some of which established similar services. The social workers I spoke to had nothing but admiration for FSUs and the way they worked. But it was the sort of admiration reserved for tightrope walkers – they thought it was wonderful but were unlikely to try it themselves. As Mary Mason said of FSUs, '*they did anything!*' But some thought FSU workers were a soft touch, easy going and odd-balls.

A different type of voluntary agency in Bolton thrived. Bolton Moral Welfare Association had appointed an outworker in 1942, Irene Wilson. In 1948 she worked with 55 unmarried mothers, 15 married women with illegitimate children, 13 matrimonial problems, 16 young people in moral danger, 16 adoption enquiries and payments of affiliation orders for 12 children. This society had, as philanthropic societies earlier in the century all had, a huge committee, there being 80 members on its council. Through the 1950s the work remained similar but with a steadily increasing number of unmarried mothers; 83 in 1953, 103 in 1955, 132 in 1960 and 137 in 1962. Two additional workers were appointed in response to this increase (BHC B/170/BOL).

The NSPCC too carried on in much the same way, the primary agency dealing with cruelty. Isobel Groves makes the comment that '*in Lancaster CCOs were happiest dealing with foster parent applications in the nice areas rather than addressing concerns about children in the big council estate behind the station*'. E.R. Braithwaite, Marian Penny, Ron Standring and Hilary Corrick confirm that Children's Departments, by and large, did not deal with cases of cruelty, leaving that work to the still largely uniformed, and still overwhelmingly male NSPCC inspectors.

Chapter 7

1948–1971: Training, Outsiders and Themes

Training

Eileen Younghusband's post-war reports about social work training (1947, 1951) revealed a patchwork of courses across England with little consistency and varying levels of exclusiveness. The most widespread courses were the university social studies certificates which had been in place since the Great War – a handful at first, a score or so by 1939 and, according to Walton, 32 in 1951 (1975). People who had taken one of those courses and had the funding could then take specialist training offered by the Institute of Almoners (only in London until after the Second World War) or a train to be a PSW (only at the LSE until 1942). The Home Office offered training for probation officers from 1937, the same year probation officers became state employees rather than CETS funded missionaries. There were also long-standing specialist courses for teachers for the blind and people working with the deaf.

In preparation for the Children Act 1948 the Home Office established what became known as the Child Care Course in 1947. Clare Britton (later Winnicott) was asked to lead it. There was also, as there was for teachers just after the war, a flurry of short-lived emergency training, which included short courses for those Poor Law workers transferring across to CDs or WDs.

Ken Powls went on an extra mural course at Leeds University in 1949 and was surprised to find out that mental defectives could learn to read and write. His previous understanding was that any formal learning was beyond them, making a life in an institution inevitable for many. This perception made him change the way he worked with people. It is also striking that, as a post-war DAO, he reports a willingness to respond to the expectation that he should maintain a relationship with mental cases both in and after hospital (Powls 2010).

C. Ross, working in the Social Welfare Department in Bolton in 1946, left a report about a short course she attended for boarding-out visitors run by the National Provisional Council for Mental Health. She mentions visits to children's organisations and discussions as well as lectures, those by an Educational Psychologist, Miss Thomas, being the most important. These emphasised the mental wellbeing of children boarded-out over traditional concerns such as cleanliness, and characterised a good foster mother as one who would create a warm atmosphere and encourage the child to converse freely. Nearly a third of her report about the course covers child development according to Freud: oral, anal, genital stages of child development, the latency period and adolescence associated with a revival of infantile instincts. This is followed by a discussion about bedwetting and punishment. No examples of practical application of this analysis are offered. But the main messages C. Ross brought back to Bolton were relevant to her work:

> It is of extreme importance that any family ties which exist should not be broken … Untold harm can be done by breaking the blood tie … every foster child and every adopted child should grow up knowing the truth about his own position (BHC ABSS/1/768).

She also noted that foster parents should be persuaded to change their attitude of secrecy; that the importance of the foster fathers should be emphasised and that boarded-out children should take part in organisations for young people in the community. The way the report is written indicates that the advice she noted chimes with her own experience. She seems to have returned from the course considerably enthused (BHC ABSS/1/768).

But no specialist qualification training was put in place for people working in the new WDs or as Mental Welfare Officers. Indeed the tide was turning against specialist training. Eileen Younghusband, having investigated training for social workers, was in a strong position to articulate a vision for training. This required, in her view, a single pattern of qualification training on which specialist skills might be grafted. She championed, with others, what became known as generic social work training. Richard Titmuss at the LSE was persuaded by this argument, funding was secured from the Carnegie Foundation for a three-year pilot of a generic training course and it began in 1954. This approach discomfited both the PSW trainers and the almoners for obvious reasons and led to a famous dispute at LSE about what was to happen once the three-year Carnegie funding ended. Should Eileen Younghusband be offered leadership of subsequent arrangements for social work training with the concomitant acceptance of the generic route as the future? Or should it be Kay McDougall, one of the champions of specialist training? I shall not go into the detail of the dispute that is available in accounts by Donnison (1975) and Jones (1984), but the conflict was obviously painful. Younghusband herself commented 24 years later '*the ashes are still hot*' (Jones 1984: 71). Kay McDougall won and Eileen Younghusband resigned from the LSE. But McDougall's victory was pyrrhic because, early on in the dispute Younghusband had been asked to chair a national review of social work training, which in 1959 resulted in a report which set the structure of social work training for a generation (Younghusband 1959). Generic training was proposed along the lines Younghusband had already championed: leaving the university courses in place and urging the establishment of non-university qualification training for the large number of unqualified workers. In-house training was proposed for those asked to undertake less sophisticated welfare roles. A social work college was also proposed and the National Institute for Social Work Training (later NISW) established. This hosted, for a short time, a one-year training course for experienced staff from WDs where numbers of trained staff were very low. These proposals were accepted by professional bodies of social workers, even the associations of PSWs and almoners, whose control of training in their specialism was to be weakened. More importantly the proposals were accepted by the political establishment, catching a mood which acceded to an expanding need for social workers, and legislation established the Central Council for Training in Social Work.

But training for many social workers from the end of the war into the 1970s comprised two stages – a social science diploma course followed up by social work training. And if numbers trained in WDs were tiny in the 1950s, numbers trained in CDs were not that much greater. These numbers only increased from the early 1960s when Younghusband's training proposals came into force.

It was Something to do With the Way he Talked …

Joyce Rimmer was a student on the pilot generic course at the LSE, which she refers to as the *Carnegie Course*. After a post-graduate certificate in social science Joyce taught for a few months at an Approved School for girls, where she lost a huge amount of weight, so demanding was this experience. She regarded the regime as degrading to the girls, who were completely deprived of affection. Although she thought the head teacher was committed, some staff were not; the psychologist for instance referred to girls not by their name but by the number of their IQ – '*that little 72*'. Traumatised but with increased commitment to help people, Joyce's placement experiences were more positive, particularly her probation placement with Rose Mary Braithwaite at Old Street Court London.

Joyce remembers a lot of law teaching and a lot of psychology on the Carnegie Course. Her tutor was Eileen Younghusband herself '*a very good tutor, who wanted the best and expected hard work and real commitment*'. Joyce remembers being pushed by her and refers to Eileen Younghusband as '*all brain*'.

Although Marian Penny felt '*liberated*' by the social studies course at Hull, she felt uneasy about her skills as she thought the casework teaching there had been weak. So she applied for the Child Care Course at LSE for 1957/58, led by then for ten years by Clare Winnicott. Marian was mesmerised by Donald Winnicott's lectures so much so, that she could not take notes, '*it was something to do with the way he talked*'. But she always remembered one thing he said: '*listen to what the mother says, she knows the child better than anyone*'. She was impressed by most of the content of the course but baffled by some parts of it. '*One woman talked about children's diets, a whole course of lectures on it. She was a joke really and she was "taken of" in the student's play*' (Penny 2010).

But she was impressed by Miss Gardner at the Institute of Education who taught child development, '*who so loved little ones she didn't get beyond the age of 11*'. Marian remembers a particular observation from Miss Gardner's experience:

> She described children playing with aeroplanes, playing at bombing. These children had been bombed out so knew the horror of it first hand and the staff

decided to take the planes off them to stop them thinking about it. Miss Gardner stopped them, saying, 'no, they're in control – leave them to work it through' (Penny 2010).

She also recalls an experience of a visit to Paddington Green Children's Hospital where she followed a ward round with a doctor. After talking to a two-year-old the doctor asked the students what they thought of her. After they had spoken he opined that '*she was a little minx*' and went on to suggest that she would not do well, implying that she would become a prostitute. Marian was shocked and thought that sort of talk was wrong and a misuse of authority. Fascinating though it all was, however, and despite the privilege she felt at being there, Marian felt aspects of the course were '*directionless, perhaps because Clare Winnicott had been ill and out of it for nearly a year*'.

Mary Hartley trained at Harris College, Preston, receiving the Home Office Letter of Recognition. Mary learned about theories of behaviour, family dynamics, and the impact of the worker on families and began to think she had done terrible things to families in Blackpool. Slowly however it dawned on her that she may have just been operating in her own way, which may well have been as effective as doing it by the book.

Isobel Groves' memories of her social studies degree in Durham at the age of 18 in 1958 are dominated by Miss Lloyd and Constance Braithwaite, both of whom she admired. Constance Braithwaite, she recalls, was the stereotypical social worker of her day, wearing a pudding-basin hat and a handbag across her bosom. Isobel also remembers practical advice from Miss Lloyd about always wearing a bolero. '*If it's hot you can take it off while you have your lunch, but to see a client you must always wear sleeves*', and wear the dowdiest clothing possible for visits to prison, '*as they have not seen a woman for a long time*'. Isobel also recalls the exhortation not to be shocked by people in the office saying funny things, '*this is just letting off steam*'. Isobel then went directly to Liverpool University where she took her Home Office Letter of Recognition. '*We were Freudian and Biestek trained*' she says, '*although Derek Jehu was just beginning his interest in behaviourism*'. Keith Hiscock's memory of the same course some years later was that it had a behaviourist slant.

Isobel's vivid memories are from her placements. One placement supervisor, Miss Jay, said that Isobel could not go to court without a hat, and showed her the office hat. Isobel was horrified and dashed down to British Home Stores to buy a proper one. A bright young woman, Isobel obviously caused something of a stir. Miss Jay suggested to her tutor Peter Boss that Isobel wore too much makeup to be a social worker. He was amused by this and made no mention of it in his report, only telling Isobel later who, understandably, was furious. This concern to maintain a conservative appearance was not unusual. Ron Standring remembers a CCO in Bolton called Judith, who was once given a dressing down by the CO, Philip Varey, for wearing a trouser suit.

I Never Missed Anything!

Brian Fox, encouraged by the Chief Welfare Officer in Manchester, Arthur Ryan, applied in 1961 for the new course run by the NISWT at Mary Ward House in London. Brian didn't think he stood a chance, but was interviewed and was accepted. Robin Huws Jones was Director of the NISWT course. He and his wife, Enid, an important partner in all his activities, and their children, were installed in a flat on the top floor of the Institute. Eileen Younghusband claims that with the warmth that emanated from that household and the training activities underway, Mary Ward House soon became a haven for international visitors and for meetings, discussions and conferences of senior administrators, social workers and academics (Jones 1984). According to Brian Fox this was not hyperbole. The course he says was a '*very threatening*' experience, which consisted of '*unwrapping you, and putting you back together again. They handled it so well*', he says '*it was brilliant*'. How could the teaching be any better with regular contributors including Penelope Hall, Eileen Younghusband and Donald Winnicott – although before he arrived the students had a pep talk during which they were told '*how important Winnicott was*'. The Huws Jones family invited students to dinner with the many visitors in their flat upstairs and there were regular social events, parties and dances. Brian recalls one student, while dancing with Penelope Hall, commenting that he had '*been to bed with her all the previous week*', she being able to take the joke. No one, he says, would have dared say anything like that to Eileen Younghusband, whose lectures were so intense. As a result of his training Brian became more confident and found that on his return in 1963 people sought his advice. But while most of his colleagues were happy to chat, others – and not just the older ones – could not see the point of training. He says that the Deputy Chief Welfare Officer noticed an essay Brian had left with one of the typists and instructed her not to type the word *non-judgmental* because it was not English.

Ruth Evans, as reflective a commentator as Marian, is very open about the starting point on her training course. '*All I brought along was enthusiasm ... and a nebulous wish to be useful. The innocence with which I conducted my happy venture at the vicarage* (offering holidays to deprived children) *was the better for being unmolested by the pressure of theoretical impedimenta*' (Evans 1977: 49). She is very specific about what she learned on placements, an example being that curing wayward youngsters in isolation from their families and peer influences was a fruitless task. She learned to pay attention to how people looked, stood and smelled, even though she said it was often misleading. She learned not to chase absconders: '*one loses face*' (Evans 1977: 54) and learned a strong lesson about sticking to doing what you think is right. She convinced herself, to her lasting shame, that she should persuade a boy to return from his home to a boarding school. As it happened he jumped from the car and never did go back but the experience ruined his faith in her. And like others the experience of being on the course itself was of key significance. '*During my training I was encouraged to look inside myself, to do accounts with myself about my motivation ... I thought it was presumptuous ... too introverted to indulge in'* (Evans 1977: 50).

But slowly she saw that previously she had been in the shadow of big personalities, her late husband and his friends, and began to see herself as '*a person in her own right'*. Through it all her confidence blossomed. '*I knew that here there was work I wanted to do and could do'* (Evans 1977: 51). Her attitude to social work literature however was stark. She found the volume of words and magnitude of related theories frightening:

> Much of it is too dry and too finely ... spun with threads of intellectualism. Despite valuable and enlightening comments and fascinating interpretations it often does not seem to touch the practicalities of everyday encounters with men, women and children ... I find the brave new world in social work literature a little synthetic (Evans 1977: 135).

Others were searching for clear guidance too. Sheila Ives grew up in Harrow and after leaving school worked at Heathrow airport on check-in. Bored by that, after helping out in a nursery she decided to be a CCO, starting her training at Bristol University in 1967. '*I knew nothing'* she says, but did not take a lot from her course:

> It was very Freudian and I could not understand why it was all so vague. Fifteen people were on the course and three ended up very distressed by the introspection of it all. They were very good at breaking you down but not very good at building you up. One student spoke of his wonderful casework with a family, his concern being marital problems. I would have concentrated on their housing problem because they were being threatened with eviction, and indeed were evicted! (Ives 2011).

Marie McNay felt she had a wide ranging course. It explored individual psychology and family dynamics, stimulated by a tutor who had been to America and was familiar with the family work developing there in the 1950s. Marie trained between 1966 and 1969 at Barking College and remembers with gratitude the teaching which included group work and community work – unusual for the time she thinks. She was gripped by it all: '*I never missed anything'* she says and has always, as a result, espoused a wide range of interventions.

Peter Hewitt responded positively to his training too, but by taking what he could use practically and occasionally showcasing the approved language of social work training. Jean Heywood's course at Manchester had a psychodynamic ethos, unsurprisingly as '*they'd all been analysed'*. Peter saw himself as '*pragmatic, focussed on the here and now and trying to help people make a difference in their own lives'*. But he admits that as a student, he used the Part C (the summary part of the national recording template used by probation officers at the time) '*to debate ego development of various clients'* (Hewitt 2011).

Invariably the social workers I spoke to made long-standing decisions based on their placement experiences. H. Clare Makepeace trained at LSE in 1967. She had been confronted on her pre-course placements in a city Welfare Department by having to use a certain formality in her relationships, to dress appropriately and to get the right forms filled in. This did not sit well but she took it because she wanted to learn. Her supervisor, a former medical social worker, provided her with a structure by being the first person to give her with the opportunity of reflecting on what she was doing in building relationships from a social worker perspective. '*I realised this was the sort of person I had got to be*' (Makepeace 2011).

Her training also confronted her with her own ignorance. On an FWA placement she had to work with a young woman and her mother with concerns about her marital relationship. '*I was out of my depth*'. She also helped a woman with three children move into a tenancy from accommodation for homeless families but did not feel equipped to offer real help. '*It was difficult to see what I was actually doing*'. Her supervisor told Clare that she was having difficulty because she came from a stable family background but she would learn. Clare felt these insights were helpful in understanding more about herself and her capabilities. She went from that experience to the more structured environment of St Georges Hospital in London. The students worked in close proximity to their supervisor and the medical social workers. She says that the consultant there valued what social workers did and because she had a year's experience as an auxiliary nurse she was familiar with the surroundings and the language. Her role was to work on two wards covered by a consultant. The work was varied and as some people had to make considerable changes to their lifestyle or living arrangements she worked with some people after discharge. She felt so positive about this experience that she looked for opportunities to work in GP practices once she had qualified.

Mary Hartley sums up the views of several people I spoke to about training: it was stimulating, but most important was the confidence and the valued status it could offer:

> Of course we did a lot of work in groups and I learned a lot about myself, I suppose partly because in a group I could never bear the silence. I don't think I did anything differently after training but I felt I belonged after that; I had my ticket.

But many social workers during this period did not get that ticket. Mary Mason, for instance never undertook qualification training, '*always being just ahead of it*', as she progressed through various more senior jobs over two decades.

Outsiders

During this period there were survivals from earlier days of limited aspirations for a child in public care's future. Mary Mason, for instance, was particularly critical of organisations such as British Boys for British Farms which placed children leaving care in farms just as they had done fifty years before. She herself placed boys in trawler work. She also recalls at least one foster couple who wanted to adopt a girl more or less as a domestic servant, but only remembers one child emigrating – a bright boy who did very well with his Duke of Edinburgh's award and whose choice was entirely voluntary. And as social workers were mostly middle class and the people they dealt with working class and often poor they were outsiders to each other's experience.

But there were people who were more outsiders than others, Catholics for instance. Part of the reason for the several moves Dennis O'Neill and his brothers endured was Newport's search for a Catholic placement. This was not unusual. Mary Mason said '*it was an unforgivable sin if a child was placed in a home of the wrong religion*'.

Social workers' responses to the needs of what were universally referred to as 'coloured' people were sometimes confused, but on other occasions very clear. Ruth Evans' comments about 'coloured' girls are restricted to what she thought of as their enchanting waywardness. Isobel Groves worked in Bradford when immigrants from the West Indies and South Asia were mostly men. Isobel reports that working with different ethnic groups was very enriching, although she encountered awful poverty, with rickets in children a real concern. She and the local Medical Officer of Health became very concerned about the welfare of a number of girls living in households made up largely of Pakistani men. One 11-year-old, Rana, whose full name Isobal can recall nearly 50 years later, was removed to a reception centre where she expressed concerns for her eight-year-old sister still in the household. When the authorities arranged for a medical examination to be undertaken the child was spirited away. Isobel still thinks about this, wondering what she could have done to help her.

But my key informant about how social workers related to 'coloured' people is E.R. Braithwaite, another social worker novelist. His approach in *Paid Servant* (1962) was similar to John Stroud's. Case stories are intertwined with observations about the work, with one child's situation followed through the whole narrative. But there are differences too. John Stroud was a career CCO, active in the Association of Child Care Officers (ACCO), conscious of his responsibilities towards the idea of social work, the emerging profession. E.R. Braithwaite had no such commitment and his stance as an outsider is maintained throughout the novel.

Braithwaite was brought up by Oxford educated parents, received a university education himself and seems to have had some sense of being a cut above the average man. He was black, from Guyana, trained as an engineer in Britain before the war and joined the RAF for the duration. Unable to get a job in engineering in 1945 because of prejudice he fell into teaching in the East End of London in the early 1950s. He did not choose to be a social worker but was seconded to the LCC Children's Welfare Department from teaching, to find placements for the increasing number of 'coloured' children they were having difficulty placing. So he had received no social work training and saw himself as different from his CCO colleagues, frequently pointing this out. He also observed parents, children and CCOs with the appraising eye of the writer. By the time he was a social worker his first novel *To Sir, with Love,* based on his experiences teaching a class of difficult, uninterested 15-year-olds had been accepted for publication. This intimacy with and immersion in the work, combined with his distance from the profession, make Braithwaite's observations especially valuable.

The children he worked with were 'coloured', or described as such, all of whom were considered difficult to place. Braithwaite's job was to find placements for them and to recruit foster parents. He went about his work with verve and imagination. From beginning to end he describes using whatever opportunities arise, preferring informal methods over what he sees as the bureaucratic approach of his colleagues. He approaches friends to foster children; recruits white couples (subsequently turned down by the department as unsuitable for 'coloured' children); recruits a woman he has only met once on a train; attempts to recruit a single woman and so on. One of the main themes is the difficulty presented by simple, blind prejudice against 'coloured' people, although all his colleagues state clearly they are not prejudiced. He wonders, for instance, why all the 'coloured' children have ethnic descriptions in their records but the white children don't, even if they are, for instance, half Irish or half German.

The boy whose story is followed through the novel is the son of a white English girl, who wants nothing to do with the child, and a US soldier thought to be Hispanic who had returned to the USA. Braithwaite cannot get across to his colleagues that culturally and ethnically he has nothing in common with either of the boy's parents or that Roddy, four by the time he meets him, is as English as the rain from the sky. And withal he rages at the off-hand racialism, as it was called, shown towards 'coloured' children – especially poor Roddy – about whom one of his colleagues muses that he is impossible to place with a family where there are girls because of '*what could happen in adolescence or later*' (Braithwaite 1962: 8).

He is also sceptical about other attitudes of his colleagues. He comments that the physical arrangements of the waiting room in the office did nothing to relieve the anxieties of the visitors. '*It's shape colour and furnishings made it a striking example of the complete lack of imagination characteristic of bureaucratic planning*'. He wondered why it was that '*although women occupied the most senior positions ... they have not been sufficiently revolted by the sterile and miserable conditions of the ... waiting rooms to bring about some worthwhile improvements*' (Braithwaite 1962: 45). He wonders too at his colleagues behaviour. '*At most interviews I witnessed officialdom and not service. The officer was the kingpin, firmly in the seat of authority*' (Braithwaite 1962: 49). He says he tried in his own interviews to reverse that and '*make the applicant conscious of being served*'. He ponders this at length, regarding black Welfare Officers for 'coloured' children unnecessary '*if only the Welfare Officers could see themselves as servants. True, they were all decent, intelligent, sympathetic people, but ... they saw themselves as officers, as people in authority*' (Braithwaite 1962: 49). He recounts a conversation with '*Jim Baxter*', one of the five male CCOs in a department of 16. Having been in the department for six years Braithwaite said Jim didn't take a step without being quite sure of all the precedents. '*He knew all the ... neuroses by name and after he had interviewed an applicant, would neatly fit him or her into the appropriate neurotic pigeonhole. He never said "child" if he could say "sibling"*' (Braithwaite 1962: 72). Jim said he started out each case convincing himself he disliked the people, so that once the case was resolved he could forget about it and have his mind free for the next problem. '*I care for my family emotionally, but I care for these others in a kind of scientific way*' (Braithwaite 1962: 174).

Themes

There are several themes that emerge from these accounts which are worth noting. First of all, for those working in child care, was the spread of Bowlby's ideas about children needing to bond properly with a mother figure in order to have basic security, and needing a loving family to develop as an independent individual. Most of those working in the 1950s took this thinking on board – slowly some of them – from their own experience, from training and what was being debated in the profession. And there were other influences. James Robertson's film *A Two-Year-Old Goes to Hospital* (1952) was a documentary in which the cruelty of separating a mother from a two-year-old girl for a stay on a ward needs little commentary. Marian Penny saw the film during her training and remembers the immense impact it had on her.

But like many ideas where the penny has to drop in each individual mind for its full impact to be felt, the spread of the idea of the importance of attachment was fitful. If there was a fulcrum for the change it may well have been John Bowlby's 1951 speech at the Association of Children's Officers (ACO) meeting, the same year that *Maternal Care and Mental Health* was published (Bowlby 1951). His ideas were so powerfully expressed that ACO changed its terms of reference as a result (Brill 1991).

But through the 1940s and 1950s although many people were persuaded of the importance of attachment, others were not. Kenneth Brill claims that his training at LSE in 1938, where Bowlby was teaching, gave him '*a thorough grounding in the concept of separation anxiety ... twelve years before it became the small change of social work thinking*' (Rimmer 1995:179). C. Ross's report on her training in 1946 confirms her understanding of it as does Mavis Smith's report mentioning '*Mother Love*' (BHC ABSS/1/768).

On the other hand Barbara Totton recalls in her early years as an almoner, just as the war was ending, having to assure mothers whose children needed some sort of treatment that they would be fine in a nursery and not to worry. She shudders at the memory. Nora Cooper regretted something that happened early in her career. A two-year-old boy had Glue Ear and although he could not be discharged home, the ENT department demanded he be moved. '*Someone suggested that "if Honor had been the social worker, Peter would be in a convalescent home by now"*'.

Under pressure Nora arranged for the child to be placed in a home by the sea on the Welsh coast, 75 miles from Wolverhampton and his family. Nora looks back on this decision to separate this child from his family with something very close to shame. She also says that only one of her supervisors, Mary Fox, emphasised that children removed from their parents should always be helped and encouraged to keep in touch with them.

In the early 1950s Mary Mason reports that her first boss in Dewsbury operated on the principle that they should sever contact between the parents and children placed with foster parents or adopted. She said '*one changed an awful lot*' and that in this regard she '*had a complete conversion*'. Her own experience convinced her of the power and need of children for their parents and vice versa. She described the case of a 15-year-old girl who had been placed with a couple as a domestic servant. They got on well and the couple started talking about adopting her. The girl was appalled by the idea of the severance from her birth family becoming final and ran away.

And spread of the idea was not firmly championed by national authority. For instance, the Curtis report anticipated boarding-out officers' caseloads as being around 150 each. The report also advised that infants in public care should be in a nursery for the first year of their lives before being boarded-out, hardly a ringing endorsement of the importance of early attachment (Brill 1991: 111). And John Moss, who had been on the Curtis Committee, produced a report for the Home Office in 1953 on child migration which had always been a contentious practice. The report endorsed migration, commenting that standards in homes were high and produced '*remarkably successful results*' (Kershaw and Sacks 2008: 217). Brill asserts that some CCOs and CDs discouraged or even prevented contact between parents and children in care well into the 1960s (Brill 1991: 208). Keith Hiscock, working in Westminster in the late 1960s, comments that at the time '*trying to keep children in care in touch with their families was reasonably novel*'. His senior colleague told him that – as late as 1961 – CCOs would take children to foster homes and leave them there, no obligation mentioned or implied about keeping children in touch with their families.

But by the end of the period the centrality of the idea was firmly established.

The second theme is a localised and variable picture of relationships between welfare agencies. Stroud's experience, as reported in *The Shorn Lamb* about his first visit to the Magistrates Court in 1948, was not positive.

> There were … two Probation Officers … Mr Bland's … dark twill trousers were always creased to a knife edge, and … hair and moustache were brushed till they shone. His colleague Miss Perret, was tall and round shouldered … They treated us in a kind but slightly condescending way, as though they were stage managers at the London Palladium unexpectedly having to deal with the winners of the Rutland Amateur Dramatic Festival (Stroud 1960: 24).

On the other hand, probation officer Joyce Rimmer reports getting on well with CCOs, but not really working with them, '*we all just got on with what we were doing*'. Nora Cooper wonders now why, as an almoner, she did not work closely with the CD. Mary Hartley says her relationship with police in Blackpool was '*cosy*'. She also had a lot to do with Health Visitors and some GPs who she respected a great deal – unlike Mental Welfare Officers. She did not respect them as they always seemed to '*muddle*' along. Relations between workers and councillors were very close in some areas. CDs were tiny, so councillors and workers had frequent opportunity to meet up. Mary Mason says of Warrington in the late 1950s: '*some councillors knew the job and the area better than the CCOs*'. One example of the greater role played by elected representatives concerns David Custance, a young unqualified CCO in Knowsley in 1970. He reports being made welcome by the team and warned that councillors sometimes rang up and, on occasion, the MP. One day he had a telephone call put through from Westminster about a case he was working on. On the line came the distinctive voice of Harold Wilson, the Prime Minister, asking after something raised in one of his surgeries. David observes drily that his career was downhill after that, 1970 being the only occasion his advice was sought by a serving Prime Minister (Custance 2010).

Maurice Ffelan reports that the Children's Officer Margery Decker in Preston County Borough faced the '*unrestrained hostility*' of the Education Chief in the early 1950s because he felt that his work had been taken away from him by the Children Act. Maurice says that a little of that hostility was still evident in the early 1960s.

The third theme is one we have noted right from the beginning of the century: each social worker relied to a certain extent on informal methods or contacts. Jack Preston says '*what made the difference*' in his career was his strong informal relationships with the police, market traders and housing officers. This allowed him, among other things, to make good attempts to get people rehoused, and helped him offer regular Christmas parties for children in care without considerable expense (Preston 2010). Ruth Evans ran informal sessions on a Sunday afternoon for a group of girls living in a hostel. She did this in her own home, much like Jo Harris 50 years before, and reports that at first the occasions were stilted, but that they soon warmed up. Mary Mason during the 1950s bent the rules a little. A mother of three children died and the father had been off the scene for a long time. Miss Mason, finding no procedure preventing her approving a 16-year-old as a foster parent, did exactly that with the older daughter who was content – for a while at least – to share the care of the younger children with relatives, and the family was not broken up. Isobel Groves reports being exasperated by a particular family in which the mother was kept short of money which led to rent arrears. One pay day she marched to the docks where the husband worked and took his pay packet so the rent could be paid. When told about this incident Isobel's supervisor, according to her, focussed on the psychological aspects of her relationship with the family, to which Isobel replied that none of that would have mattered had they not had a roof over their heads. Hilary Corrick appears to have operated in this manner all the time. On one occasion, in preparation for taking a group of children away for the weekend, she was having difficulty getting the funding from one of the fathers. She went to the pub she knew he was in and extracted the cash there and then. His wife reported later: '*you really showed him up. He's been much better since then*'. Hilary also recalls one family in a terrible state, the gas and electric both being off: '*there were potties with poo in them and they were all drinking sterilized milk*'. In a fit of enthusiasm she offered to come and decorate for them, but when she arrived they had done it already. '*That was a relief. I'd never decorated in my life!*' (Corrick 2011).

The fourth theme is pride. Peter Hewitt and Isobel Groves both reported that in the early sixties new workers shared a sense of excitement about what they were doing. '*We were going to win the world*' says Isobel, and Peter still enthuses about the agitation there was at the time for prevention initiatives to be recognised by statute, finally achieved in 1963. Ron Standring's comment is more prosaic: '*It was a privilege to be a Child Care Officer*'. Mary Mason agrees and was '*glad I was in that sort of social work. You saw super people as well as the difficult situations*'. Several remember *The Shorn Lamb* with great affection, suggesting it gave them a fillip, seeing their own experiences in print. Maurice Ffelan felt proud of the preventive work he did. Isobel is still proud of the foster carers' group she started in Bradford. Mary Hartley sums it up with: '*feeling satisfied at having achieved something ... seeing families who were at the point of breaking up who stayed together*'.

She also tells a tale from much later, when she was a very senior figure and was seeing a group of carers. She was asked by one of the young people if she had been a CCO in Blackpool and had she placed a particular boy for adoption. Mary concurred, slightly apprehensively, wondering what was coming, but was told that the boy placed had settled well, was now a doctor and that the family still talked about her work with them with fondness and gratitude.

Along with this there was a feeling from those who became social workers in the middle of this period that they were entering a profession on the cusp of significant change. Young people entered the work with commitment and passion, but they who wanted to live family lives as well as have a career. Isobel Groves remembers working in Nelson in Lancashire, in the late 1960s under the Area Officer Miss King, who had been a moral welfare worker. Miss King's view was that workers should always be available. Isobel, as a newly married woman, was acutely conscious that these old-school single ladies worked deep into the night and had difficulty accepting people who wanted to carry on a family life as well as being a social worker.

The fifth theme seems barely worth mentioning: these people cared about their clients and when things went wrong they hurt. Sometimes they felt bad about parts of the job which were horrible but unavoidable. Marie McNay says that in the later 1960s children with learning disabilities were still excluded from mainstream schooling and one of her tasks was to take a letter to parents informing them of this. She describes it as one of the worst tasks she ever had to do as a social worker, made worse because alternative provision was very poor. Isobel Groves reports spending a lot of time with Jimmy, brought up in difficult circumstances and whose mother was a prostitute. He went off the rails at 13 and Isobel feels she failed because she could not reach him. This feeling was made more poignant as his aunt bought her a present, so highly did she think of Isobel's work. Marian Penny is haunted by the memory of Pamela, 14 and in a local mental hospital when Marian got to know her. Removed from her mother, '*a vagrant*', at the age of two, Pamela had been subjected to placement after placement. Marian was advised straightaway that there was nothing wrong with Pamela and when she was discharged from hospital, the chairman of the Children's Committee offered her a job. This broke down as a result of Pamela '*letting rip, with appalling destructive outbursts*', and the pattern of placement break downs continued. Marian left Bolton in 1967 but kept in touch with Pamela. Marian continued to try and support her until, after having her own child removed, Pamela committed suicide at the age of 31. Marian does not know what she could have done differently, but she is still baffled and pained by the memory of this failure. These feelings of failure edge into a more general sense of regret with some people about the things they missed. Hilary Corrick says '*I'm ashamed for the children; the ones I didn't notice*'. Maurice Ffelan still feels a sense of guilt, reporting that he never felt he had enough time to devote to individuals. Peter Hewitt says something very similar about children who were sexually abused. Ron Standring sums it in his comment: '*Looking back there were many things I could have done better*'.

The sixth theme is that nearly all drew immense support from colleagues and supervisors. Isobel Groves thought it '*was like a big family*'. Nora Cooper says the best part of the work was being part of a team, being able to talk about what she was doing. Marian Penny makes it clear that being in a supportive team was very important: '*you need that sort of support*' and she reports being part of an '*amicable*' team. Ron Standring remembers a '*good family atmosphere*'. Joyce Rimmer found everyone '*very, very supportive*'. Keith Hiscock reports that in Westminster '*the team leader was wonderful ... the team was everything*'. Barbara Totton thought the team in Lewisham was '*wonderful*'. And all the Bolton workers, especially in the CD, thought the teams they were in were supportive and safe. In many CDs the close involvement of the CO was crucial to this inclusive feeling. '*All the teams were in one place*' says Sheila Ives of the CD in Southampton, '*and everyone was very supportive. We all had coffee together. The Children's Officer, a lovely man, came out and made the coffee*' (Ives 2011). Mary Hartley says a key feature of Blackpool CD in the 1960s was its leadership. '*Jack Earl, the CO, always accompanied the CCO on any final visit or just prior to a case going to committee*'. He was also very skilled and set the tone for a group of people '*who shared everything*', each knowing their colleagues' clients and offering all the support that implies. So everything, from the trauma of having to move a child from an adoptive placement to the daily inconvenience of nits, was dealt with in the context of a comprehensively supportive team (Hartley 2010). Even E.R. Braithwaite praises the willingness of his colleagues to explain things to him. '*This was ... characteristic of Welfare Officers ... whenever I needed help or advice it was always there, without exception*' (Braithwaite 1962: 128).

But he was not so happy with senior people and in *Paid Servant* uses a senior officer, Miss Conley, as a device for outlining all the bureaucratic hurdles that stopped him placing children where they would thrive; all the organisational rules which responded to the colour of a child's skin first and the actual needs of the child second. Others, universally, report regular detailed support from senior people. Jane Sparrow for instance, the pseudonymous author of *Diary of Student Social Worker* (1978), describes her final placement in a CD around 1959. She reports a demanding but supportive supervisor, an increasing amount of work, starting with arranging short-term placements, but concentrating on three cases where she has to negotiate the interface between long-term private foster carers and the parents of teenage children. But Jane also reports to her surprise the CO's interest in her cases and how much time he commits to discussing them with her. In Somerset nearly ten years later Hilary Corrick reports that every two weeks the Assistant CO would come down to Yeovil and go through their cases with each CCO (Corrick 2011). This support from the top was also available in Merton, London, when Hilary moved there in 1967. She said there was a message book and sometimes there'd be a note from the CO about a court report Hilary had written saying something like '*I saw that report and it was very good*'. Keith Hiscock, when he moved to Bedfordshire, says that the CO always paid attention to individual cases. Barbara Totton remembers similar support. Working for LCC before it was abolished in 1965: '*there were always specialists in County Hall you could ring up*'.

The support experienced by social workers existed on a broader canvas too. The establishment of the journals the *British Journal of Psychiatric Social Work*, and *The Almoner* in 1947 and 1948 and *Case Conference* in 1952 attest to an expansive confidence (Rimmer 1995); and the establishment of ACO in 1948 and ACCO in 1949 and the Institute of Social Welfare in 1954, along with the long established APSW, Institute of Almoners and NAPO ensured constant debate about the issues nationally.

Chapter 8
1971–1979: Seebohmising

Diagnosis and Treatment

When Marian Penny left Bolton in 1967 she was interviewed by the local newspaper. Asked for her view of social work she said '*skill in diagnosis has outstripped the facilities to treat children in need*' and that '*several social workers might be visiting the same family, overlapping wastefully*' (BEN 1967: 4). Marian thought social work agencies should be brought together in one organisation but nevertheless was confident of the effectiveness of what social workers did. Their professional efforts were certainly valued; numbers of social workers in child care more or less doubled in five years both in Bolton (from five to eleven) and across England after the fillip of the 1963 CYP Act (BHC AB/32/1/[2]). Numbers of probation officers employed were increasing too and their work now encompassed discharged prisoners and a greater proportion of adult offenders. Probation work also achieved a higher national profile with the TV series *Probation Officer*, with Honor Blackman, which ran between 1959 and 1962 (Bochel 1976).

But despite this expansion, confidence and higher public profile, traditional themes were still apparent in the late 1960s. Hilary Corrick for instance had no desire to be a social worker, but as the daughter of Harry Mapstone, CO of Somerset, her career path was probably inevitable. She did sociology at LSE which she hated. But Hilary loved living in a settlement while studying. In the mid 1960s Bede House in Bermondsey had 24 residents, each of whom had to contribute to one of the club activities. Hilary ran a club for children aged 5–7 and one for teenage boys. Having found no real direction after that, while she was at home in Somerset, Hilary's father invited the Deputy Children's Officer to tea. The officer begged Hilary to help out at the Yeovil office for a fortnight. How could she refuse? Forty-five years later, when speaking to me, she still had not completed that fortnight's work. From the start she thought the work was '*engaging, intriguing*'. The Area Officer was Juliet Berry, '*very posh and very classy*' according to Hilary.

> She used to have me in her office every day and asked me what my plans were, and like everyone else she was immensely supportive. She was also into feelings and silences. Sometimes with a client she would just stop ... and say nothing. I would feel the sweat trickling down the back of my neck: the anxiety of it all (Corrick 2011).

Another feature of the work Hilary appreciated was the '*wonderful admin support*' in Merton CD when she moved there in 1967. '*The admin officer would tell us that a review was due on a child in a fortnight and here are the forms for it, or she'd say it's a particular child's birthday soon, here's a card and here's some money for a present*'. Carol Clark was similarly grateful for the administrative support in the CD she worked in. '*It was so well structured and organised I never had to fill a form in*' (Clark 2011). Keith Hiscock says the same.

For Hilary there was a down side. She thought some family work lacked focus, and says '*we were very judgemental, talking about people's inadequacies and problem families*'.

One Man Intake Team

In addition to this traditional work in CDs, innovative roles were appearing. In 1967 Clare Makepeace, having been attracted by work in a medical setting, started in the integrated Health and Welfare Department in Buckinghamshire. The team had a Senior Social Worker, a qualified worker, a social work assistant and two trainees. The Senior Mental Welfare Officer offered her induction and soon after appointment she was undertaking a full range of responsibilities. This included being on call two or three nights a week and one weekend a month. She remembers this as a '*baptism of fire*', as the work covered all the department's responsibilities including homeless people, for half the county. But she felt support systems were in place and recalls '*some good practice out of hours*'. Sometimes a doctor would leave a completed form for an individual's compulsory admission to hospital with '*a responsible person*' before she arrived. Clare always felt she should do a proper assessment and explore whether there was an alternative, feeling the weight of responsibility for removing someone from home. As the ambulance service monitored her whereabouts and provided transport to hospital she did not feel on her own. As part of her responsibilities Clare took over from the Area Officer, an experienced medical social worker, work with a GP group practice. Clare shared work and recording with an experienced Health Visitor whose caseload included children under five and people over 75. Clare took on patients with social problems arising from physical illness and disabilities, mental health, learning disabilities and family problems. She was supported to maintain her own networks with social workers and local welfare agencies and contributed recommendations to the multi agency '*problem families meeting, where rent arrears and potential evictions were addressed*' (Makepeace 2011).

In 1970 she moved to the North West and was appointed as Medical Social Worker for Cheshire Health Department, as part of a team of OTs, volunteer organisers and an employment service. '*The service had been developed around the needs of young people with physical disabilities in transition from residential school to adult services*'. Her previous experience, in particular with the rehabilitation staff at Stoke Mandeville hospital, helped as '*I began to work with people with complex needs set up home, and to offer a wider range of support services and after care services than currently existed'.*

Peter Hewitt had an innovative role as well. He left probation in 1969 and was appointed as Diagnostic Social Worker in Hattersley, a Manchester overspill estate, which had few shops and amenities. Peter describes the job as a '*one man intake team*'. He was jointly managed by a WO, who was qualified and positive, and a very traditional CO. Working out of an advice centre he was the front door for the CD and the Welfare Department. He established good working relationships with all agencies, making sure he had lunch regularly in the CD and Welfare Offices. He took referrals for both departments and was consciously community-oriented in his approach. He was determined that no family should be evicted on his watch, so worked with families where there were notices to quit, developing a strong partnership with the housing department, with an Environmental Health Officer, Bob Young. He also ran a campaign to treat dampness in the poorly constructed Wimpey houses. He tried hard to support older people in their own homes, lamenting the very limited range of resources available. '*If the offer of meals, the local Darby and Joan club, or Home Help was not enough you could not offer anything*'.

Massive Structural Reform

There was in the late 1960s a political consensus that large state organisations were both effective and benign and a strong trust in the experts tasked with making the state work. There were several such expert occupations, new ones, on whose skills people increasingly relied: town planners, nuclear scientists, architects working on public housing, pharmaceutical scientists, psychiatrists, teachers in state secondary schools, social workers and probation officers. These people, using what might seem to lay people, incomprehensible wizardry, helped make the world more predictable, safer (Beckett 2009).

As the nation's health was improving and housing needs were being met other problems emerged. Immigration from the New Commonwealth countries fuelled economic expansion, but led to social tensions (Green 1979). The continued existence of poverty was brought to public attention in the 1960s, as well as the idea of relative poverty (Abel Smith and Townsend 1965). The revelation about how limited the range of care offered to poor older people was and the continued reliance on residential care caused a stir (Townsend 1962). The rise in juvenile crime from 1956 was noted and mainstream society was bemused by promenading Teddy Boys and later Mods and Rockers fighting (Sandbrook 2005). The political establishment pondered all this and in the early 1960s the Ingelby Report (Ingelby 1961) confirmed that support of the family was a legitimate role of the state and encouraged greater coordination between welfare services. The Labour Party Study Group report *Crime: a Challenge to us All* (Labour Party Study Group 1964) suggested there should be a family service as part of the response to crime and the

White Paper *The Child the Family and the Young Offender* (Home Office 1965) proposed that family support was the way to reduce juvenile crime. As a result of these deliberations and pressed by a social work lobby, Frederic Seebohm, a banker, was asked in 1965 to chair a committee to look into personal social services (Cooper 1983).

The Seebohm Committee found uncoordinated, under-resourced services and proposed that social work and welfare services should come under a single local authority department in which '*a family or individual in need ... should, as far as possible, be served by a single social worker*' (Seebohm 1968). The new Social Services Department (SSD) in each area should be freestanding (i.e. separate from the NHS) and have a role in ensuring reciprocal support across communities. The report gained sufficient political support to see the proposals accepted.

Peter Hewitt recalls younger POs being in favour of the proposed amalgamation of social workers, including POs, into one organisation, but remembers older officers being horrified at the prospect. But other traditional social work groups – the APSW and the Institute of Medical Social Workers – supported the recommendations, even though they implied a dilution of their specialist function (Means and Smith 1998: 302). In the end probation officers stayed out and medical social workers went in.

This Man Just Spoke to Me for Hours and then Went Silent

Through all of this thousands of individuals were still offering their time as volunteers. In the London Care Committee system, where Geraldine Aves and Lucy Faithfull worked before the war, old attitudes persisted. Willmott reports that while a Care Organiser was in conversation with someone from outside the care committee, a volunteer walked into the office. The Care Organiser stood up automatically, not to greet her, but out of ingrained respect. This incident, from the 1960s, was interpreted, surely correctly, as a survival from COS days of Harry Snell, when volunteers were the key people and organisers mere functionaries (Willmott 2004). Another care committee worker was frustrated by volunteers.

> Voluntary workers, Great! But ... the only ones I ever met were the wives of politicians ... of senior officers in various things. Another thing, I really didn't like – you'd go to a dinner party and you'd hear them chatting away about how they did their social work that day. To me that was totally unprofessional (Willmott 2004: 104).

Qualified workers at the time had a thin view of volunteers. Peter Hewitt comments ruefully: '*we had an exaggerated sense of our own professionalism – we were setting up a profession, and inadvertently ignored a lot of voluntary effort*'.

As well as individual volunteers, a new more assertive voluntarism had been emerging. Aneurin Bevan, who steered the NHS bill through Parliament, commented on its implementation in 1948 that '*after tomorrow the weak will be entitled to clamour*' (The Times 1948: 3). Even under the NHS there were groups not properly catered for and some did begin to clamour. One of these was Judy Fryd, a mother whose little girl had a learning disability and who, in 1946, had been declined admission to her primary school as unsuitable for mainstream education. She wrote a letter to the Times, to which scores of parents in similar circumstances replied. As a result the National Association of Parents of Backward Children was established, flourished and is now known as Mencap. Similarly in 1952 four parents of spastic children and a social worker, Jean Garwood, called a meeting, advertised their presence and the Spastic's Society (now Scope) was born. Sometimes gaps in the welfare state were spotted and filled by social workers. One example is Cruse, the bereavement counselling and support service. Margaret Torrie, a social worker, had a simple inspiration in 1959 to do something for widows and publicised her idea. Within weeks Cruse was issuing advice leaflets and within a year a national branch structure was in place with counselling and less formal support being offered (Torrie 1970).

Another voluntary organisation established in 1950s was the Samaritans. A curate in Stepney, Chad Varah, received 100 responses to an article he wrote about the suicide of a 14-year-old girl, a number from people he considered might be suicidal. As there was an emergency telephone number for Police, Fire and Ambulance he thought there should be one for suicide. He set up a service where people could call in for help. Soon, people he at first regarded as '*useless amateurs*' began to offer help and he let them keep the people occupied while they were waiting to see Varah himself. He soon realised that these amateurs were connecting with people and helping them as effectively as he was. He dubbed them *Samaritans* and operated from then on mostly with telephone advice using only volunteers (samaritans.org).

This easy going approach had hardened somewhat by 1972 when Lynn Baxter volunteered to be a Samaritan as a 17-year-old. She was stimulated by the unsympathetic response from many people on the death of her father when she was 15. She remembers weeks of training. '*There were some set phrases to use, particularly for sex callers, but we were taught mainly to listen and avoid questioning or giving too much information about ourselves.*' What she found difficult was the fact that confidentiality was all. '*We were told we must not try and trace people's whereabouts even if we thought they had taken something and were dying as we spoke to them. I'm sure that happened to me once, this man just spoke to me for hours and then went silent*' (Baxter 2011).

If the Samaritans represented something of a continuation of the classic pattern of volunteering, self help became a theme in the 1960s. In all parts of society individuals and groups were trying to take back responsibility for their lives; whether it was shop stewards challenging the machine politics of big unions, beer drinkers taking on big brewers in the Campaign for Real Ale (1971), Gingerbread (1971) which offered mutual support to single parents or MIND questioning the efficacy and legitimacy of the power of psychiatrists (Curtis and Sanderson 2004).

Minority groups began to cajole government to let them live as they wished and individual freedoms were extended as a result. National Service ended (1962), hanging was abolished (1965), abortion legalised (1967), homosexuality decriminalised (1967) and divorce made easier (1969). Pressure groups sprang up focussed on a range of social ills; the Child Poverty Action Group and Shelter being among them (Curtis and Sanderson 2004). Such thinking spurred on groups who experienced daily oppression within mainstream society and in the early 1970s young women banded together demanding an end to the casual exclusion of women from so many roles in society and confronted the hearty sexism which dominated many workplaces and much entertainment.

It was through the women's movement that Hannah McCarthy became involved in social work. Hannah got involved in the women's refuge in Oxford in the 1970s. Funded by Urban Aid, a government regeneration fund, with links to Oxford University, the refuge was well set up. *'We met a lot of prejudice from agencies such as the police and social workers and lawyers, and the housing department would not always accept any responsibility for rehousing the women'*. Hannah remembers exciting times challenging stereotypes, encouraging the women to become independent and getting them to help. *'And some did get involved in the administration of the place'* (McCarthy 2011).

Why Am I With Old People?

Something else was happening at the end of the 1960s. The Robbins report in 1963 proposed that university entrance should be available to all who were eligible, and by the late 1960s after several new universities had been set up in response to the recommendations, increasing numbers of graduates were entering the job market. Expansion of social work training was bringing in more young people, some no longer willing to accept the wisdom of their elders. Sheila Ives, on placement in a CD in 1968, noticed that all those around her were in their 50s yet she was 25. She wondered *'why am I with old people?'* This unease was compounded by being told that she had to have a handbag and had to call everybody in the department 'Mrs' or 'Miss'. Sheila also remembers one occasion when she and a friend were buying fish and chips. She was careful that no one from the office saw them as that would have been unacceptable for a CCO.

Routes into social work were changing too and Hilary Corrick's choice of living in a settlement while training was by then unusual. Although the grim allure of moving to a poor area to learn how others lived may have still been strong for idealistic young people, by the mid 1960s many students had experienced living in rundown areas anyway, for there were no longer enough halls of residence to accommodate them. Moreover those bravehearts seeking to test themselves against the reality of poverty were more likely to do a year with Voluntary Service Overseas, established in 1958, or work with Community Service Volunteers (1963), than live in a settlement (Curtis and Sanderson 2004).

Although for some the route in was via a few hours' voluntary work a week – Lynn Baxter and Jennie Polyblank's work as Samaritans for instance – others who had to earn a living found employment which required no qualification, no experience and not much checking into your background; work in residential homes (Polyblank 2011). Robin Hobbes is plain that his motivation in 1973 for taking a residential care job in Kent after completing his degree was money (Hobbes 2011). Amanda Brown took another route and after her degree at York spent 15 months working as a home help (Brown 2011). One who did live for a time in a settlement was Ian McHugh, who stayed at Oxford House in Bethnal Green for six months in 1977. Coming down from Cambridge and taking a job in London he followed a friend who had become a resident there – one of five. Ian paid board, not rent, and as part of his contribution he helped out once a week in a youth club. He also remembers that homeless families lived on another floor of the settlement and that a welfare rights service was based there. His job required a lot of travel so he could not get as involved in settlement led community work as he would have liked, although he felt disappointed there was not more activity. Nevertheless he was mindful of the legacy of Oxford House and fascinated to be in Bethnal Green – by then famous amongst socially aware students as the land of *Family and Kinship in East London* (Willmott and Young 1957). He was conscious of following in the footsteps of reforming pioneers and of current racial tensions being exploited by the National Front. But despite this his need for accommodation in London was as much a motivation for being there as anything else (McHugh 2011).

The New World: Enthusiasm and Chaos

So into this world where big structures were lauded, where minority and oppressed groups were beginning to flex developing muscles and where people entering social work had different aspirations and backgrounds from their predecessors, SSDs were born. Peter Hewitt, in his own words a '*zealous enthusiast*' gave me this quote from the report, which encapsulated the breadth of the ambition for SSDs:

> A new local authority department, providing a community based and family oriented service that will be available to all. This new department will … reach far beyond the discovery and rescue of casualties, it will enable the greatest possible number of individuals to act reciprocally, giving and receiving service for the wellbeing of the community (Hewitt 2011).

The emphasis on community echoed Peter's experience in Hattersley and as a result the new Director of Social Services (DSS) in Cheshire, Maurice Speed appointed Peter as one of his new Area Officers. Peter got on well with his older deputy a – former MWO – and managed a team of ten social workers and assistants with two seniors. There were some initial problems. Peter recalls that the Medical

Officer of Health, uneasy about patient confidentiality in the SSD, ordered that all medical letters should be removed from files. This painstaking task done, Peter's MWO deputy who oversaw it, said '*don't worry too much. If we need any of the information I've kept copies in a drawer*'. Overall Peter thinks the transfer went well, with everyone bringing in their caseloads and the team being able to collate for the first time all the local resources available to them.

Clare Makepeace too became a manager, one of three seniors in an area team. A lot of preparation was done and when the appointed day came she remembers '*tremendous enthusiasm*'. Clare had a team of five social workers and one of her tasks was to develop confidence, ensuring the team shared ideas about practice and worked in a community focussed way. Her team included two former child care workers, but their experience with teenagers and in court was very limited. This presented the biggest challenge, especially as with the 1969 Children and Young Person's Act, the SSD had to work with more teenagers, who had previously been the preserve of probation officers. The Area Officer and one of the other seniors, both ex CD, offered considerable support initially, but ultimately the Area Officer said, '*you'd better manage this ... I don't want them coming to me*'. Clare realised that she had wide experience to offer the team, but understood that if she was to work effectively she had to gain experience and confidence in court work. She did become involved and supported staff but was never comfortable working in court. Nevertheless she became very committed to generic work, although she says some of the staff were less enthusiastic than her.

Keith Hiscock remembers in 1969 thinking Seebohm '... *had great potential, but I could not quite see how it was going to work. I felt that the SSD would be organisations coming together and had no feeling that it would affect the way we worked*'. He also remembers a series of meetings between those groups of workers about to be amalgamated into the SSD, something that seems to have happened everywhere. Carol Clark remembers a series of '*love-ins*' between the different groups of social workers. Hilary Corrick refers to similar meetings as '*Seebohmising*'.

In 1970 Keith had moved jobs for family reasons and was appointed as a senior CCO in Bedfordshire. He was immediately involved in planning for Seebohm implementation and began to realise that the way the work was done and what was expected of social workers might change. The plan, when implemented, mixed the managers of the old departments. The social workers were put all together in geographical patch based teams. Keith remembers his own realisation that the old CD had been ambitious but insular and that there were distinct elements of Poor Law thinking still present in the Welfare Department.

These three, Peter, Clare and Keith all found themselves managers for the first time as SSDs came into being. All were university educated. All thrived on the experience. All, at the time of their appointment, were not quite 30 years of age. This was a national pattern. The new DSSs wanted qualified, forward thinking people as leaders. But there were limited numbers of experienced, qualified people to do this, so hundreds of relatively young people found themselves in key positions.

As Clare Makepeace pointed out at around the same time the 1969 CYPA was implemented. This introduced ideas such as Intermediate Treatment, which led to many initiatives attempting to keep children out of care and shifted the legislative paradigm towards a welfare approach to troubled youngsters, away from punishment. In addition the Chronically Sick and Disabled Person's Act 1970 (CSDPA) required each SSD to undertake a local survey of disabled people and introduced a range of new services to support people in the community. This being the case, memories of the introduction of SSDs are mingled with these other changes.

So while Mary Hartley welcomed the 1969 CYPA because, in her view, it made space for imaginative ways of working with young people, her attitude to her transfer to the SSD is clouded because:

> … overnight and with no training I became a generic worker. As my new boss had an older people's background he had no knowledge or sympathy with family work. In the first week I had to visit every house on a large council estate to meet the requirements of the CSDPA – this in addition to my own child care caseload (Hartley 2010).

Her survey work identified a number of people with disabilities and she arranged in one instance for a hoist to be installed in a disabled person's house, not, of course, having any experience of such things. Something went wrong and the disabled person was nearly injured. Mary came very close to leaving as a result. Carol Clark remembers that the different approach of the newly merged sets of workers grated. The ex WD workers, she says, clocked in at 8.30 and out again at 16.45, while the ex CD staff came in later but often worked late into the evening. There was some anger at ex MWOs being paid for doing duty which ex CCOs had been obliged to do for nothing. When the transfer took place Carol was told to go to a particular office with eight other workers where there were four desks and one telephone, and then … nothing. *'Eventually the new Area Officer turned up. It was chaos'* (Clark 2011).

Before Seebohm, Marie McNay had a joint appointment with Croydon Health Department, working in both a psychiatric hospital and the community. In 1971, Croydon SSD selected workers from each of the three former Departments to form an intake team, which she joined. She did visits with CD workers, to familiarise herself with the work, having already worked in a Welfare Department. She was excited by the possibilities, particularly as she had heard Peter Leonard, a member of the Seebohm Committee, speak at a university. But she became disenchanted as Croydon operated four huge area teams which were not locally based and to her that was not what Seebohm intended. So she moved to Islington where there were ten small teams operating in small geographical patches. She thought there were too few workers in her team, though others were larger, to make it really viable and they were quite stretched. But she loved it. She had a big range of work, including community work and was active in the union. The whole Department had regular meetings and it attracted some very dynamic people whose ideas and energy made for a very creative service.

An older worker, Ruth Evans regretted the passing of the CDs, feeling that the CCO had been allowed a single-minded contemplation of the needs of children, which disappeared in SSDs. She was also very unhappy at the burning of files because of a lack of space – this practice being by no means restricted to Oxfordshire. Ruth also thought the 1969 CYPA took away the punitive edge in working with young children, an authority she thinks was necessary. Isobel Groves agrees. '*The 1971 amalgamation was a bad move. The best time was when we stood alone. All the weight went into adult services afterwards*'. Away child rearing at the time of reorganisation, Isobel returned to a generic team in 1977 and on her first day was thrust into the unknown to deal with a violent man who had to be sectioned. Sheila Ives was not looking forward to the SSD either. In Southampton three teams were created: one for older people, one focussed on mental health and one for children. So she had to move offices and lost the wonderful senior colleague she had relied on. The new one with a mental health background could not help at all. The most stressful thing was overnight duty, which each worker had to do for a week at a time for no extra pay. '*Nobody knew you'd gone wandering off to nasty situations. You were exhausted working all day and all night. Not good for the nerves*'. But she persevered and stayed in social work for the next 25 years.

It has been suggested that female COs did not get the new DSS jobs because the local authority tradition was to appoint men to big departments (Cooper 1983). But in 1970 CDs were still very small compared to Welfare Departments which, with their residential homes and home helps, had more staff and fabric to manage, so Chief Welfare Officers were more experienced in big operations. In Bolton George Taylor, pre-Seebohm Chief Welfare Officer, was appointed DSS. The ex CO Philip Varey soon left.

For front line workers in Bolton the transfer seems to have been as it was elsewhere – a mixture of enthusiasm and disarray. Maurice Ffelan thought the reorganisation was a complete shambles and claims that over a twelve month period about 20 people left Bolton SSD. Maurice himself moved to Oldham. Ron Standring said there was a lot of nervousness that those from the old Welfare Departments, accustomed to '*pleasant visits*', would struggle. Ron thought they came through well. But in Manchester Tom Daniels, a very young trainee social worker, reports that after the reallocation of work across the new staff group, two experienced ex WD workers returned in tears from a visit to two 15-year-old girls after being sworn at and threatened (Daniels 2011). Mary Mason became DSS in Bolton in 1972, replacing George Taylor, and she said that of all the staff coming into the SSD, medical social workers were the most difficult to absorb.

> They came kicking and screaming into SSDs. We inherited … a group of almoners in the geriatric and child psychiatric department very much … under

the consultant's thumb. They felt they were part of the NHS. Also they had no idea about child protection (Mason 2009).

Howard Syddall, taken on in Bolton just after implementation as an unqualified trainee social worker, had worked for three years as a psychiatric nurse, so he was familiar with mental health but not child care. At the end of his first week in which he had received no induction, no training and not much advice, he was at a review of a child in care and understandably did not know what was expected of him. An Assistant Director came up to him after the meeting, very agitated, and told Howard that he had better get up to speed pretty quick. All in all Howard thought '*it was bloody chaos*' (Syddall 2011).

For Some it Became a Lifeline

Whether seen as benign or chaotic the new SSDs were big departments and began to operate like big organisations with in-house training sections, workload management experiments and research programmes. And the new SSDs themselves were researched. In an early study of SSDs Satyamurti identified reduced admin support, people walking into offices more regularly, staff shortages and more work arising from the 1969 CYPA and the 1970 CSDP Act as characteristic of the new SSDs (Satyamurti 1981). Stevenson and Parsloe's *Social Services Teams: The Practitioner's View* (DHSS 1978) investigated how social workers operated in several local authorities across the whole of the United Kingdom. The report looked at how different teams managed duty processes, took referrals, allocated and undertook work. It also commented on specialisms, casework methods and supervision. It reveals a divergence in the way SSDs operated; some having intake teams for new work and long-term teams for longer term involvement; some operating on a generic patch basis where teams took on all the work in a smallish geographical patch; some using social workers completely generically and others having social workers operating in traditional specialist roles.

The overall impression from the report is of overworked teams, whose primary focus is on children and families with fear of non-accidental injury to children high on the agenda. The researchers found little evidence of group work. A few authorities had taken the Seebohm aspiration to support communities seriously enough to employ community workers and accept referrals for marital counselling. Common features included dingy reception areas and interview rooms, erratic supervision and inadequate administrative support. Some local authority social workers gloomily compared their working conditions to probation officers, each of whom had their own office, a secretary and nationally prescribed patterns of recording and supervision.

The researchers comment that, generally, there was no expectation that the workers should approach their work in a particular way. Neither were practice methods as taught on qualification courses much in evidence. The researchers reported that social workers were uneasy about discussing the theoretical frameworks they used. Some denied that in-depth casework was possible in a local authority because of the constant minor demands including '*referrals to collect walking aids from the homes of clients who have died ... or driving a woman with bunions to the doctor*' (DHSS 1978: 107). When pressed social workers often explained their approach as 'intuitive' or 'eclectic' or mentioned using particular methods which, in the researchers' view, they did not fully understand. The researchers comment that the report '*makes somewhat depressing reading for the social work teacher*' (DHSS 1978: 339).

And there was more depression. Younghusband's review of social work over the previous 25 years (1978) included a section on a number of studies of the impact of social work interventions, a new phenomenon. Her commentary is somewhat defensive. I found this odd, as all the reports she quotes were positive about social work interventions, indicating effectiveness in nearly all of them, even if mostly on a moderate scale. Perhaps Younghusband was expecting success to be more comprehensive. The language social workers used in the 1960s, the language used by Marian Penny in 1967, '*diagnosis*' and '*treatment*', implies certainty in the likely outcomes of intervention which the impact studies demonstrated was not the case. So moderately positive findings, in the face of unrealistic expectations, were interpreted as failure.

But in spite of this those coming into SSDs after 1971, introduced to generic work from the start with no baggage and no certainty of positive outcomes, accepted the generic role and thrived. One such was John Dunkerley. Brought up in north east London, he only realised in later life how much he took from his parents' commitment to helping others. Both Christians, his father throughout his life was involved in the YMCA and his mother worked as a volunteer with blind people. Aware of this or not at the age of 18 he wanted to give something back to society. After realising that a career in nursing was not for him, he enrolled on the BA in social administration at Manchester University. His commitment to social work was confirmed in Manchester as was a commitment to Dinah Cooper, Nora Cooper's daughter. They both then took the one-year post-graduate course in social work at Exeter University. John particularly remembers Bill Jordan's approach to learning about relationships. Each week a student chose a book, everyone read it and the group discussed it, teasing out from literature psychological insights about how people behaved and related to society. What he remembers most however was learning a set of principles – to respect people as themselves. He found the experience inspirational and later if ever he was stuck or in a dilemma he would think to himself, '*what would Bill Jordan do in this situation?*'

He started work in Cheshire SSD in 1975, the youngest member of a generic team. It was '*a very mature team, some people had come from each of the forerunner departments. And it was Northwich ... three of the women had double barrelled names*'. John loved it, getting involved in all aspects of the work. '*I put myself forward for everything*' he says and is particularly proud of a group he led for mental health clients, the Russett Club. They met, talked, got to know each other and sometimes went on weekend visits to places like the Yorkshire Dales. The group included young and old, male and female and he knows that '*for some it became a lifeline, even though the thinking behind it was not very sophisticated*'. Not a boastful man, John says he knows he was successful, partly because of the feedback he got from people: '*where would I be without you?*' But it was also because he thinks he was clear what he was doing. '*My approach was to use my resources to help people use their resources, so I had to make sure people learned from me how they could help themselves*'. At the heart of this was their trust in him, which of course meant that he had to be reliable; turn up on time, go the extra mile, always respond. But in the end it became too much.

> I wasn't as tough as I thought I should have been and ended up overwhelmed. Until you get involved in this work you have no idea of the emotional demands of other people's distress, or how you will be able to cope with it. Having children and other responsibilities outside work helped me realise that I had to look after myself in order to offer anything of value to other people (Dunkerley 2011).

Others report being radicalised by the work. Lynn Baxter for instance trained as a teacher but as there were no jobs in south London when she qualified in 1976 she took a job in Lewisham SSD as a trainee social worker. The scheme involved weekly sessions with Peter Ruben the staff development officer. He advised on books to read and encouraged the trainees to voice doubts and ask questions. Lynn was hooked and when offered one turned down a teaching job because she liked the '*variety in social work; learning about children, race, older people, mental health*'.

She started out in an intake team where she did a lot of six monthly reviews of old people, '"*dormant cases" they were called, cup of tea and a bun, that sort of thing. I had a checklist of questions about how they were coping but I soon learned to weave those into the conversation*'. And she had a formative experience when sent out to enquire about three children who were not being sent to school.

> I went out on my own. It was an Asian lady with three kids. She did not speak English and was agitated; agitated about me being there more than anything else … I felt completely out of my depth. What was going on? What could I ask her? What was I looking for? In the end I left her a card and mimed her telephoning me. I went back to my boss straightaway. I felt this huge sense of responsibility. I knew there was pressure on social workers to know which parents would hurt children and which would not and it started me wondering how I could get hold of the Magic Fairy Dust that could help me differentiate between the two (Baxter 2011).

There were external pressures too. The area Lynn worked was rough, with drugs and organised crime and some of her colleagues put on tough, cynical fronts. To local voluntary organisations the SSD were '*the pimps of the poor*' and questions about race were everywhere, prompting the lapel badge defence '*I'm a racist but I'm working on it*'. Lynn took her CQSW between 1978 and 1980, which coincided with the national social work strike, which she supported. But she lost respect for some of the people in the union as she thought the power implicit in strike action had gone to their heads. She also thought the Socialist Workers Party's take on the class struggle was cute: '*we're winning the battle, they'd say, they're having to use brown envelopes now instead of white!*'

Lynn returned to Lewisham after her training more confident, pushed to do group work, and when required to carry out duty interviews where conversations could be overheard, she refused. She also devised her own social work theory; Christmas Pudding theory. One of her clients, a deserted mum with two sick children, needed re-housing, but she could never talk to the Housing Department without shouting and threatening to dump the children. The client gave herself permission, Lynn felt, to lose it with officials as she was adamant she was never going to get what she wanted. Trying to convince her that it was possible for things to go right for the client one Christmas, Lynn ordered one of the mayor's Christmas Hampers but lied to the client saying she had entered all her client's names into a raffle for the hamper and she had won it. This change of 'luck' boosted the woman's confidence enough to enable Lynn to work on her approach to officials and after a few months she was successfully rehoused. One of Lynn's hard line colleagues lectured her about the perfidy of charity and lying to her client being a betrayal. Lynn later felt able to defend herself by explaining her actions as being underpinned by elements of cognitive behavioural thinking, psycho-social analysis and loss theory. So she could always fall back on Christmas Pudding theory, as it seemed to work!

That social workers would go on strike anyway was novel, unthinkable before the establishment of SSDs had created workforces big enough for unions to have real influence. But such activity attracted a raft of young workers many of whom, like Marie McNay, were as committed to collective action as to individual change strategies. Marie herself had been involved in unions from her first job and also with the iconoclastic social work magazine *Case Con* nurtured at North London Poly. The title was a satirical take on the casework journal *Case Conference*, set up in 1953; and *Case Con* contained material deeply critical of individual approaches to clients which did not raise awareness of their subservient political position or propose radical direct action to change society.

Hannah McCarthy had similar political views and chose to train at Ruskin College in Oxford, with its socialist tradition. She found the psychoanalytical framework difficult and was more sympathetic to the ideas about attachment and the impact of environmental factors on people. Hannah says '*I really had a thing about individual pathology. That was my background in Women's Aid, I suppose; women, by implication, being blamed for being beaten. I hated it*'. She also hated her placement in hospital.

It was very boring. I don't think I saw anyone who needed a social worker in six months and didn't feel part of the team, yet I was told off for talking to a consultant who wanted to work with me. And there was endless process recording (McCarthy 2011).

Process recording was the requirement to record an interview in complete detail, including the workers thoughts and feelings and changing perceptions of the subject at hand; a different requirement for someone accustomed to pressing practical demands. And Hannah felt medical social workers were a different breed '*and my presence challenged them because I had a different approach*'.

But she had a similar approach to a female colleague, with whom on one occasion she went on a joint visit to a client's house. When they arrived the woman opened the door, looked them up and down and said, '*you two could be bleedin' twins*'. They looked at each other in their matching duffle coats, CND badges and fingerless gloves and looked behind at their tinny French cars parked nose to nose; the classic image of radical seventies social workers. Radicalism of course is a relative concept. Maurice Ffelan worked in Oldham in the early 1970s and thought the social workers there were really left wing. He says that at one of the frequent group meetings he opposed some sort of direct action that was being proposed: '*I was shouted down being called a capitalist lackey*'. A couple of years later, by then working in Lancashire, a '*more formal and authoritarian place, I was regarded as a dangerous radical*'.

Elsewhere traditional themes were still being played out. Sue Moya, from a middle class background, reports for instance that '*the Chief Lady Almoner who appointed me as a medical social worker did so, I think, on the basis of my accent alone. She always insisted that we never disagreed with a doctor*' (Moya 2011). Judith Niechcial came from a similar background. After having children wanting to do something useful, she took a job in housing and then signed on for what she called the '*CQSW course for married women*' in 1973. This course had short teaching days, no teaching in school holidays and lasted three years – to attract women with children. She says '*it was fantastic. We were introduced to psychodynamic concepts, but then, like the third degree, these were focussed on us, most traumatic. I had a personal tutor and a weekly two hour session, all of which was about personal development*'. Particularly demanding was her experience of a group sculpt. One member of the group took charge and carefully placed the rest of the group together or separately in positions which for the sculptor represented each individual and the group as a whole. One member of the group placed Judith in a chair above the others, '*because they thought I was snooty, and considered myself better than others. It was very distressing*'. Judith had been brought up in South Kensington, London with a formidable father and an artistic mother and had taken an English degree at Birmingham University. Though she was in her own words '*very posh*', she did not find anything she could excel at as a young woman. It was 15 years after this, when doing a placement in a generic team in Croydon SSD, she remembers thinking '*I've found what I want to do*'. Her mother's reaction was like that of Eileen Younghusband's mother 50 years before: *'I don't know why you want to work with those smelly people'*.

In 1976 Judith started work in an intake team in Croydon and quickly took on mental health work, using a psychodynamic approach in her practice. Interested in family dynamics, she picked up on the ideas of Salvador Minuchin and trained as a family therapist just as these ideas were spreading across the UK. But then she moved to better resourced Lewisham and worked in a generic patch based team, doing mostly child care work. She loved it … *'really, it was a golden age'*. If she has one regret about that time, it is that in her family support work she thinks she blamed parents for the child's predicament. This she thinks may have been to do with the psychodynamic, that is, childhood trauma basis of her approach. In later life she came to know a boy with ADHD and through him understood fully that some children bring deep challenges which remain, no matter what nurturing or skilled parenting is brought to bear.

Another trained on a *'married women's course'* was Jennie Polyblank who like Judith came to social work late after a career in television, having children and experience of voluntary work as a Samaritan. *'I did not really know what social workers did but the course sounded interesting and I wanted to work with troubled families because I did not come from a "Perfect Family"'*. The course was, she feels, an enlightening experience for women in her position. Immediately the course opened her eyes to the relatively unboundaried way she had operated in the Samaritans and she realised the professional training gave her a more secure basis for work with clients than she had had working as a volunteer (Polyblank 2011).

John Mercer had been a teacher but did not think he could earn enough so after a period in a factory in 1976, he fell into a six-month temporary contract as a child care worker in Accrington.

> My first case was about fuel bills, all new to me, and I had to go back time and again to get the full story. It was an introduction to clients trying to pull the wool over your eyes and I imagined the others thought I was a right pillock (Mercer 2011).

But John soon found his niche working with teenagers, or *'raggy arsed street arabs'*. Using behavioural techniques, star charts and so on, ideas taken from his teaching experience, John persisted with these boys. He began to work in more informal settings; in turn the boys used to wait for him in various places and he came home one night to find one of them sitting on his sofa. Wendy Leach's initial experiences in the mid 1970s were epitomised not by informality but by being overwhelmed by procedures. A Cardiff University psychology graduate who had intended to train as a clinical psychologist, she married instead and moved to Burnley. There was no relevant training for psychologists there, so as a *'second best, because I wanted to help people solve their problems'*, she joined a child care team in Nelson. She says that she knew about social work but did not know quite what it was. *'On my first day I was handed a small filing cabinet with 50 cards in it, 50 child care cases. But then I was taken through the forms that had to be filled in. No one talked about the people, just the forms I had to fill in'.* But as with most social workers she found everyone '*really friendly and supportive*', although she described the team as '*a funny bunch with a diversity of politics, attitudes and approaches; some old stagers, some lefties, some theorists'.*

The emotional pressures of the work experienced by the people I interviewed showed themselves in many ways. Judith Neichcial recalls being kept awake at night wondering whether she was good enough, whether she had done the right thing with the children she was working with. Hannah McCarthy accepts she made, in her early days, mistakes with boundaries: '*I gave a drunken husband of a client of mine a lift home, that was stupid'.* Lynn Baxter says she had a problem with boundaries too. On returning from her course she threw herself into work and knows now she became too emotionally involved. As a result she felt sucked dry by all the demands. She says to carry on she had to recognise her own limitations, be up-front with clients about personal boundaries and stop feeling guilty. Jennie Polyblank was overwhelmed by having too much to do. She took a part time job in 1979 in Child Guidance but within six months her manager and experienced colleague had moved on, leaving her with 38 cases – six being statutory. She also had responsibility for removing children into care. '*I was really green anyway and completely out of my depth'.* The Deputy Area Manager was as helpful as possible, she says, but she was not supervised for several months and within two years began to distance herself from and became inured to the distress all around her.

Others found themselves reacting in odd ways. Hilary Corrick, working on a ward where many of the children had cancer, began dreaming that her own children had cancer. This became unbearable and she had to leave. John Mercer reports that after two colleagues left his workload became very heavy and he began to experience '*a sense of doom*' that always came on strong on a Sunday afternoon. And he was sick of experiencing the same cycle of behaviour and going through it all again. So he broke the cycle by moving across to work with older people.

Training, Weak Tea and Alcohol

Although the research exercise *Social Services Teams* (DHSS 1978) reported limited use of group work, most of the 1970s social workers I spoke to ran groups. John Dunkerley's description of the group he ran is strikingly similar to Val Burnham's view of her group a decade earlier: '*not very sophisticated'.* But he like Val knew it helped people cope with their world, offering a bit of fun and friendship. Isobel Groves ran a foster carers group and girls life skills group with two teachers. This was encouraged and enabled by the 1969 CYP Act, which allowed social workers to fund Intermediate Treatment – group work as part of an alternative to institutional care. Keith Hiscock remains very proud of his involvement in an early pilot for Intermediate Treatment in the early 1970s.

But there were other ideas around. Unbidden, several of the social workers I spoke to mentioned writers and theorists who influenced their practice: Salvador Minuchin (family therapy), Tom Douglas (group work), Carl Rogers (person centred counselling). This was new: social workers from the previous generation mentioned individual teachers or tutors as influential rather than writers. And training involved more imaginative teaching methods. Hilary Corrick was involved in a group experience on her course. A group of 14 met every Friday for two hours. They sat in a circle and what happened happened. This was a T group, as described and proposed by A.K. Rice: structureless, ruleless, a group discussion (or prolonged silence) in which anything might happen or nothing (Rice 1965). Hilary found it absorbing. *'It was such fun ... but what I learned from it heaven only knows'*. The training on group work was a very significant aspect of Lynn Baxter's course too, although it included sensory awareness sessions which included *'relaxation and hugging people'*. Lynn did not want to hug everybody, nor did she know what it was supposed to achieve and clashed with the leader when he hugged her against her wishes. Simon Armitage's memoir *All Points North* (2009) contains derisive and ribald comment about similar training games and exercises which he experienced at the hands of Manchester Probation Service in the 1980s.

John Mercer brought back a less hasty approach from his training and learned that his opinions were as valid as others. But he was *'bored to tears by the social work theory crap. None of it helped you get through the day'*. On the other hand he thought highly of some of his teachers, Tim Lang for instance, and had his eyes opened by the social policy teaching. Others report having had little time for their training. Howard Syddall had been a psychiatric nurse and found the psychodynamic aspects of the casework training very unimpressive, in his own words *'weak tea'*. When I asked Carol Clark what she learned she simply said *'not much'*. Others like Wendy Leach said her training broadened her understanding of wider political pressures. She learned a lot about the importance of understanding family dynamics for success in fostering and adoption, but *'got fed up with the trendy lefty stuff ... and what Karl Marx had to do with anything I don't know'*.

Lynn Baxter said that people said one of three things would happen on the course to everyone: divorce, a breakdown or an affair. This feeling that life on a social work course was slightly out of kilter was hinted at by others too. Jennie Polyblank wondered if the course would make her *'less of a nice person'*. What was predicted on Lynn's course happened to Judith Neichcial: *'the course helped me move on faster than my husband. He wanted me to be as I had been, but I was no longer that person. We divorced'*.

Finally, something about the typical social worker's lifestyle had changed. Across England in the 1970s social workers drank. In his first week John Mercer was sent out with a worker who had two years' experience. He learned from her to be persistent about getting into a house where there was a referral about a child. But he wondered why a 25-year-old, like her, would talk about needing a sherry every night when she got home. Howard Syddall says *'we'd pile out to the pub at 12, have a couple of pints and see what we could make of the afternoon'.* Lynn Baxter in Southwark says '*alcohol was very much part of the scene*' and can remember seeing one of her '*dormant*' old ladies when she was somewhat the worse for wear (her not the old lady). Michael Murphy talks about '*horrible*' parties, by which he means drunken ones. (Murphy 2011). John Dunkerley says a great deal of his social life was tied up with work colleagues, and lot of that social life went on in the pub where he thinks there was too little account taken of the need to present a positive image of the social work profession and occasionally of the importance of confidentiality.

Chapter 9

1980–1989: This is Alright

Expert Failure

As SSDs were being introduced in 1971 big state initiatives led by experts were coming under scrutiny, with problems emerging across society. Most obvious was the failure of much of the post-war housing programme. Millions of houses and flats had been built since 1945, but council estates were often built with few amenities and high-rise blocks could be lonely and riddled with damp. In 1969 one corner of an East End tower block, Ronan Point, collapsed. New towns, pedestrianed town centres and motorway systems may have been inspired by Le Corbusier but were despised by ordinary people even while being built. In 1969 the Poulson scandal revealed architects, builders and politicians lining each other's pockets at the same time as building shoddy housing (Beckett 2009). Medical science got it wrong with the sale of Thalidomide, an untested drug which caused serious harm to thousands (*Sunday Times* 1979). Psychiatry was another big disappointment. Intrusive procedures and wonder drugs seemed to produce results, but growing understanding that such drugs were often used as symptom suppressants and not much more coincided with criticism of ECT as unethical and ineffective (Kesey 1962). The Ely Hospital scandal of 1969 brought to public attention the easy brutality some staff in some institutions could mete out to mentally handicapped patients (Butler and Drakeford 2003). And finally analyses which demonstrated how poverty was still embedded in parts of society such as Coates and Silburn's in Nottingham (1970) questioned all that had supposedly been achieved since the war.

These perceived failures of the welfare state and the experts involved with it demonstrated, for some, that state leadership was ineffective. In 1965 Iain McLeod, a Conservative politician, first used the phrase '*Nanny State*', heralding a political analysis which envisaged individuals taking more responsibility for their lives; state machinery humming in the background rather than orchestrating so much of daily life (McLeod 1965). So it should have been no surprise that social workers were found wanting too. Two broad themes, expert failure and ordinary people taking action themselves coincided in the scandal around the homicide of eight-year-old Maria Colwell in Brighton in January 1973. Maria had been placed voluntarily with her mother's sister as a baby. Once settled with a new husband, her mother asked that Maria, by then seven, should be returned, much to the distress of her sister. After careful consideration and a phased introduction to her mother's new family, Maria was returned in November 1971. Underweight and having been regularly beaten by her stepfather she died in January 1973 (DHSS

1974). Butler and Drakeford's (2003) persuasive view is that the public profile of the death was raised by a group of local women, angered by what they saw as failure by the welfare authorities. Their skilful use of the media and persistence created the atmosphere in which an enquiry into the death was unavoidable, although Parton points out that an enquiry was also politically convenient for the government (Parton 1981).

The report of the enquiry gives a clear account of the events leading to Maria's death. The SSD, in its very early months of operation, was swamped with work, so social workers had too much to do. Nevertheless considerable effort went into considering first whether to, and then how best to, return Maria to her birth mother. The report argues that there seemed to be a greater emphasis in the social worker's mind on the primacy of the '*blood tie*' than the needs of the child (DHSS 1974). As marked a feature was the confusion, throughout 1972, between the NSPCC worker, the SSD worker and the Education Welfare Officer (EWO), about whose responsibility it was to check on the progress of the placement once made. This partly explains the relatively limited emphasis given to monitoring the family once the placement was made. There were also continuities with the past:

- The SSD Duty Officer took a call about suspected child abuse in 1972 and suggested that this was NSPCC territory, not considering the SSD had prime responsibility for protecting abused children.
- A WPC was sent to warn Maria's mother and new husband about going out drinking and leaving the children alone, a standard WPC function at the time, and the role we saw Ethel Jeeps taking on in the 1930s. This action was not followed up by any liaison with the SSD.

A key theme noted in the Colwell report is repeated in subsequent child death enquiries; poor communication between social workers and other professionals. At least as significant was something Eileen Munro's analysis of 45 child death inquiry reports between 1973 and 1995 revealed. She identified that, in the 19 cases where blame was lodged with social workers' activities, a persistent error was being in thrall to an idée fixe; social workers were slow to revise initial judgements about a family, becoming fixated on one interpretation, which tended to remain unchanged by external evidence to the contrary (Munro 1996).

Even before the Colwell report was published the DHSS issued guidance that Area Review Committees should, in each locality, provide coordinated leadership for child protection practice, obliging all relevant organisations to contribute and take responsibility. And the 1975 Children Act imposed restrictions on removing children from care. While some commentators regretted this focus on child protection (as against a broader preventative approach with children), the management and activities of social workers in SSDs was still a primarily a local affair, with few national procedures and protocols imposed by central government until the end of the 1980s (Parton 1981, Thorpe 1994, Butler and Drakeford 2003).

The background to these events was the burgeoning professional interest in baby battering. Radiologists in the USA drew attention to the possibility that a long bone fracture in a child or a subdural haematoma, brought to the attention of medical authorities by parents, could have been inflicted by the parents themselves. Henry Kempe in the early 1960s coined the term 'battered child' to describe harm done by parents. British paediatricians were debating the issue in the late 1960s and at the same time Joan Court translated these primarily paediatric concerns into material for social workers and the NSPCC for whom she worked. Her approach included strong advice that social workers and medical practitioners should behave in the face of suspicions so as to protect the potential of a therapeutic relationship with the suspected attackers. '*Any type of investigatory proceedings will only lead to hostility and prejudice*' (Court 1969: 19). In this she was following Kempe's view that the investigative and therapeutic function of caseworkers should be separated.

The NSPCC set up the Battered Child Research Project in 1967, partly as a result of the debate about battered babies, but also in an effort to find a role. The soon-to-be established SSDs were in a much stronger position to respond to and work with cases of child abuse than a relatively small, increasingly old fashioned looking anomaly that the NSPCC had become. In an imaginative move the NSPCC began to amalgamate its resources in special units which offered specialist therapeutic help. John Pickett led the first one in Manchester in 1967.

He Pushed Things Back to the Team Asking, 'OK, What's Your Solution?'

In the preface to Ruth Evans' memoir Olive Stevenson comments: '*Everyone remotely interested in social work in this country must realize that it has been heavily under attack in the last few years*' (Evans 1977: 9). She was referring to the disparagement of social workers associated with the death of Maria Colwell, but also to critical analyses from both left and right and disenchantment with traditional social work methods. The academic social work literature worried at all these issues (Lymbery 2001). In wider society a dismissive attitude to social workers hardened as the 1970s progressed, especially from the political right. Paul Johnson wrote about '*the burgeoning bureaucrats of local and central government; the new breed of administrators ... the so-called social workers with their glib pseudo-solutions to non-problems*' (Beckett 2009: 288). The stereotypical young social worker driving a Citroen 2CV and dressed as Hannah McCarthy had been on her joint visit, was lumped by some commentators in the same box as hippies: '*floppy, shambolic ... obsolete and suffocatingly ubiquitous*'. Peter York, the style commentator, wrote that in some circles '*you only had to talk about a social worker or an ethnic print dress ... to get a laugh*' (Beckett 2009: 285). Brewer and Lait's diatribe *Can Social Work Survive* (1980) pulled much of this thinking together, castigating social work as impertinent, ineffective and pretentious. And there were in the 1980s more child deaths followed by high profile enquiry reports;

Jasmine Beckford, Kimberley Carlile and Tyra Henry among others (Blom Cooper 1986, 1987, Sedley 1987). Then later were the investigations about the removal of significant numbers of children which were perceived to be, in the main, hasty and misguided; Cleveland, Orkney and Rochdale (Butler Sloss 1988, Clyde 1992, La Fontaine 1997). Criticism piled upon criticism. There was also critical commentary from the left about social work supporting an inegalitarian status quo in both the short-lived, radical magazine *Case Con*, its probation equivalent *Probe*, and in academic literature (see Bailey and Brake 1975). But only one social worker I spoke to who worked during this period mentioned the tension between care and control. That was Hannah McCarthy who says '*I don't know if I ever resolved that. People didn't want you in there but you had to carry out your responsibilities, and sometimes it felt uncomfortable as you were offering support ... but could instigate legal proceedings and remove their children*'. Only two of my interviewees referred directly to fears associated with critical enquiry reports, Keith Hiscock and Penny Hindle (Hindle 2011) and they only tangentially. For despite this atmosphere of criticism, even ridicule, the memories of social workers I interviewed who worked in the 1980s were almost all positive, and by the end of the decade new attitudes, philosophies and techniques were being incorporated into their practice.

But at the beginning of the 1980s people I spoke to reported a lack of structure and rigour in what they were expected to do. The formless nature of the work is well articulated by two Bolton social workers: Eileen Gallagher and Wyn Haslam. Eileen started out as an unqualified worker in Bolton General Hospital and after training at Manchester University joined a generic team. '*It was a good course with a strong therapeutic element, gestalt for instance, but it did not equip you for confrontational and tense situations*'. This sense of not being prepared did not dissipate once she was working. Eileen praised the managers she had in that they would always accompany social workers should they ask; but knowing the pressures the managers were under, social workers mostly got on with it on their own. On reflection both she and Wyn Haslam question the off-hand way managers expected staff to go out on mental health sections or child abuse investigations on their own – and the brio with which the workers did it: '*I was learning as I went along, but*', says Eileen '*could not shake the feeling that I did not quite know what I was doing. The idea of such a young woman assessing adopters ... is hilarious: scandalous!*' She looks back at some experiences ruefully.

> On a section once I was walking up the garden path and noticed a grave shaped
> hole dug in the front lawn, but I didn't wait for the police, I just went straight in.
> It was OK, he was upstairs hiding in a wardrobe. In the end I was only locked in
> a house with a madman once (Gallagher 2011).

Wyn joined that team in 1982 after qualification and remembers there being '*no structures for the work*'. But Wyn, a natural enthusiast, had been deeply disappointed by her course. '*There was no connection between the teaching and what it's like going through someone's front door'*. Only one lecturer, on family therapy, gripped her. *'You could tell she had practiced it. She talked about how to interview people, how to talk to people, calm them down'*. But this woman was only with the students for two sessions. So despite having good, well supported placements Wyn started work in 1982 *'not having a bloody clue what I was doing'*. Early on, as a particular foster placement had to end, Wyn was asked to rehabilitate the little girl concerned to her parents, at whose hands she had suffered a skull fracture.

> I couldn't work out how I was supposed to know if the child was safe to go home. There was no clear model. I tried to use common sense, but I was very worried. I knew I was worried 'cos I was visiting two or three times a week in the evenings! (Haslam 2011).

No connections were made within the SSD either. Wyn reports taking social histories in some detail in mental health cases – a practice presumably surviving in mental health social work from PSW days. *'But we never used the technique in children's work. We worked in a vacuum'*. One of the few examples of structured work was the family therapy sessions run by two workers. Eileen thought the approach was clear and that they had negotiated protected time to undertake this work. But Eileen thought the potential was limited *'because they only worked with nice families'*.

Penny Hindle experienced a similar lack of structure. She went straight to university from school, to Bradford in 1982, taking a four-year combined social studies degree and CQSW. She thought it could have been done in three years and that the learning was on placement, particularly the practical work with families she did during the miner's strike of 1984–85. In the mid 1980s, CQSW courses were producing more social workers than local authorities could afford to employ and Penny had difficulty getting a job. Her first experience was a temporary job in Rochdale in 1986 to which her introduction was: *'there's your drawer, there's your caseload; get on with it. But it was a really nice way to start work. It was in an elderly long term team; the work was very practical; people liked you to turn up every week on time'* … much like Brian Fox's volunteers in the 1950s and Mr Watkinson's rounds in the 1920s. But in September that year she started in a generic team back in Leeds. *'We dealt with everything, although individual workers could swing towards their own preferences. There was a real sense of team togetherness and the two qualified people were very supportive'*. Looking back there is a tinge of embarrassment, *'I was very naïve, very enthusiastic but very questioning'* and recalls black and white views. *'I volunteered to do group work with Probation and I was very pro children's rights, always taking their side against their parents'*. By then her focus and passion was entirely on children. Being assaulted by a client put her off working in mental health and she thought work with older people, epitomised by assessments for bath aids, was tedious. A key memory was that in Leeds no parents were ever invited to child protection conferences, nor were they told about any care plan and certainly not involved in developing it. Nor was she expected to record in great detail and cannot remember many procedures. In the mid 1980s Penny moved across the Pennines to Blackburn, and experienced something entirely different. One of the differences was that the intake team manager, Tom Daniels, '*was inspirational*'.

> He wanted to do things and never just accepted what he was told. He pushed things back to the team asking, "OK, what's your solution, how should we develop this service?" By the late 1980s with the Orange Book (a national framework for comprehensive assessments in work with children published in 1988) we had a clear framework, we had plans and structures, children and families were involved in planning, we knew how to use chronologies with families, there were high expectations about recording and we worked well with other agencies (Hindle 2011).

'I Understood That Not Everyone White is Racist'

Another newcomer was Nirmal Singh. He arrived in the UK in 1978, was looking for any type of job and fell into a part time social worker role – the first deliberately appointed worker in that authority from an ethnic minority, funded under section 11 of the Local Government Act 1966. '*The myth in the team that "they look after their own" was strong*', says Nirmal, implying that this attitude was self serving as the social workers could not really work with the Muslim, Hindu and Sikh families because they had neither the language nor any interpreter service. Cases were just closed so from the start Nirmal realised he had a role to play. He remembers his first four cases. Closed previously, they were reopened and allocated to him: someone who was blind, a bedfast man, one family with three mentally handicapped children and one other mentally handicapped person. His Area Manager briefed him about services and Nirmal briefed the Area Manager about cultural expectations and somehow they got through. '*It was the blind leading the blind*' he says. But within eight months he had a caseload of 55 and had recruited four ethnic minority foster parents. '*We began to build up trust with the communities. Some people came to see me at home and not in the office*'. When the Area Manager secured additional funding and created a full time post Nirmal understood that '*not everyone white is racist*'. Although he did not experience overt racism from his colleagues he was aware immediately who had difficulty with him. '*They were over polite and stilted with me and asked questions like, "why are we doing this for these people?" or "why don't they learn English?"*'

Nirmal loved his training, all the ideas and practice methods thrown at him, but he had considerable difficulty with one placement, which he failed. '*It was aimless*' he said '*and I didn't get on with the practice teacher for whom I was the first student and from an ethnic minority too*'. The furore that followed included a letter to the university staff signed by all the students about the racist attitude to him. Subsequently all the teaching staff had to undergo anti-racism training. Newly confident after that battering, on returning to his role as a qualified worker, Nirmal said to his manager '*I'd like a mixed caseload*'. His manager said no, he had to work only with ethnic minorities. Nirmal countered by closing all his cases except half a dozen and his manager relented. But Nirmal's thinking had moved on by then and he asked to be given a role advising and developing services for ethnic minority communities. By that time groups within ethnic minority communities were beginning to articulate specific needs and demand responses to those needs from local government. See, for instance, Irene Lynn's careful analysis of the needs of the welfare Chinese community in Liverpool, which contributed to Liverpool City Council's decision to establish a qualified Chinese Social Worker post and two unqualified posts (Lynn 1982).

Amanda Brown's early experience in Cheshire was characterised by long hours, informality and just getting on with it. In 1980, aged 25 after training, she started in a generic team. The team she says was:

> … brilliant, very supportive, as was the District Officer. He knew all the children in care. One girl wanted a motor bike and he asked to see her in person with me to discuss it. It was so much more informal then, but we worked so hard. If I got home at five o'clock I thought I was skiving (Brown 2011).

The informality extended to expectations about recording which were neither stringent, nor authority-wide, with each worker having a different approach.

Heather Cameron's early experiences were also characterised by informal methods (Cameron 2011). As a newly qualified worker she joined, in 1981, a Mental Health/Mental Handicap sub group in an Area Team. Heather's memories are of an immense support where innovation was actively encouraged. Her analysis of the caseload of 70 she was bequeathed was that '*there was a lot of loneliness*'. Accordingly she ran one group for depressed younger women, one for depressed older women, a drop-in facility on a Friday for both mentally ill and mentally handicapped people and a social club, '*the Tuesday Club*', for mentally handicapped people.

> We had three staff on that and provided transport. It was so successful we asked the council for a house and the club became a day centre. We saw people so regularly and so informally that we could tell immediately if someone was becoming ill. A man called Norman, who had schizophrenia, used to walk differently if he was getting ill, so we could intervene at an early stage (Cameron 2011).

The cooperation between staff was not just within Heather's sub group. '*We used to stand in for child care colleagues if there were gaps and mucked in if there were trips out for older people, to York, I remember, and Liverpool Garden Festival. And we all used Mrs Anderson's volunteers*'. Mrs Anderson ran an entirely independent volunteer service which was used by everybody … '*and every six months we got together, social workers and volunteers, for a cup of coffee and a piece of cake to make sure we knew who we were. We also invited everybody – GPs, police, housing officers, Mrs Anderson – to our Christmas parties*'.

The social workers also used to do sponsored walks and cycle rides to raise money for the amenity fund. '*We all gave of our time. We had a real team identity*'. But Heather was shocked by some of the attitudes which accompanied support for the mentally handicapped. In 1986 she assisted in setting up reviews of the needs of mentally handicapped trainees in a day centre.

> The staff all wore overalls and the trainees had to refer to them as Mr or Mrs and be quiet in the workrooms. At lunchtimes the staff sat on a higher table than the trainees with a white tablecloth on it. And they did not want us coming doing reviews of the trainees (Cameron 2011).

Heather thinks the survival of such controlling attitudes was because no one had challenged them. This paternalistic approach was by no means unique to Heather's area, but during the 1980s was being confronted by increasingly articulate, coordinated and angry representatives of disabled groups and disabled people themselves. And they were developing muscular philosophies to support their demands. Michael Oliver and Vic Finkelstein's analysis of society and the state's oppressive response to disabled people (Oliver 1990, Finkelstein 1980), and Wolf Wolfensberger's exposition of the idea of normalisation (Wolfensberger 1972) were immensely challenging to social workers. The new philosophies demanded that society accommodate the needs of disabled people, supporting them to lead ordinary, independent lives rather than maintaining people in isolated ghettoes and imposing limited aspirations and second class citizenship on people. The criticism from the new philosophies was as much of the inclusive approach Heather's team took with their clients as it was of the 'white table cloth' people. Social workers decided when to run clubs, who should be invited and so on, and organised everything. Ingrained attitudes and society's requirement that they should take charge of disabled people's care meant that social workers, even those captivated by the ideas behind the social model of disability and normalisation, had to rethink their role completely.

Some social workers could make that shift, or begin to – relating as equals to their clients and offering more nuanced, negotiated brokerage and support. Two years after her experience at the white table cloth day centre Heather was involved in setting up a supported tenancy for a group of people with a learning disability. This involved negotiating with parents of the future tenants, the clients themselves, service providers and neighbours who were not keen to share their street with such people. A year later, as more houses were secured under dowries released as part of the resettlement programme for people with a learning disability living in long stay hospitals, those reluctant neighbours came forward to convince other prospective neighbours that living next door to people resettled was not the end of the world.

'My Dad's Been Shagging Me Since I was Six'

Something else happened, it seems, at more or less the same time all across England. In 1983 one of the social workers I interviewed says a lad told her his stepfather had been having sex with him; she asked her senior if she should ring the police. The senior replied '*why?*' This response, epitomising the bafflement and fastidiousness towards sexual abuse of social workers of an earlier age was about to pass. Hannah McCarthy's first experience of an allegation of sexual abuse, that same year, reflected a brave and determined attitude. A ten-year-old girl disclosed that her uncle had been having sex with her. Hannah and her boss went through the child protection procedures, talked to the police, secured the medical evidence and the man was arrested. Soon after, while on duty, Hannah took a referral from a girl alleging sexual abuse by her father, a doctor, and from then on such allegations came more frequently. Brenda Ryan tells a story, from a little later, of a 13-year-old girl on supervision who was extremely difficult to engage. '*The family was very dysfunctional and colluded with the children's bad behaviour in front of them. I was uncomfortable with the girl but she kept turning up and I stuck at it. Then out of the blue the girl said "my dad's been shagging me since I was six"*'. And the two children of an older learning disabled sister, who were wards of court, were in the father's care. Brenda worked with the older sister to keep the children. In the end she had to give them up, but Brenda guided her through choosing adopters and letting them go. The father '*hung himself out to dry*' in the care proceedings, but the Crown Prosecution Service decided not to prosecute as the two girls were not seen as credible witnesses (Ryan 2011).

From this time on as allegations were dealt with head on, the idea of sexual abuse became news. This resulted in a spate of allegations about the experiences of children in children's homes, residential schools and so on and also resulted in the establishment of *Childline*, a telephone service offering comfort, advice and protection to children who feel they cannot talk to anyone around them, who may be at risk or just lonely. Run by the NSPCC, it was set up in 1986, emerging from editions of a consumer affairs TV programme *That's Life*, fronted by Esther Rantzen. Volunteer counsellors offered a 24-hour a day telephone service, similar to the Samaritans.

'It was as if a Lightbulb had Gone On'

Penny, Hannah and Heather all report moving on in their thinking and approach to their work. This also applied to Brenda Ryan. She was a bright girl, but left school to earn a wage before taking her O levels. Three years later she had two children and by the age of 27 was working as a dinner lady. In September 1978 she did a course for women designed to broaden their job opportunities, which was '*life changing*' (Ryan 2011). From that Brenda got a job in 1979 as a clerk typist in Bolton SSD. The four clerk typists' desks were at the crossroads between social workers' rooms. '*There we sat with our card index boxes, carbon paper, india rubbers, and two cards for each case, one for the team and one for central records*'. Brenda realised she could make a go of being a social worker herself when a student she typed for talked to her about his work. '*It was like supervision – me supervising him. I thought, I could do this*'. A considerable part of the motivation for her, a single parent by this time, was financial, so she applied for a job as an assistant social worker in the team. She remembers how nervous she was carrying her diary into the social workers' room the day she started, '*the diary being the symbol of being a professional*'. She need not have worried as all but one of the team were supportive. Initially she worked mostly with older people and like so many others Brenda felt she had been '*let loose on the community; no manual handling training, no guidelines, no procedures*'. But she soon got her confidence. '*I loved it. I could connect with people*'. She also loved her training between 1983 and 1985 for which she was funded by a local education authority grant. Although the teaching disappointed her, what she learned on her placements easily made up for that; a key experience being a placement in Rochdale FSU in 1984. The approach deployed was classic FSU; regular, occasionally intensive contact and often very practical engagement with families in a range of difficulties. '*For some families it was about having someone to fall back on. It is a necessary role and this was the first time I had seen clients involved in meetings*'. It was here that Brenda first came across family therapy, with which she was not impressed. '*To my way of thinking social work is about connecting with people and family therapy, with its paradoxes and carefully derived questions, is very contrived, manipulative and pseudo scientific*'. Later in my conversation with her she pulled back from her original statement, commenting that she probably took against some of the people drawn to become family therapists as much as the method itself. Brenda reports responding negatively to other practice methods she was introduced to as well: psychosocial theory and gestalt for instance. On the other hand she was also introduced to Vera Fahlberg's ideas on the FSU Placement. Fahlberg's *Attachment and Separation* (1979) and more comprehensive later work *A Child's Journey Through Placement* (1994) outlines the harmful effects of moving children in public care to different placements, then essays ways of preparing for such moves and mitigating their impact. Brenda took the lessons to the centre of her practice. '*Attachment had a truth and a heart to it*' she says, '*the only theory I ever believed in*'.

On completing her training she returned to Rochdale as a member of a long-term child care team. It was a small team with five staff. Like others, Brenda reports that there were no real procedures, '*although we talked a lot about values and sustained each other*'. And when the senior left '*we were like a group of siblings without parents*'. Seniorless Brenda nevertheless benefitted from the active support of the Area Officer, who '*held the team; made us feel safe*'. One Christmas Eve he even accompanied her to take two children into care.

But there were problems. '*We had difficulty with the intake team, who used the NSPCC model of working*'. What Brenda meant by that was a perception on her part that the intake team was more likely to precipitately and '*coldly*' remove children rather than work with families. When she had first moved to the team, her senior too had been '*besotted by the NSPCC. He wanted me to remove, remove, remove. I operated on the basis that children need their parents and once I knew the senior was leaving I hung on to several children I had been instructed to remove until the new senior came, when we reassessed the situation together*'.

In the FSU placement and in the child care team in the mid 1980s Brenda was working next to the Rochdale NSPCC Special Unit. Developing from John Pickett's NSPCC unit in Manchester, specialist assessment and therapy units were the NSPCC's new direction. In Rochdale a special unit was established and in an agreement with the SSD took on the management of both the child protection register and ran child protection case conferences. From the beginning the five workers in the unit showed imagination and ambition. They developed an analysis of what contributed to child abuse and devised a model for assessing risks to children and what might be factors contributing to dangers to children. This was allied to an approach to discern the capacity of the parents to change. They proposed small therapeutic teams to work with families supported by a network of all the relevant workers known to the family. Their analysis also suggested that professional behaviour could inadvertently condone abusive behaviour in families, making the system designed to protect children itself dangerous. This approach was revolutionary, took protecting children more seriously than any prior practice and required more staff resource than was previously thought necessary. It was also associated, in situations where risks were high and parental capacity low, with early removal of children. The group who devised this model and drove its implementation were all men: Tony Morrison, who had trained as a probation officer; Peter Dale, a PSW; Murray Davies, Jim Waters and Wilf Roberts. The first four were in their twenties or thirties, while the latter was an older man with a traditional NSPCC background.

The members of Rochdale Special Unit were articulate, practiced what they preached and put on training courses. In 1984 Eileen Gallagher went on one of their courses and returned to Bolton on fire with enthusiasm about this framework for assessing families. She persuaded a few colleagues and, as importantly, a couple of managers that there was something in these ideas. A project was set up and an authority-wide child abuse assessment model devised, using family histories, consideration of family dynamics and careful consideration of the responsibility taken by parents, their capacity to change and the risks posed to children. Social workers operated in pairs, sometimes with a third offering support. Therapeutic work with families and individual work with children was initiated. The wave of enthusiasm amongst those involved was infectious and many workers followed the wave. '*It was as if a light bulb had gone on*' says Wyn. '*We got very excited *and the team fed off each other'*. It did as Eileen suggests *'change the way we thought. The culture changed from "we've got to help these hapless people look after their children" to protecting children being paramount'*. Although workers central to the project had time for the project protected, Eileen and Wyn, both involved, accept that they also worked hugely long hours. Wyn is clear that – as well as having a framework to help understand family dynamics and a clear process for considering risk – this period taught her empathetic, compassionate and comprehensive interviewing. The idea of joint working confronted the idée fixe shortcomings identified by Eileen Munro as contributing to child protection tragedies. Workers were more alert to what might go wrong and according to Eileen Gallagher recognised the potential of a single worker being sucked into distorted family dynamics.

When Elizabeth Mannion arrived fresh from training in 1985, she slotted into these structures and practices. *'It just worked for me from the beginning'* (Mannion 2011). The detailed, multi-faceted interviews with pairs of workers which latterly took place in well appointed premises, with interviews being video recorded and analysed with the help of a third worker, tended to reveal more of what had gone on in a family. *'This was very unnerving as you knew how children had been harmed. But that openness, with parents offering more detail, indicated parents were becoming "safer". You knew the worst and could properly assess risk'*.

Slowly a large slice of the workforce were skilled up, earlier permanency decisions were made, and earlier rehabilitation decisions taken. Eventually at the end of the decade the whole approach was mainstreamed and a permanent Child Protection Unit set up (Murphy 1996).

Training and Learning

But enthusiasm for the Rochdale NSPCC approach was not universal. Eileen, Wyn and Elizabeth, strong proponents of that approach, were clear that there were harsh elements in it. Brenda Ryan, on the other hand, accepts that the ideas were immensely influential and recognised they were onto something with the notion of *'dangerousness'*. She was also very impressed by the determination Rochdale Special Unit workers showed in identifying networks of professionals and the skill demonstrated in working with these networks. But she detested aspects of it. *'They excluded people by the language they used, created hurdles poor people could not overcome and posed challenges without enabling people'*. Brenda remembers one client who was required to walk all the way to the centre where the unit was based, in order to be observed making a meal, a particular burden for the young woman which angered Brenda a great deal. There was also academic criticism of the focus on child protection to the exclusion of broader family support (Parton and Parton 1988). But the ideas the Rochdale Special Unit developed spread, helped by their book *Dangerous Families* (Dale et al. 1986) and in some places this approach became the benchmark for child protection work.

Another Bolton social worker, Dave Seaber, thought that the ideas which came over from Rochdale were '*central, crucial. It opened up difficult to work with families, finding out how they ticked, offered an analysis*'. Dave Seaber was, like Marian Penny a generation before, a seeker, determined to live a good life, influenced by eastern philosophy and in the 1970s an unashamed hippy. He trained at Huddersfield Polytechnic between 1983 and 1985 and then worked in a generic team in Bolton, doing a little of everything although he felt, because he was a bloke, initially he had more than his fair share of teenage lads. Dave articulated perhaps better than anyone else the step-by-step learning approach which so many social workers in the 1980s seem to have engaged in:

> I learned most from colleagues. You'd pick up some ideas, like TA, or system approaches from someone and then read up a bit, try a couple of things out, talk to people. I can remember learning David Finkelhor's stuff on sexual abuse through colleagues, picking up on the importance of reflective supervision from articles by Tony Morrison (Seaber 2011).

This self directed, mutually supporting approach trumped for some people what was offered on formal training. While Nirmal Singh '*buzzed with enthusiasm*' at being introduced to gestalt and family therapy on his CQSW course, Amanda Brown seems more typical of people who trained at this time. She thought her course at Liverpool was '*not brilliant*', partly because:

> they were obsessed by the systems model, using Pincus and Minahan (1973). Everything had to be based on the idea that social workers were intervening in systems: family systems, client systems, target systems. You could fail a piece of work if you did not reference it. It was twaddle. I didn't learn anything expect on placements, apart from odd snippets; the need to avoid NAA section 47 compulsory removals, the importance of hair care for African/Caribbean children in care, that sort of thing (Brown 2011).

Two features of Dave Seaber's approach to practice coalesced in his four years in Bolton: the importance of remaining true to, while continuing to reflect upon, his values and remembering the impact of his actions on the people he was working with. So, a few years later when working for the NSPCC and delivering multi-agency child protection training, a senior manager arrived and said bluntly he did not want anything about values on the training and was more interested in procedures. So Dave decided to withdraw from that sort of work. And this relates to the second feature of his practice – being reflective. Although he prided himself on intervening creatively with children he knows he made mistakes. '*The best of people make mistakes, you have to be honest. And because people are the raw material when you make mistakes it affects people's lives. That's why it's so important to be reflective and strive to get it right*'. He thinks the model of working with families and children developed in Bolton supported self reflection. '*We were learning from and supporting each other all the time, striving to develop and improve practice...and more experienced workers played a crucial role'*. But ...

> In the end ... I began to wonder if family therapy had got overcomplicated. Sometimes professionals over complicate things to sustain their status. Perhaps we over-professionalised it and people got the balance wrong ... started thinking they were therapists rather than child protection social workers (Seaber 2011).

And there were greater dangers in getting the balance wrong. The confidence engendered by focussed assessment models and a new toughness about removing children became intertwined with the exhortation to take what children said very seriously in sexual abuse allegations. There are examples of actions SSDs took which were influenced by allegations made by a lone child about dozens, or scores more children. The removals of children in Orkney, Rochdale and Nottingham in the later 1980s and early 1990s were triggered, it has been suggested, when social workers became entangled in the distorted worlds of children, themselves traumatised by experiences of abuse (Clyde 1992). I am aware of one authority in which allegations of sexual abuse made by a single child about a considerable number of other children led to concerted action between the SSD and Police. Simultaneous raids were planned on a number of houses to remove all the children at once, the logic being that a single raid would destroy the network, whereas individual investigations would alert those involved who could then cover their tracks. As the secret preparations developed social workers were instructed not to travel to the briefing police station by the same route twice and were issued with mobile phones, outlandish and expensive equipment at that time. The worker concerned reports anticipation at first, being involved in something so extraordinary. But then came creeping unease at the secrecy. This was followed by a feeling of not being in control as the numbers of children concerned rose, then deep disquiet that something was not quite right. A series of discussions then confrontations and arguments led, in the end, to a drastic reduction in the numbers of children to be removed in the planned raids. Once the scaled down raids were completed, although children were found to have been abused, the scale of the abuse was limited compared to what was expected and many allegations were baseless. So the decision to curtail the ambition of the intervention was right. The confidence of the workers to argue for caution may have saved many families from pointless distress and the SSD from severe embarrassment.

Working with the Forgotten and Dispossessed

Stevenson and Parsloe's (DHSS 1978) finding in the 1970s that work with older people was the least popular was still the case when Amanda Brown trained, her decision to study work with older people being viewed as unusual. That was part of the reason that Julia Pither was attracted to it. Julia is Barbara Totton's daughter and was brought up in a household dominated by the CCO work her mother was involved in. Julia says Barbara chose her, of all her children, to be a social worker. Julia kicked against this and considered training to be a teacher, but got married and had a baby instead. However, at a loose end after her marriage broke up in her mid twenties, she followed a friend into social work training, even though she had no experience (Pither 2011). On her course child care work had a very high profile but there was never any doubt that she wanted to work with older people with mental health problems, '*people who were least valued*'. This was something to do with both her grandmothers having developed dementia. Her training brought her out of her quiet shell and taught her the two things that underpin her practice. The first was '*Don't make judgements, but stand in their shoes*'. She reports that the probation officers on her course drove her mad because of the constant judgements they made about people. The second lesson was that if you get stuck in a conversation '*always reach for the feelings*'.

She started work in 1989 and made it clear she wanted to work with older people with mental health problems. '*No one else was interested in this and from the beginning I was on my own. There were no resources for this group, I had to fight really hard to get onto the Approved Social Worker training* (a pre-requisite to practice in mental health under the 1983 Mental Health Act) *and residential care was always seen as the only route*'. From the beginning psychiatric nurses were her allies, although her constant refrain of '*one more try at home*' was sometimes interpreted by risk averse NHS staff as '*wicked and cruel*'. From the beginning Julia's strategy was precise: '*you have to help keep people in their own homes so they can make their own choices*'.

Despite feeling isolated with the people she had chosen to work with, she remembers with affection times when strangers came to her aid. One lady who was very confused lived in a big house on her own. It had always been her home and, despite difficulty in articulating what she wanted, to have moved her on account of a bureaucratic interpretation of safety would have been hideous. But she became anxious and wandered about outside. One of the strategies to keep the lady at home, which Julia stumbled on, was the people next door.

> They were students, all young men. They looked out for her. If she got confused
> at night or came out, they'd reassure her, take her back indoors and tuck her up.
> In the end she died in her armchair, surrounded by all her lifelong possessions
> just as she would have wanted (Pither 2011).

If Julia struggled initially to raise the profile of work with older people with mental health problems, she was not alone in standing up for the needs of forgotten or dispossessed groups in the 1980s. Ray Wyre, a former Probation Officer, carried on the work he started in Albany Prison, by founding the Gracewell Clinic in 1988, a commercial enterprise and the world's first residential clinic for sex offenders (Guardian 2008). Another Probation Officer, Philip Priestley, working with the National Association for the Care and Resettlement of Offenders, piloted the idea of Victim Support Schemes in 1973 in Bristol. The idea spread from locality to locality and by the mid 1980s there were 100 schemes nationally, all operating on the classic model of paid members of staff coordinating and supporting a group of volunteer visitors (victimsupport.org). Another forgotten group were child migrants. Margaret Humphreys, a Nottingham social worker, met someone in the mid 1980s who was looking for a relative who had, as a child in care, been forcibly migrated to Australia in the 1950s. Margaret followed this up, discovered the huge extent of the practice of child migration in post-war Britain and set about finding child migrants and reuniting them with their families. Her tale is well known, the subject of a sympathetic feature film *Oranges and Sunshine* (Loach 2011), as well as her own book *Empty Cradles* (1994).

More Freedom, More Status and More Money

Employees of large organisations were, of course, not forgotten or dispossessed, but there were few enough employers who took their employees' emotional needs seriously until the 1980s. After the Second World War two weeks paid holiday as a minimum (1948), industrial injuries compensation (1957), tighter workplace safety legislation (1961 and 1963), and in the 1970s maternity leave, equal pay and flexible working all made working life more secure (Russell 1991). But the emotional pressure of some work, in the police or fire services for example, could cause considerable distress to staff, leading to absence, ineffectiveness, high staff turnover and even litigation against the employer. During the 1980s, with a heightened interest in organisational efficiency, discussion about management methods began to include a focus on the commercial advantage of better trained and supported staff (Peters and Waterman 1982). Thus employers began to consider their responsibilities for the emotional support to staff. As it happens Bolton SSD was one of the first to do this for social workers themselves. In 1987 Michael Murphy, a social worker, was asked to establish a staff care scheme, an initiative in part stimulated by the emotional demands of the child protection work considered above. Michael himself took calls and helped people decide what support they might need. He did some of the counselling work himself, which might involve three or four sessions, but he also secured the services of a number of counsellors independent of the SSD and paid them commercial rates for work undertaken. Michael recalls there being a dozen counsellors he could call on by the early 1990s and remembers receiving about 150 referrals a year in the late 1980s (Murphy 1997).

This phenomenon of people setting themselves up as professional counsellors was relatively new in the 1980s, with the British Association for Counselling only offering membership to individual counsellors as late as 1977. What was on offer from these practitioners was different from classical psychoanalysis. People had been paying psychotherapists to be analysed since the 1920s, although in tiny numbers. Psychoanalysis is a long process, demanding a regular commitment by the analyst and the patient to meet weekly or more frequently over a period of months if not years. This restricted the constituency for analysis to those with time, money and emotional staying power. Many who put themselves through this did so because they themselves wanted to be analysts, Clare Winnicott for instance (Kantor 2004). We have seen how psychoanalytical ideas were closely associated with social work from the early days of the mental health course at the LSE in the late 1920s and how their influence remained strong in social work training into the 1970s.

Sue Moya for instance, a social worker who qualified in the 1970s, had undergone psychoanalysis in her teens '*so I was familiar with the idea that it is helpful to understand behaviour and feelings when they are getting in the way of being able to live one's life*'. Later as a social worker she remembers stimulating discussions with colleagues about how best to understand people, which led to more reading and more study. She took a course which reintroduced her to these ideas and then underwent a full analysis alongside training to be a psychotherapist. '*I wanted to be able to understand someone else and then help them to understand themselves, so they don't keep on tripping over the same obstacle. This is just very satisfying*'. Sue thinks that the relationship is the key and says '*the relief, for client and therapist, of arriving at something which feels genuine and which offers a way to understand what has gone wrong has always felt like the real thing*'. And she says '*social work didn't get me there*'. She became a psychotherapist (Moya 2011). Judith Niechcial also went into therapy after her training course although she remained in social work.

But the general appeal of this approach waned. As early as 1959 Barbara Wootton (1959) questioned the efficacy and ethics of psychodynamic casework. And many social workers training in the 1970s were dismissive of the psychodynamic ideal, sharing Hannah McCarthy's thinking that this approach implied that whatever difficulties people were in, the starting point for the psychodynamically inclined was that it was their own fault. In addition the 1960s and 1970s saw the emergence of alternative therapeutic ideas in which people are invited to be the arbiters of their own lives; the psychology of thinkers such as Carl Rogers (Person Centred Therapy) Eric Berne (Transactional Analysis) and Ellis and Beck (Cognitive Behavioural Therapy).

Robin Hobbes read Bertrand Russell's *History of Western Philosophy* when he was 18 and was struck by the chapter on Freud. From then on he was determined, however incoherently at first, to become a therapist. In the late 1970s, when working for Kent SSD, he took part in a Transactional Analysis course and was hooked. He trained and passed the exams of the UK Institute of Transactional Analysis. He began offering training, part time at first, took individual clients and then trained and supervised other practitioners. Around 1982 he resigned as a social worker and became a therapist full time.

It meant more freedom, more money and more status. At that time social workers were hated and at parties, once I had made the break, I no longer hid what I did.

When I told people I was a therapist I would get asked questions like, 'can you read my mind?' (Hobbes 2011).

Brenda Mallon worked as a teacher rather than a social worker, but took a similar path. After experience in a primary school she took a job in the local child guidance clinic, teaching in the morning and visiting children and their families in the afternoon. In the late 1980s she did a counselling course, to add an extra string to her bow rather than as a distinct career choice. But a change in direction was stimulated by a teacher whose colleague had died. She was visibly distressed in class when a child came up to her asking if it was alright to cry. Questioned, the boy said that after his father had died by suicide, his mother, in her grief, had told him not to cry – it was not allowed. Brenda had always been interested in '*children on the margins*', and from then on her focus was work with bereaved children. She wrote a book and, taking her courage in her hands, gave up work to write, to offer training and to offer counselling for individuals. At first she advertised in a local alternative magazine *Cahoots*, attracting clients from a particular cultural milieu. From the beginning 60 per cent of her work was counselling with a lot of work being about stress, relationship difficulties and a lack of a sense of direction in life. Her philosophy and methods she characterises as Rogerian and Jungian.

Both Brenda and Robin recall how few therapists were practicing in the 1980s. Brenda was involved in a feminist therapy group for a while but all the other women were employed by the NHS or local authorities.

Typical Bloody Social Workers, All Talk, Nobody Actually Does Anything

On Saturday 11 May 1985 Michael Stewart agreed to go to a football match with a friend. For some reason his friend called the arrangement off and Michael spent the afternoon elsewhere. Later his wife, a nurse, who had been on duty all afternoon, came home raging at him for not letting her know he was safe. The match he had not gone to was Bradford City v Lincoln City. The main stand had burned down. Fifty-six people had died and hundreds more were injured.

At the time Michael was a social worker in an alcoholic unit in Bradford. He started out with a religious vocation but at 21, after an abusive experience in a Dublin monastery, he fled to London. He rattled around for a couple of years, working for a while with homeless people and alcoholics in St Martin's in the Fields, where Eileen Younghusband had become enthused 50 years before. In 1975 serendipity led him to Leeds, to a job in a children's home and from there to CQSW training. His strongest memory of training is of a weekend away with a group of students. Each took on the mantle of a different physical disability, and each had a buddy, helping one another as they could. Michael had his arms tied behind him for the whole weekend and his buddy was blind. '*It was heart breaking, funny and useful all at the same time*' (Stewart 2011). After three years in a generic social work team in Bradford Michael joined the multi-disciplinary unit working with alcoholics and loved it. '*We had enormous independence, good relationships with the doctors and we ran therapy groups*'. He also underwent psychotherapy himself partly, because like Sue Moya and Robin Hobbes, he harboured an ambition to be a therapist. And he wanted to learn how better to help people. He says '*there's always a temptation to become cynical about the system we work in. I didn't want that. I wanted to get better at what I did*'.

It is fair to say that on the day the football stand burnt down at Valley Parade, Michael was looking for something. Partly as a result of having narrowly missed being at the match himself, he went to a meeting called by the Director of the SSD the following Monday evening, at which the response to the fire was discussed. About 30 staff turned up. At one point a message came through that a couple from Lincoln wanted a lift to Bradford to identify and collect the effects of their father who had died. But the discussion just passed over that. Michael thought, '*typical bloody social workers, all talk, but nobody actually does anything*'. He got up, got his car keys out and said '*OK, if no one else will do it, I'll drive over there now*'. He had to ask a colleague to borrow a fiver to pay for the petrol, but made the journey. Spending time with those people seeking out charred remains of a cardigan and not much else affected him deeply.

He applied for and was appointed to a three-year SSD post established to work with those bereaved and injured by the Bradford fire. '*I learned a bucketful*' he says. One of the first things to decide was how to approach people. Most SSD clients for one reason or another could not avoid the social worker. In this new job Michael knew he had to have something to offer and convince people the offer was worth having. He used the device of wondering what his mother would do faced with this sort of offer and developed a successful approach. He worked with individuals and families, published a newsletter and helped establish a support network. But latterly he was often called away. Those last five years of the 1980s were marked by a peculiar litany of civil disasters: the Piper Alpha oil platform explosion, the King's Cross fire, the sinking of the Herald of Free Enterprise, the Clapham rail crash, Lockerbie, Hungerford, Dunblane. Michael was called to advise in several of these tragedies and '*by the end of the 1980s I was hot property*'. When his three years working with bereaved families was up, he tried but could not go back to the work he had done before. He consulted a solicitor about setting up a charity, but was told that he would be better setting up his own business.

Michael Stewart is an engaging character with a commanding presence and became a successful businessman. With a partner (Peter Hodgkinson) he set up Crisis Psychology, a company offering support when there was a civil disaster, but also taking on work with post offices and banks helping prepare people for the eventuality of a robbery. Just as Victim Support claims to have been the first such service in the world, Crisis Psychology, when they started getting calls from across the globe, understood they were at that time alone in the market. Michael should have realised it because although there was literature about trauma counselling and supporting military personnel after action, he could find only one book about supporting people after civil disasters – *Disaster Strikes* by Beverley Raphael

(1983). That's part of the reason they wrote their own book in 1991 (Hodgkinson and Stewart).

Michael is candid about their approach. '*We didn't develop new values, just a few new methods*'. When they started appointing staff Michael says he was shocked by some people's attitudes, both social workers and psychologists. They might not turn up on time, or overpromise what was offered, or in some cases did not respect other staff in the business. '*We only employed people who could get those basics right and who did not need chivvying*'. As far as practice methods were concerned Michael says '*we just tried things out*', explaining that after a bank raid for instance the common sense response was to send people home, where nobody would be in and the person would be on their own. Michael concluded that the workplace was the optimal place for recovery – people were together and could start processing the experience, going back on the front desk for example to try out how it felt. '*It was an amazing time*', he says, '*there were no barriers, you could be so creative*'.

To others however, because he ran a successful business and was getting a lot of attention, he was a traitor. '*There was a lot of resentment from former colleagues. I was accused of losing my moral compass and betraying my profession*'.

Michael Stewart made a good living from Crisis Psychology, but he was also following in the footsteps of many others whose tales have been sketched in these pages. He had done what Mrs Greg and Mary Haslam had done 80 years before. He had seen a need and tried to meet that need using his own imagination, skill and compassion to get a service up and running. He was following Mary Mason, Brian Fox, Margaret Torrie, Nirmal Singh, Eileen Gallagher, Wyn Haslam and Julia Pither in working out better ways of helping people in distress.

He was doing the same in his day-to-day work as Heather Cameron:

> I was on secondment in a different job and while I was away the children of one of my clients were removed. She had long term mental health problems and always struggled. I went to see her when I returned and she was at rock bottom, lost and angry. Things got worse and in the end I had to section her under the Mental Health Act. But I spent a lot of time with her and she managed to get on a more even keel. We were able to re-establish a visiting schedule with her children. One day a group of social workers took several people out for the day to Blackpool and I just remember being in this double helter skelter alongside her. I looked at her, thinking how much she had been through and how well she was dealing with life. It was amazing. I looked at the smile on her face and that felt OK. Yes, I thought. This is alright. This is alright (Cameron 2011).

Afterword

The Landscape in 1989

It's a June morning in 1989 and if you were to travel down Wigan Road into Bolton as Mary Haslam had done 85 years before you could not travel by tram. The tracks had been pulled up half a century before. White Bank, Mary Haslam's home, was no more. Her family had donated the land on which the house stood to the council in 1923 shortly after she died, and it had been turned into a park and play area. A mile down the hill on the left you would pass the butcher's shop where Alice Kearsley had been brought up, still a butcher although a Halal one by then. And looking across town you would have been able to see barely half a dozen chimneys ahead of you, a sparse reminder of the cotton mills which had dominated the Edwardian skyline. Despite all of that Mary Haslam and Alice Kearsley, had they been travelling with you, would have recognised the town's street layout. A bus station had replaced an engineering works behind the town hall and the warren of streets in front of it had been pedestrianised. But they would have noticed that the muggy cowl of smog over the town was no more. Local mines had been closed as well as mills and the biggest employer in town was a baker establishing a regional reputation.

And what had been the most significant changes across the UK? The UK was no longer a net exporter of emigrants but since the war had become a net importer. In 1989 the overwhelming preponderance of housing tenure was owner occupation which in 1901 had stood at only ten per cent of the total. But the greatest changes were in health. Between 1901 and 1991 the UK population rose from 38 million to 57 million. Life expectancy in 1901 for both men and women was less than 50. In 1991 it was nearly 80 for women and nearly 75 for men. Infant mortality had dropped from 140 deaths per 1,000 births in 1901 to less than ten per 1,000 in 1990. So many fewer children died, but due to the almost ubiquitous use of birth control, the number of children under 16, nationally not just in Bolton, was not much different in 1989 from what it had been in 1904. The numbers of people over 65 on the other hand had trebled, a cause for social comment from mid century onwards. In 1901 the great majority of deaths were caused by infectious diseases. The control of fatal infections through antibiotics in the latter half of the century meant that by 1989 70 per cent of deaths were due to circulatory illness and cancer (Parliamentary Papers 1999).

While the structure of the population was changed the geography of social work in Bolton was still recognisable. The Bolton Poor Law Union building in Maudsley Street where Mr Cooper, Alice Kearsley and George Knowles had worked was still there in 1989, housing a firm of solicitors. Ada Wainer's office in Wood Street had become a branch of Pizza Express. Silverwell Street, always a haven for charities, was still that in 1989. Here were the offices of the Guild of Help, long devoid of its throng of visiting Helpers, being instead the first port of call for social workers seeking furniture and domestic appliances for families being rehoused. But the Moral Welfare Association was gone and the NSPCC had withdrawn their inspector from Bolton in 1983. Age Concern had a base near the market and the local Gingerbread Group had a welfare officer, as well as offering mutual support. A Victim Support Scheme had started in October 1984, and while the workshop for the Blind had gone – its work incorporated into the responsibilities of the SSD – a voluntary group called Vision Aid, started by parents, offering support to families with blind and partially sighted children was just getting into its stride. Queen's Street Mission, although continuing, commanded a moderate income of around £15,000 annually and the equivalent minor expenditure, the Mission Hall in Central Street having been sold off. A great deal of voluntary effort was coordinated by the Council for Voluntary Service, a direct organisational descendent of the Council for Social Welfare established in Bolton in 1911 (BHC BCF/7/1/26).

Plus Ca Change ...

But in 1989 the SSD was the biggest show in town by a margin. In 1904 Bolton Union employed seven relieving officers, a couple of assistant relieving officers, a Relieving Officer for Lunatics, an Infant Life Inspection Visitor and a handful of Vaccination Officers and Registrars. And there were around a score or so volunteers helping out with the boarding-out visiting coordinated by Alice Barlow and the after care service managed by Alice Kearsley. In Bolton SSD in 1989 there were 113 social workers and assistants employed by the local authority. The number of people on the caseloads of the 1989 social workers is not directly comparable with the work of the Poor Law early in the century because of the Guardians' responsibility for out relief (i.e. financial support for the poor) which the SSD did not have, and the huge increase in numbers of people surviving beyond 65. But the numbers of children in care in 1989 (368) was somewhat more, by my admittedly crude estimation, than the low hundreds of children cared for by the Poor Law in the cottage homes or boarded-out in 1914 (BHC BCF/7/1/26).

The work of the SSD in 1989 showed some consistencies with the past although most things were new. In January 1989 the Social Services Committee (SSC) had agreed to the resettlement in the town of the first 24 people with mental health problems from Prestwich Hospital (BHC BCF/7/1/25). Social workers were already managing the resettlement of people with a learning disability into the community from long stay hospitals (Kirkpatrick 2011). Extra funding was agreed in February 1989 to establish three social worker posts for a Child Abuse Team (BHC BCF/7/1/26). These were in addition to those working with abused children in the area teams who, like their colleagues across the UK, were at the heart of the increasingly successful system for protecting vulnerable children, as Pritchard's work suggests (Pritchard 2010). Bolton was involved in a wrangle with the Home Office about funding for more ethnic minority social workers. The committee had asked for funding for nine, but the Home Office thought that was a bit steep and asked for further evidence of need. Discussions were underway about the future care of 140 very vulnerable older people then resident in Hulton long stay hospital which the NHS had decided to close, part of the NHS strategy to withdraw hospital care from any older people but the acutely ill. Also an AIDS strategy had just been agreed (BHC BCF/7/1/28). Recording practices for social workers were being tightened up in response to the Access to Personal Files Act 1987, which allowed citizens access to their social services files (BHC BCF/7/1/27). And in July 1989 the SSC agreed to the purchase of ten word processors, an addition to the 13 already owned by the department. These, it was argued, were much more efficient than typewriters (BHC BCF/7/1/29). If any aspect of the social worker's life and experience is bookended within this volume it is this. 1904 saw the Poor Law Guardians agree to introduce buff cardboard folders for the records of each individual person visited or allocated out relief. The decision in 1989 by the Union's successor body about word processors was an early harbinger of the cardboard folder's demise.

The ever demanding focus on child protection meant that the proportion of non-child centred work being dealt with by the three area teams was, according to my several informants, about 20 per cent of the total. Work with children was still the favourite destination of newly trained social workers and there was a view that people with learning disabilities or mental health problems, people with physical disabilities and older people were getting a raw deal; this within a structure which was still supposed to be generic. The committee had agreed to a reorganisation, creating specialist teams which would mean a greater focus on services for disabled adults. Associated with this was a deliberate change in terminology, with the committee beginning to refer to teams of workers for people with physical disabilities rather than physical handicap and to the team working not with mentally handicapped people but with people with learning difficulties (BHC BCF/7/1/29).

The specific problems identified in the 1988 annual review of social services in the town included the increasing number of very old people, the levels of poverty in the Borough, poor housing, the social isolation of single parents and difficulties of minority ethnic communities. In all this, as the 1980s came to an end Bolton SSD faced the same problems as many others. And were those key pressures much different from what they had been 85 years before?

Observations

One general observation about social workers across the century is that the pattern of attitudes expressed by individuals matches the natural life course. By and large young people entered social work with energy and enthusiasm, learned their trade and brought their own take on the world to the task. They then toiled away and towards the end some became disillusioned with the world changing under their feet. So Isobel Groves' comment *'we were going to win the world'* (2010) epitomises the enthusiasm of the twenty-something social worker she was in the 1960s. Similarly Mr Watkinson's jaundiced view of the mechanical approach to welfare introduced by the Attlee government, replacing the more human management of distress he remembered from his forty years as a relieving officer in the East Riding, can be seen as typical of an old-stager ill at ease with innovation (1955).

But people from different traditions and generations sometimes delighted young workers as much as they frustrated them. Val Burnham for instance much admired one ex Poor Law colleague. Brian Fox reported old ROs as being, in his words, *'chalk and cheese'*. On the other hand some young or new workers were critical of the tradition they entered (or amused by it), attempting to throw over previous attitudes and practices. Geraldine Aves in the 1920s, Isobel Groves in the 1960s and Penny Hindle in the 1980s were all aware, as young workers, of things changing, leaving the attitudes and practices of some of their older colleagues behind.

We have also seen that there have been a number of separate gender and class traditions amongst social workers. ROs, NSPCC Inspectors and SAWOs were traditionally male until 1948, were predominantly working class and their vocation was often picked up on the way rather than guiding their choice of work. Almoners were traditionally female (setting aside the male working class tradition which Thomas Cramp represented). Probation officers from 1908 were traditionally male, but women, in smaller numbers were always involved. Affluent, educated women dominated the pre-war elite social worker groups, although some middle class women were to be found in publically funded social work in the 1930s, Lucy Faithfull for instance. And, as we have seen, boarding-out visitor and child welfare visitor posts in PACs in the inter-war years attracted women from across the class divide. The establishment after the Second World War of local authorities as the home of social workers as public servants completed this pre-war trend. By the early 1970s, people from well educated or affluent backgrounds were drawn as ever to social work but people like Sue Moya and Judith Niechcial were by then in a minority compared with the numbers of younger people joining the new SSDs who were often the first in their families to have any secondary education beyond the age of 14. And although from the end of the war until the 1980s men trained as social workers in increasing numbers, the number of men coming forward dropped in that decade as a different social and political dynamic replaced the welfare ideals of the post-war period (Christie 1998).

Finally, as well, we have seen continuities across the boundary years of 1948 and 1972, hardly surprising when the majority of workers in the new systems had worked in the old. Moreover, lauded initiatives often reprised previous practices. For instance, the boarding-out of children in public care was common (though not primary) practice by 1900. Rolph was surprised that in the 1950s MWOs were working 'generically' (2003), but Ken Powls and Cyril Bustin although mostly working with mental cases worked with both older people and children in the 1930s, as did Robert Robbie, Relieving Officer for Lunatics, in 1918. Ian Brown's family group homes, new in Manchester in the 1950s, were very similar to the use of the in-house foster parent couple employed by Bolton in 1904.

The Problem of Technique

But it is what Macadam referred to as the problem of technique which characterises a considerable amount of what social workers report, especially, but not only, in the latter half of the century (Macadam 1925). Although one of the regular features of the narratives in this text is the worker's reported enjoyment of qualification training, for many the techniques they were presented with were at a tangent to their understanding or experience of their work. Some like Joyce Rimmer and Nirmal Singh were excited by their training. Others, like Howard Syddall and Carol Clark were unimpressed. But a lot viewed their training with a sort of frustrated gratitude. Here are Ted Perry's observations reviewing his training of the late 1960s. He is referring to his lecture notes of the time and a text book, *Casework in Probation* (1964) by Mark Monger, who was his tutor.

> I have read through a number of passages in his book and I regret to say that my fantasies about the casework based training are still … justified. Apart from his writing still being gobbledegook to me, I cannot believe that, at the time, we all seemed to believe that offending was an irrelevance to the task of supervising offenders. There is one particular passage in Monger's book where he devotes 7 pages to providing a model for casework recording on a case that spanned some 6 months of work and where the offender's offending is not mentioned at all.
>
> But the lecture notes were clear, concise and, by my standards, surprisingly well written. With hindsight, I can see that the lectures all had practical application and were a key to my survival as a practitioner working in isolation. So, when it came to practice, my training had … prepared me … better than I had..given it credit for. Even the casework began to make a little more sense when Mark Monger concentrated in lectures on the practicalities of the subject. His lectures helped me to grasp the value of the empathic relationship with the offender – no matter what he had done – and how to interview with sensitivity. He helped me to gain confidence in my ability to record my thoughts in writing and facilitating an effectiveness in providing useful reports to the Courts … and Mark Monger was a wonderful man. He was kind, sensitive, considerate and

supportive. He was a man who I admired and respected and this was possibly
the reason why I worked so hard to follow his conventional wisdom of the day
(Perry 2010).

Some social workers no doubt started with the naive assumption that their
training would turn them into experts, a not unreasonable aspiration until the
1970s, when confidence that social workers could be predictably successful took
a battering. And some training courses, like the one Amanda Brown experienced
where Systems Theory was thrown at her, seem to have offered 'the answer',
the 'big idea'. What most social workers, in the end seem to have understood is
that learning, as Dave Seaber articulates so well, is a brick by brick endeavour,
self directed, reflective, career long – a melding of personality, work setting,
procedural requirements, technique and the courage to take responsibility.

But also thinking about social work and doing it are so different as to be almost
antithetical activities. Breaking down and analysing the causes of an individual's
or family's inability to cope and identifying their needs requires a different sort
of thinking from that required to relate to people, influence them and help them.
Jonathan Sacks explains the distinction well in his essay on the difference between
scientific thinking and religious thinking. Scientific thinking he describes as a left
brain activity; taking things apart to see how they work. Religious thinking he
sees as a right brain activity; putting things together to see what they mean (Sacks
2011). The metaphor is hardly precise, but social workers all know that analysing
a family's problems is very different from establishing an empathetic relationship
with them. The psychiatrist Val Burnham worked with, described in Chapter Six,
certainly understood that he could analyse and interpret but he took Val along
to interviews because she could empathise and relate. Talking and walking are
different functions and have to be learned in different ways.

More Tales to Tell

I have only mentioned or quoted something like 90 social workers in these pages;
that's less than one a year for the twentieth century. And while I have tried to cover
a broad range of activity, making sure publically funded workers are given a voice
through the first half of the century and that voluntary and commercial sector
workers are covered in the second, there are still many gaps. As well as groups of
social workers I admitted to being absent from the text in the introduction I have
also come across tantalising hints of stories not told. The tradition of employing
men to act as Outpatient Inspectors in voluntary hospitals at the turn of the last
century needs investigating. In Willmott's book about Geraldine Aves (1992) there
is a photograph of a score or so uniformed Canadian social workers brought over
to help in the war. Who were they? What did they do? In a Humphrey Jennings
film *Welfare of the Workers* (Jennings 1940) there is mention of the Welfare Board

which employed social workers to support young munitions workers. What was that? I did not have time to follow up any of these or other hints.

On a more significant level I cannot find any detailed commentary on the impact of Seebohm on social workers. And where is the history of the attitude to and use of practice methods by social workers? Where is there comment about the role eugenic ideas have played in social work thinking? Where is the history of the care committee systems? And Ramesh Chandra Mishra's first class review of the history of relieving officers was completed in 1969. Since then there has been nothing … so where is the history of relieving officers?

There are many more tales to tell.

Appendix 1

Chronology of Circumstances and Events Relating to the Activities of Social Workers During the Twentieth Century

1889   Children Act sanctions removal of children to a 'place of safety'.

1892   Poor Law Journal established.

1895   Thomas Cramp taken on as Outpatient Inspector at the Metropolitan Hospital, London and Mary Stewart taken on as Almoner at the Royal Free Hospital, St Pancras, London.

1896   Superannuation for Poor Law Officers introduced.

1898   Infant Life Protection Act.

1899   Poor Law (Amendment) Act clarifies Board of Guardians' right to assume parental rights over children.

1902   Boer War ends. Education Act raises school leaving age to 13, and transfers control of schools from school boards to local authorities. Central Midwives Board established.

1903   Almoner's Committee established by eight voluntary hospital almoners. Formal training at Urwick's School of Social Work begins with both COS visitors and ROs participating.

1904   First Guild of Help set up in Bradford. University based training for social workers in Liverpool begins.

1906   Education Act allows schools to offer free school meals. London care committee system established.

1907   Probation of Offenders Act allows magistrates to appoint probation officers.

1908   Children Act establishes separate Juvenile Courts for children. Bolton School for Mothers and Babies Welcome established. Old Age Pensions Act.

1909   Royal Commissioning on the Poor Law reports.

1910   Local Government Board requires unions to use female visitors for children boarded-out.

1911   National Insurance Act introduces sickness benefits and unemployment benefits.

1913   Mental Deficiency Act. National Association of Probation Officers established. Welfare Workers Association for factory welfare officers formed.

1914   Great War begins.

1915   Munitions of War Act encouraged the steady flow of women into munitions factories. Debate about the status and care of men suffering from shell shock heightens interest in mental distress.

1918   Maternity and Child Welfare Act. Local Church of England Moral Welfare committees set up around this time and over the next decade.

1919   Ernest Jones founds British Psychoanalytical Society. First Women Police appointed.

1920   Blind Person's Act. Marie Stopes publishes *Married Love*. Hugh Crichton-Miller opens Tavistock Clinic.

1922   Severe financial problems lead to reduction in government spending by 20% between 1922 and 1931.

1924   Sybil Clement Brown, and subsequently many others, visits USA to study child guidance and social work training.

1925   Criminal Justice Act requires courts to appoint probation officers.

1926   Adoption Act.

1927   London School of Economics begins the Mental Health Course to train Psychiatric Social Workers. First Child Guidance Clinic established in London.

1929   Local Government Act transfers Poor Law powers to local authority from Poor Law Unions. Public Assistance Committees set up.

1930   Mental Treatment Act permits outpatient treatment.

1931   Huge increase in unemployment and introduction of means tested 'Transition Benefit'.

1933   Children and Young People's Act introduces cognisance of the welfare of the child.

1935   British Federation of Social Workers established.

1939   Board of Education proposes local authorities set up local Youth Committees. Second World War starts. All hospitals become subject to central direction. Evacuation of vulnerable from major cities.

1940   Old People's Welfare Committees (OPWCs) set up. Nazi bombing of major UK cities begins. Cambridge Evacuation Survey published. Hostels set up for hard to place evacuated children. Regional Welfare service established.

1942   Beveridge Report published. Pacifist Service Units begin working with 'problem families'.

1944   Education Act. Curtis Committee investigating children in public care set up.

1945   Death of Dennis O'Neill. Second World War ends. Monckton Report into the death of Dennis O'Neill published. Family Allowances Act.

1946   NHS Act. National Association of Mental Health set up. Curtis Committee reports. COS becomes Family Welfare Association.

1947   Clare Britton asked to lead a qualification course for the new Child Care Officers.

1948   National Assistance Act, Criminal Justice Act and Children Act. Local Authority Children's Depts and Welfare and Public Health Depts set up.

1949   Association of Children's Officers established. Association of Child Care Officers established.

1953   Samaritans set up. Ministry of Health requires local coordination arrangements for problem families.

1954   Generic 'Carnegie' Social Work Course started at LSE.

1959   Younghusband report on social work training.

1961   National Institute of Social Work Training qualification training course for workers in Welfare Departments, to increase numbers of qualified staff there.

1962   Health Visiting and Social Work (Training) Act amalgamates all training for social workers. Standing Conference of Organisations of Social Workers established.

1963   Children Act legitimises expenditure on 'prevention'. Robbins Report proposes increase in number of university places. Community Service Volunteers started.

1965   Remit of Probation Officers expands from the mid sixties. Seebohm Committee set up to investigate how social services operate. Child Poverty Action Group established.

1966   Shelter launched.

1967   NSPCC Special Unit set up in Manchester.

1968   Seebohm Committee reports.

1969   Children and Young Person's Act introduces the facility for Intermediate Treatment, as an alternative to care/custody.

1970   Chronically Sick and Disabled Person's Act obliges local authorities to survey population of disabled people.

1971   Womens' Aid branches set up and spread across the country. *Better Services for the Mentally Handicapped* published, proposing community care for people with mental handicap. *Case Con* magazine begun, offering a critical analysis of social work as a tool of state control of poor people.

1972   Social Service Departments come into being. Former workers in local authority Mental Welfare and Public Health, Welfare and Children's Departments and almoners formally managed within the NHS are all transferred to SSDs.

1973   Maria Colwell dies. Victim Support experiment operates in Bristol.

1974   DHSS requires Area Review Committee in each area. Report of the enquiry into the death of Maria Colwell published.

1975   Children Act tightens rules on parental responsibility.

1976   Financial pressures curtail regular increases in funding for a SSDs and Probation. Union of the Physically Impaired Against Segregation publishes definition of impairment and disability.

1977   British Association of Counselling accepts individual members.

1978   National social worker's strike over pay and conditions.

1979   Conservative government elected and is associated with subsequent tight control of public spending.

1982   Resettlement of people with a learning disability begins. Barclay Report published.

1983   Mental Health Act requires social workers to be 'Approved' to work in mental health. Child Sexual Abuse is 'discovered' around this time.

1985   Jasmine Beckford dies.

1986   Jasmine Beckford enquiry report (*A Child in Trust*), followed by a number of similar reports about child deaths. Childline begins operation.

1987   Access to Personal Files Act passed.

1989   Children Act requires social workers to work in partnership with parents. Cleveland inquiry into the large number of 'diagnoses' of sexual abuse by paediatricians in Middlesborough.

1990   NHS and Community Care Act. Controversy over a number of cases of coordinated removals of children by social workers (Orkney, Rochdale, Nottingham).

1992   Memorandum of Good Practice in interviewing children where there was a suspicion of abuse was published.

1993   Implementation of NHS and Community Care Act.

List of Applicants for the Post of Child Welfare Visitor Advertised by Bolton Poor Law Union in 1925

The application forms did not require considerable text. Claims made by applicants about qualifications are sometimes slim, so what is recorded here is limited. CMB refers to the certificate of the Central Midwives Board. SRN status was consequent upon the Nurses Registration Act 1919. The Royal Sanitary Institute ran training courses for Health Visitors and Child Welfare Workers in the 1920s.

(Table begins on next page.)

Name	Age	Marital status	Current role (and whether Private, Commercial, Voluntary, Local Authority or Poor Law)	From …	Previous experience (and whether Private, Commercial, Voluntary, Local Authority or Poor Law)	Qualification claimed in application form
Annie Hancock	38	S	Woman Visitor (Poor Law)	Birmingham	Paddington School For Mothers (Voluntary)	Health Visitor Certificate
Lizzie Poole	47	S	At home	Bolton	Work in a children's sanatorium/slum rescue work (Voluntary)	
Sarah Dewhirst	45	S	Undertaker (Commercial)	Bolton	Bank Street Chapel school (Voluntary)	
M. Buchanan	42	S	Mental Nurse (Poor Law)	Manchester	District Nursing (Voluntary)/Sick Attendant, presumably in a Poor Law infirmary	State Registered Nurse [SRN]/Central Midwives Board certificate [CMB]
E. Brennan	35	S	Private Nurse (Private)	Bolton	Sanatorium ward	Nursing Qualification
A.M. Godrich	36	S	Foster mother (Poor Law?)	Birmingham	Salvation A/U/M mother visiting	
E. Kidd	34	M	Nursing sister (?)	Bolton	Maternity sister/Staff Nurse/ District Nurse (Voluntary)	SRN/CMB
H. Davey	44	S	Private Nurse (Private)	Macclesfield	Children's home matron/ Canadian children's home assistant matron	Nurse
H.D. Hughes	52	S	Woman Visitor (Poor Law)	Grimsby	Probation officer	CMB

Name	Age	Marital status	Current role (and whether Private, Commercial, Voluntary, Local Authority or Poor Law)	From ...	Previous experience (and whether Private, Commercial, Voluntary, Local Authority or Poor Law)	Qualification claimed in application form
Doris May	24	S	Welfare Supervisor (Commercial)	Bolton	St Johns Nurse (Voluntary)/ kindergarten (Voluntary)	St Johns Nursing
E.J. Wolstencroft	45	S	Midwife (Local Authority)	Bolton	Guild of Help Visitor (Voluntary)/Auxiliary in Military Hospital	SRN/CMB
M. Lewis	33	S	Private Nurse (Private)	Rhos	District Nurse (Voluntary)/ Maternity Nursing	SRN
A. Turton	29	S	Woman Visitor (Poor Law)	Birmingham	Visiting widows with dependent children (Voluntary?)	Sanitary Inspectors certificate/Health Visitor training
Esther Chance	35	S	Mental Nurse (Poor Law?)	Bradford	Nursing and Child Welfare in Stockport and Warrington	
S. Anderton	47	S	Health Visitor (Local Authority)	Bolton	Health Visitor (Local Authority)	
E.A. Jobling	41	S	Woman Visitor (Poor Law)	Burnley	Removal of Lunatics in Birkenhead (Poor Law)	CMB/ Royal Sanitary Institute certificate
Ada Simpson	34	S	Woman Visitor (Poor Law)	Devon	Matron in nursing home (Private)/informal sick visiting (Voluntary)	
M. Dawson	53	S	Sick Nursing (Private)	Burnley		Nurse

Name	Age	Marital status	Current role (and whether Private, Commercial, Voluntary, Local Authority or Poor Law)	From ...	Previous experience (and whether Private, Commercial, Voluntary, Local Authority or Poor Law)	Qualification claimed in application form
Ada Holt	32	M	Midwife (Local Authority?)	Bolton	Welfare Visitor 'Holbeck school for mothers' (Voluntary)	CMB
K. Primold	39	M	Junior Infant Ward Attendant (Poor Law?)	Chorley	Welfare Nurse at White Lund Fillings [munitions] factory (Commercial)	
Margaret Kay	46	S	Sewing machinist at Hospital (Poor Law)	Bolton	Guild of Help/Rounders Association/wartime nursing experience with Voluntary Aid Detachment (VAD)	
F.E. Wood	51	S	Woman Visitor (Poor Law)	Barrow	Assistant matron (Voluntary)	Health Visiting certificate
E. Leyland	50	S	Assistant District Nurse (Voluntary)	Farnworth	Farnworth Guild of Help (Voluntary)/foster mother (Poor Law?)	CMB
E. Fletcher	49	S	Sister in St Austell Infirmary (Poor Law)	St Austell	District nurse (Voluntary)/ Health Visitor (Local Authority)	CMB
M. Hindley	51	S	Employment Exchange (Civil Service)	Bolton		St John's Ambulance nursing certificate
M. Lenne	37	S	Health Visitor (Local Authority)	Newcastle	Maternity and Child Welfare Visitor/Health Visitor/industrial training	CMB/ Royal Sanitary Institute certificate

Name	Age	Marital status	Current role (and whether Private, Commercial, Voluntary, Local Authority or Poor Law)	From ...	Previous experience (and whether Private, Commercial, Voluntary, Local Authority or Poor Law)	Qualification claimed in application form
S. Farnworth	54	S	Welfare supervisor (Commercial)	Bolton	Welfare & Musgrave's globe iron works	Nurse training
M. Mellody	47	S	Woman Visitor (Poor Law)	Liverpool	Health Visitor/food control inspector/matron in a Canadian children's home	CMB
M.J. McCricken	58	S	Moral welfare visitor (Voluntary)	Dewsbury	Spen Valley Moral Welfare Association Staincliffe	
S.A. Broome	49	S	Welfare supervisor (Commercial)	Bolton	William Walker Tannery/ staff nurse in military hospital	SRN/CMB
Ada Wainer	39	S	Woman Visitor (Poor Law)	Oldham	Ran a creche in Hammersmith	CMB/ Sisterhood SW
Patience G. Baggallay	38	S	Undertaking training in Rescue Work	Liverpool	YWCA/War Pensions Committee	
T.K. Gibbon	43	S	Woman Visitor (Poor Law)	Wakefield	Bath Poor Law Union Boarding-Out Officer	Certificate of Sanitary Inspectors
M.E. Seward			Infant Life Protection Visitor (Poor Law)	London	Sister of Mental Ward	CMB
A. Hollingworth	34	S	Health Visitor (Tuberculosis Nurse) and District Nurse Inspector (Local Authority)	Bolton	Nurse Wirral/Rochdale/ Leigh	SRN/CMB

Name	Age	Marital status	Current role (and whether Private, Commercial, Voluntary, Local Authority or Poor Law)	From ...	Previous experience (and whether Private, Commercial, Voluntary, Local Authority or Poor Law)	Qualification claimed in application form
M. Wilbraham	40	S	Private Nurse (Private)	Bury	Army Nurse/Health Visitor/ Welfare Superintendent, presumably in industry	Certificate in General Nursing/CMB /Health Visitor Certificate

Bibliography

Abel Smith, B. and Townsend, P. (1965). *The Poor and the Poorest: a new analysis of the Ministry of Labour's Family Expenditure Surveys of 1953–4 and 1960.* Occasional Papers on Social Administration No. 17. London: Bell.

Abrams, Rebecca (1993). *Women in a Man's World.* London: Methuen.

Alexander, Leslie B. (1972). Social Work's Freudian Deluge: Myth or Reality? *Social Services Review*, 46 (4) December: 517–38.

Anon (1898). 'A Barrister at Law'. *Shaw's Manual of the Vaccination Law.* London: Shaw and Sons.

Anon (1912). *The Cruelty Man, Actual Experiences of an Inspector of the NSPCC Graphically Told by Himself.* London: NSPCC.

Armitage, Simon (2009). *All Points North.* London: Penguin.

Ashdown, Margaret and Brown, Sybil Clement (1953). *Social Services and Mental Health, an Essay on Psychiatric Social Workers.* London: Routledge.

Atkinson, D., Jackson, M. and Walmsley, J. (1997). *Forgotten Lives: Exploring the History of Learning Disability.* Kidderminster: British Institute of Learning Disability Publications.

Attlee, Clement (1920). *The Social Worker.* London: Bell.

Aveling, Henry F. (1909). *The History Sheet or Case Paper System.* London: P.S. King.

Bailey, R. and Brake, M. (1975). *Radical Social Work.* New York: Pantheon Books.

Barham, Peter (2004). *Forgotten Lunatics of the Great War.* Newhaven, Connecticut: Yale University Press.

Barraclough, Joan (ed) with Dedman, G., Osbourn, H. and Willmott, P. (1996). *100 Years of Health Related Social Work 1895–1995, Then ... Now ... Onwards.* Birmingham: BASW.

Bartlett, Peter and Wright, David (eds) (1999). *Outside the Walls of the Asylum: The History of Care in the Community 1750–2000.* London: The Athlone Press.

Bartley, George (1876). *A Handy Book for Guardians.* London: Chapman and Hall.

Basque Children of '37 Association. Available at: http://www.basquechildren.org/ articles. [Accessed 14/11/11].

Baxter, Lynn (2011). *Personal interview.*

Beckett, Andy (2009). *When the Lights Went Out: What Really Happened to Britain in the Seventies.* London: Faber and Faber.

BEN (1964). *Chief Welfare Officer Leaves.* 24 December, 4.

BHC (1989). *Social Services Committee Minutes.* BCF/7/1/28.

Bolton History Centre [BHC]. *Children's Committee Minutes*, AB/32/1/[2].

BHC. *Billeting Advisory Committee*, AB/36/1/[1].

BHC. *Wartime Nurseries*, ABCF/17/37.

BHC. *Maternity and Child Welfare Sub Committee*, ABCF/17/39.

BHC. *Police Staffing Records*, ABJ/23.

BHC. *After Care Boarded Out Case Papers*, ABSS/1/768.

BHC. *Social Services Committee Minutes 1989*, BCF/7/1/25, 26, 27, 28 and 29.

BHC. *Annual Reports of Bolton Moral Welfare Association*, BHC B/170/BOL.

BHC. *Guild of Help Annual Reports*, 361. BOL.

BHC. *William Tomlinson's personnel record*, GBO/28/4.

BHC. *Jonathon Carrodus' personnel record*, GBO/28/46.

BHC. *Neville Nuttall's personnel record*, GBO/28/50.

BHC. *Henry Sumner's personnel record*, GBO/28/300.

BHC. *George Knowles' personnel record*, GBO/28/306.

BHC. *Ralph Bates' personnel record*, GBO/28/308.

BHC. *Robert Robbie's personnel record*, GBO/28/312.

BHC. *Alice Barlow's personnel record*, GBO/28/527.

BHC. *Alice Borland's (nee Kearsley) personnel record*, GBO/28/569.

BHC. *Samuel Kinley's personnel record*, GBO/28/799.

BHC. *Annie Higginson's personnel record*, GBO/28/1104.

BHC. *Fred Crossley's personnel record*, GBO/28/1117.

BHC. *Ada Wainer's personnel record*, GBO/28/1290.

BHC (1888). *Annual Report of the Bolton Benevolent Society*, NUB/2/6/33.

BHC. *Mary Haslam's working diary*, ZHA 17/17.

BHC. *William Walker and Son; Interesting Centenary Review*, ZWKG/8/1.

Bibby, Colles, Petty and Sykes (1910). *The Pudding Lady: a New Departure in Social Work*. Westminster: National Food Reform Association.

Blom Cooper, Louis et al. (1986). *A Child in Trust: The Report of the Panel of Enquiry into the Circumstances Surrounding the Death of Jasmine Beckford*. London, Brent Council.

Blom Cooper, Louis et al. (1987). *A Child in Mind: Protection of Children in a Responsible Society. The Report of the Panel of Enquiry into the Circumstances Surrounding the Death of Kimberley Carlile*. London: Greenwich Borough and Greenwich Health Authority.

Bochel, Dorothy (1976). *A History of Probation*. Edinburgh: Scottish Academic Press.

Boehm, W. (1958). The Nature of Social Work. *Social Work*, 3 (2): 10–19.

Bolton Chronicle (1904a). Bolton Guardians Meeting, 15 June, 3.

Bolton Chronicle (1904b). Police Court, 1 October, 4.

Bolton Chronicle (1908a). Probation of Offenders Act, 1 January, 8.

Bolton Chronicle (1908b). Probation of Offenders Act, 18 January, 3.

Bolton Directory (1904). Tillotsons [in Bolton History Centre, B901 BOL].

Bolton Evening News (1904). Queen Street Mission Annual General Meeting, 27 October, 2.

Bolton Evening News (1915). Tragic Fate, 21 April, 4.

Bolton Evening News (1922). Fine Citizen, 7 January, 4.

Bolton Evening News (1937). Juvenile Court, 19 May, 3.

Bolton Evening News (1940). Appreciation of Mr Popplewell, 12 April, 8.

Bolton Evening News (1954). Children's Committee Disappointed, 16 February, 1.

Bolton Evening News (1955). Mr Freeman Leaves, 14 October, 1.

Bolton Evening News (1967). Off to new job, 19 July, 4.

Bolton Journal and Guardian (1907). Waifs and Strays home, 15 February, 3.

Bolton Journal and Guardian (1913a). Bolton Women Workers; Mrs A. Greg, 7 February, 10.

Bolton Journal and Guardian (1913b). Bolton Women Workers; Miss Sarah Reddish, 18 February, 10.

Bolton Journal and Guardian (1913c). Bolton Women Workers; Mrs H. (Mary) Barnes, 4 April, 10.

Booth, C. (1903). *Inquiry into the Life and Labour of the People in London.* London: Macmillan.

Bosanquet, Helen (1914). *Social Work in London 1869–1912.* London: E.P. Dutton.

Bowder, B. (1980). *The Children's Society.* London: Mowbray.

Bowlby, John (1944). Forty-Four Juvenile Thieves: Their Characters and Home Life. *International Journal of Psychoanalysis,* 25: 19–53.

Bowlby, John (1951). Maternal Care and Mental Health. *Bulletin of the World Health Organisation,* 3: 355–534.

Bowlby, John (1953). *Child Care and The Growth of Love.* Harmondsworth: Penguin.

Braithwaite (1962). *Paid Servant.* London: The Bodley Head.

Brewer, Colin and Lait, June (1980). *Can Social Work Survive?* London: Temple Smith.

Briggs, A. and Macartney, A. (1984). *Toynbee Hall. The First Hundred Years.* London: Routledge and Kegan Paul.

Brill, Kenneth (1991). *The Curtis Experiment.* Unpublished PhD Thesis, University of Birmingham.

British Film Institute (2011). *The Humphrey Jennings Collection Vol 1.*

Brown, Amanda (2011). *Personal interview.*

Brown, Michael (2000). *Evacuees: Evacuation in Wartime Britain.* Stroud: Sutton.

Burlingham, D. and Freud, A. (1942). *Young Children in War-Time. A Year's Work in a Residential War Nursery.* London: George Allen and Unwin.

Burnham, David (2011). Selective Memory: A Note on Social Work Historiography. *British Journal of Social Work,* 41 (1): 5–21.

Burnham, Valerie (2011). *Personal interview.*

Bustin, Cyril (1982). *From Silver Watch to Lovely Black Eye.* Typed manuscript held in Southwark Library.

Butler, Ian and Drakeford, Mark (2003). *Scandal, Social Policy and Social Welfare.* Bristol: The Policy Press.

Butler Sloss, Elizabeth (1988). *Report of the Inquiry into Child Abuse in Cleveland 1987*. HMSO.

Cameron, Heather (2011). *Personal interview.*

Cavanagh, Winifred E. (1954). *Four Decades of Students in Social Work.* Birmingham: Research Board of the Faculty of Commerce and Social Science, University of Birmingham.

Chance, William (1897). *Children Under The Poor Law*. London: Swann Sonnenschein.

Christie, A. (1998). Is Social Work a 'Non-Traditional' Occupation for Men? *British Journal of Social Work,* 28 (4): 491–510.

Clark, Carol (2011). *Personal interview.*

Clement Brown, S. (1939). The Methods of Social Caseworkers, in Bartlett, F. C. et al., *The Study of Society; Methods and Problems.* London: Kegan Paul, Tench, Trubner and Co., 379–401.

Clyde (1992). *The Report of the Inquiry into the Removal of Children from Orkney in February 1991*. Edinburgh: HMSO.

Coates, Ken and Silburn, Richard (1970). *Poverty: The Forgotten Englishmen.* Harmondsworth: Penguin.

Cobbold, Helen (1935). *The District Visitor: A Practical Guide for the Inexperienced.* London: SPCK.

Colcord, Joanna C. (ed) (1930). *The Long View.* New York: Russell Sage Foundation.

Cole-Mackintosh, Ronnie (1994). *A Century of Service to Mankind: The Story of the St John Ambulance Brigade.* London: Benham.

Coles, Adrian (2003). *Counselling in the Workplace.* Oxford: Oxford University Press.

Collingwood, R.G. (1939). *An Autobiography.* Oxford: Oxford University Press.

Collins, C.D.E. (1965). The Introduction of Old Age Pensions in Great Britain. *Historical Journal,* 8 (2): 246–59.

Connor, Betty (1989). *A Pauper's Palace: A History of Fishpool Institution 1860–1948.* Manchester: Neil Richardson.

Cooper, Joan (1983). *The Creation of the British Personal Social Services.* London: Heinemann.

Cooper, Nora (2009). *Personal interview.*

Corrick, Hilary (2011). *Personal interview.*

Corrigan, P. and Leonard, P. (1978). *Social Work Practice Under Capitalism: A Marxist Approach.* London: Macmillan.

Court, Joan (1969). The Battered Child, Part 1: Historical and Diagnostic Reflections. *Medical Social Work,* 22: 11–20.

Cox, Pat (2003). *WRVS in the Community: Sixty Years of Voluntary Service in Bolton.* Bolton: Felton Books.

Cree, V.E. (1995). *From Public Streets to Private Lives. The Changing Task of Social Work.* Aldershot: Avebury.

Cree, V.E. (2002). Social Work and Society, in Davies, M. (ed). *Blackwell Companion to Social Work*, 2nd edition. Oxford: Blackwell.

Crowther, M.A. (1981). *The Workhouse System 1834–1929.* London: Batsford Academic.

Curtis, Helene and Sanderson, Mimi (2004). *The Unsung Sixties.* London: Whiting and Birch.

Curtis Report (1946). *Report of the Care of Children Committee,* Cmd 6922. London: HMSO.

Custance, David (2010). *Personal communication.*

Dale, P., Davies, M., Morrison, T. and Waters, J. (1986). *Dangerous Families: Assessment and Treatment of Child Abuse.* London: Tavistock Publications.

Daniels, Tom (2011). *Personal communication.*

Dearden, Basil and Relph, Michael (1952). *I Believe in You.* Ealing Studios.

Department of Health (1988). *Protecting Children: A Guide for Social Workers Undertaking Comprehensive Assessment* (known as the 'Orange Book'). HMSO.

Department of Health and Social Security (1974). *Report of the Committee of Inquiry into the Care and Supervision Provided in Relation to Maria Colwell.* HMSO.

Department of Health and Social Security (1978). *Social Service Teams: the Practitioners View.* HMSO.

Donnison, David (1975). *Social Policy and Administration Revisited.* London: Unwin Hyman.

Dumsday, W.H. and Moss, J. (1936). *Hadden's Relieving Officer's Handbook Sixth Edition.* London: Hadden, Best and Co.

Dunbar, Aileen (2009). *Personal communication.*

Dunkerley, John (2011). *Personal interview.*

Edgerton, David (2011). *Britain's War Machine.* London: Allen Lane.

Eisenstadt, Naomi (1998). *50 Years of Family Service Units.* London: Routledge.

Ellison, Mary (1934). *Sparks Beneath the Ashes.* London: John Murray.

Evans, Ruth (1977). *Happy Families.* London: Peter Owen (quoted by permission of Peter Owen).

Fahlberg, Vera (1994). *A Child's Journey through Placement.* London: British Association for Adoption and Fostering.

Ferguson, H. (2004). *Protecting Children in Time: Child Abuse, Child Protection and the Consequences of Modernity.* Basingstoke: Palgrave.

Ffelan, Maurice (2010). *Personal interview and correspondence.*

Finkelstein, V. (1980). *Attitudes and Disabled People.* New York: World Rehabilitation Fund.

Foley, Alice (1973). *A Bolton Childhood.* Manchester: Manchester University Extra Mural Dept and NW Worker's Educational Association.

Forman, Charles (1979). *Industrial Town: Self Portrait of St Helens in the 1920s.* London: Paladin: Granada Publishing.

Fowler, Simon (2007). *Workhouse: The People, the Places, the Life Behind Doors.* London: National Archive.

Fox, Brian (2010). *Personal interviews.*

Francis, James (1987). *Harwood Friendly Societies: Sick and Burial.* Bolton: Turton Local History Society.

Glasby, John (1996). *Poverty and Opportunity; 100 Years of the Birmingham Settlement.* Studley: Brewin Books Ltd.

Green, J.R. (1892). *A Short History of the English People.* London: Macmillan.

Green, J.R. (1892). *The District Visitor, Stray Studies from England and Italy.* London: Macmillan: 269–82.

Green, S. (1979). *Rachman: the Slum Landlord whose Name Became a Byword for Evil.* London: Michael Joseph.

Greenwood, Ernest (1957). Attributes of a Profession. *Social Work,* 2, July: 45–55.

Gregson, Keith (1985). Poor Law and Organised Charity: the Relief of Exceptional Distress in North East England, 1870–1910, in Rose, M.E. *The Poor and the City: The English Poor Law in its Urban Context, 1834–1914.* Leicester: Leicester University Press.

Groves, Isobel (2010). *Personal interviews.*

Guardian (2008). *Obituary of Ray Wyre,* 8 August, 16.

Guardian (2010). *On the Front Line: Then and Now. An Archive of Video Interviews with Social Workers.* 3 November, 4.

Haldane (1911). *The Social Worker's Guide.* London: Sir Isaac Pitman and Sons.

Hall, Gwen (2004). *The Pacifist Service Unit (PSU),* BBC, People's War. Available at: http://www.bbc.co.uk/ww2peopleswar/stories/37/a2810837. shtml. [Accessed: 08/05/11].

Hamer, Harold (1938). *Bolton 1838–1938.* Bolton: Bolton Corporation.

Harris, Jo (1937). *Probation, a Sheaf of Memories: Thirty-Four Years Work in the Police Courts.* Lowestoft: M. F. Robinson, The Library Press.

Hartley, Mary (2010). *Personal interview.*

Haw, G (1907). *From Workhouse to Westminster: The Life Story of Will Crooks M.P.* London: Cassell.

Hay, J.R. (1975). *The Origin of the Liberal Welfare Reforms 1906–1914.* Macmillan.

Hayworth, Phillip H. (2007). *Bolton Poor Protection Society.* Bolton: Halliwell History Society.

Hendrick (1994). *Child Welfare: England 1872–1989.* London: Routledge.

Hewitt, Peter (2011). *Personal interview.*

Heywood, Jean (1959). *Children in Care: The Development of the Service for the Deprived Child.* London: Routledge and Kegan Paul.

Higgs, Mary (1904). *The Tramp Ward.* London: John Heywood.

Higson, Jesse (1955). *The Story of a Beginning: An Account of Pioneer Work for Moral Welfare.* London: SPCK.

Hindle, Penny (2011). *Personal interview.*

Hiscock, Keith (2011). *Personal interview.*

Hobbes, Robin (2011). *Personal interview.*

Hodgkinson, P. and Stewart, M. (1998). *Coping with Catastrophe: A Handbook of Disaster Management.* London: Psychology Press.

Hodgson, Vere (1971). *Few Eggs and No Oranges, The Diaries of Vere Hodgson 1940–45.* London: Dennis Dobson.

Hodson, Alice Lucy (1909). *Letters from a Settlement.* London: Edward Arnold.

Holden, Sheila (undated). *The Bolton and County of Lancaster Industrial School (1854–1924).* Bolton Borough Archive.

Holman, Bob (1986). Prevention: the Victorian Legacy. *British Journal of Social Work*, 16 (1): 1–23.

Holman, Bob (2001). *Champions for Children.* Bristol: The Policy Press.

Home Office (1965). The Child, the Family and the Young Offender, Cmnd 2742. HMSO.

Horn, Pamela (ed) (1983). *Oxfordshire Village Life: the Diaries of George James Dew (1846–1928), Relieving Officer.* Abingdon: Beacon Publications.

Housden, L.G. (1955). *The Prevention of Cruelty to Children.* London: Jonathan Cape.

Humphreys, Margaret (1994). *Empty Cradles.* London: Doubleday.

Ingelby Report (1961). *Report of the Committee on Children and Young Persons*, Cmnd 1191. HMSO.

Isaacs, Susan (ed) (1941). *The Cambridge Evacuation Survey: A War-time Study in Social Welfare and Education.* London: Methuen.

Ives, Sheila (2011). *Personal interview.*

Jackson, Louise (2003). Care or Control? The Metropolitan Women Police and Child Welfare (1919–1969). *The Historical Journal*, 46 (3): 623–48.

Jennings, H. (1930). *The Private Citizen in Public Service: an Account of the Voluntary Children's Care Committee System in London.* London: Allen and Unwin.

Jennings, Humphrey (1940). *Welfare of the Workers.* British Film Institute.

Jones, Kathleen (1984). *Eileen Younghusband: A Biography.* Occasional Papers on Social Administration, No 76, London: Bedford Square Press/NCVO.

Jones, Kathleen (1993). *Asylums and After.* London: Athlone.

Kanter, Joel (ed) (2004). *Face to Face with Children: the Life and Work of Clare Winnicott.* London: Karnac.

Kershaw, Roger and Sacks, Janet (2008). *New Lives for Old: The Story of Britain's Child Migrants.* London: The National Archive.

Kesey, Ken (1962). *One Flew Over the Cuckoo's Nest.* New York: Viking.

Kidd, J. Alan (1984). Charity Organisation and the Unemployed in Manchester c.1870–1914. *Social History*, 9 (1): 45–66.

Kidd, A.J. (1985). Outcast Manchester: Voluntary Charity, Poor Relief and the Casual Poor 1860–1905, in Kidd, A.J. and Roberts, K.W. (eds). *City, Class and Culture: Studies of Cultural Production and Social Policy in Victorian Manchester.* Manchester: Manchester University Press.

Kilbrandon Report (1966). *Social Work and the Community: Proposals for the Re-Organisation of Personal Social Services*, Cmnd 3605. London: HMSO.

King, Steven (2004). 'We Might be Trusted': Female Poor Law Guardians and the Development of the New Poor Law: The Case of Bolton, England, 1880–1906. *International Review of Social History*, 49 (1): 27–46.

King, Steven (2006, 2010). *Women, Welfare and Politics 1880–1920: 'We Might be Trusted'*. Brighton: Sussex Academic Press.

Kirkman Gray (1908). *Philanthropy and the State or Social Politics*. London: King and Son.

Kirkpatrick, Karyn (2011). A Home of My Own – Progress on Enabling People with Learning Disabilities to have Choice and Control over Where and With Whom they Live. *Tizard Learning Disability Review*, 16 (2), April.

Kornitzer, Margaret (1952). *Adoption in the Modern World*. New York: Putnam.

Kynaston, David (2007). *Austerity Britain, 1945–1951*. London: Bloomsbury.

Kynaston, David (2009). *Family Britain, 1951–1957*. London: Bloomsbury.

Labour Party Study Group (1964). *Crime – a challenge to us all: report of the Labour Party Study Group*. London: Labour Party.

Lady Margaret Hall 'Brown Book', Annual College Journal (1963). Obituary of Alice Lucy Hodson, LMH College, Oxford.

La Fontaine (1997). *Speak of the Devil: Tales of Satanic Abuse in Contemporary England*. Cambridge: Cambridge University Press.

Lancashire Record Office. *Lancaster and Morecambe District Moral Welfare Association,* DDX 1952.

Langan, M. (1993). The Rise and Fall of Social Work, in Clarke, J. (ed). *A Crisis in Care*. London: Sage.

Laybourn, K. (1994). *The Guild of Help and the Changing Face of Edwardian Philanthropy: the Guild of Help, Voluntary Work, and the State, 1904–1919*. Lampeter: Edwin Mellen Press.

Leach, Wendy (2011). *Personal interview.*

Lees, Ray (1971). Social Work, 1925–1950: the Case for Reappraisal. *British Journal of Social Work,* 1 (4): 371–80.

Lewis, Jane (1991). *Women and Social Action in Victorian and Edwardian England*. Aldershot: Edward Elgar.

Lewis, Jane (1995). *The Voluntary Sector, the State and Social Work in Britain: The Charity Organisation Society/Family Welfare Association Since 1869*. Brookfield, Vermont: Edward Elgar.

Lewis, Jane (1996). The Boundary between Voluntary and Statutory Social Service in the Late Nineteenth and Early Twentieth Centuries. *The Historical Journal,* 39 (1): 155–77.

Liman, S. (2001). *What I valued about being a PSW: Compilation of contributions from retired PSWs,* personal archive.

Loach, Jim (2011). *Oranges and Sunshine*. See-Saw Films.

Longden, Kathryn (undated). *Iron Fist Beneath a Velvet Glove: Middle-Class Women's Representations of Philanthropic and Voluntary Work Amongst the*

Poor, Working-Class, and Indigenous Peoples in the Nineteenth Century. Working Papers on the Web. Available at: http://extra.shu.ac.uk/wpw/femprac/ longden.htm#1. [Accessed: 19/10/11].

Lymbery, Mark (2001). Social Work at the Crossroads. *British Journal of Social Work,* 31 (3): 369–84.

Macadam, Elizabeth (1925). *The Equipment of the Social Worker.* London: George Allen and Unwin.

Macadam, Elizabeth (1934). *The New Philanthropy.* London: George Allen and Unwin.

Macadam, Elizabeth (1945). *The Social Servant in the Making.* London: George Allen and Unwin.

McCarthy, Hannah [pseudonym] (2011). *Personal interview.*

McHugh, Ian (2011). *Personal interview and correspondence.*

Mcleod, Iain (1965). 'Quoodle'. *The Spectator,* 3 December.

McNay, Marie (2011). *Personal interview.*

Mahood, Linda (1990). *The Magdelenes: Prostitution in the Nineteenth Century.* London: Routledge.

Manchee, Dorothy (1946). *Whatever Does the Almoner Do?* London: Bailliere, Tindall and Cox.

Mann, Horace (1853). Census of Great Britain 1851: Religious Worship, *British Parliamentary Papers LXXXIX, Religious Worship (England and Wales) Report*, London.

Makepeace, Hilary (2011). *Personal interview.*

Marwick, A. (1967). *After the Deluge.* Harmondsworth: Penguin.

Mason, Mary (2009). *Personal interviews.*

Maugham, Somerset (1915). *Of Human Bondage.* New York: George H. Doran.

Mayer, John and Timms, Noel (1970). *The Client Speaks.* London: Routledge and Kegan Paul.

Means, R. and Smith, R. (1985). *The Development of Welfare Services for Eldery People.* London: Croom Helm.

Mercer, John (2011). *Personal interview.*

Middlebrook, Martin (1971). *The First Day of the Somme.* Harmondsworth: Penguin.

Middlebrook (2004). The Writing of The First Day on the Somme. Weblog [Online]. Available at: http://www.fylde.demon.co.uk/middlebrook2.htm. [Accessed 13/03/2011].

Mind, History of 'Cam Mind'. Available at: http://www.cam-mind.org.uk/About/ History. [Accessed 13/09/2011].

Mishra, R. (1969.) *A History of the Relieving Officer in England and Wales 1834–1948.* Unpublished PhD Thesis, London School of Economics.

Moberley Bell, E. (1961). *The Story of Hospital Almoners: The Birth of a Profession.* London: Faber and Faber.

Monckton, Sir Walter (1945). *Report of the Inquiry into the Death of Dennis O'Neill,* Cmd 6636. HMSO.

Monger, Mark (1972). *Casework in Probation.* London: Butterworths.

Moore, Michael (1977). Social Work and Social Welfare: The Organization of Philanthropic Resources in Britain, 1900–1914. *Journal of British Studies,* 16 (2): 85–104.

Morrison, Kathryn (1999). *The Workhouse: A Study of Poor Law Buildings in England.* London: English Heritage.

Morton, Reverend A. (1954). *The Early Days.* London: NSPCC.

Mowat, Charles Loch (1961). *The Charity Organisation Society 1869–1913: its ideas and work.* London: Methuen.

Mumm, Susan (1996). 'Not Worse than Other Girls', the Convent Based Rehabilitation of Fallen Women in Victorian Britain. *Journal of Social History,* 29 (3): 527.

Munro, Eileen (1996). Avoidable and Unavoidable Mistakes in Child Protection Work. *British Journal of Social Work,* 26 (6): 793–808.

Murphy, Michael (1996). *The Child Protection Unit: its History, Function and Effectiveness in the Organisation of Child Protection Work.* Aldershot: Avebury.

Murphy, Michael (1997). Delivering Staff Care in a Multi-Disciplinary Context, in Bates, J., Pugh, R. and Thompson, N. (eds). *Protecting Children: Challenges and Change.* Aldershot: Arena.

Murphy, Michael (2011). *Personal interview.*

National Association of Probation Officers (Burroughs, V., Falcon, K., Fletcher, H. [eds]) (2007). *Changing Lives: an Oral History of Probation.* London: National Association of Probation Officers.

National Society for the Protection of Cruelty to Children, Bolton (1909). *Annual Report.* Bolton History Centre, 179.2/NAT.

Niechcial, Judith (2010). *Lucy Faithfull, Mother to Hundreds.* London: Niechcial.

Niechcial, Judith (2011). *Personal interview.*

Oliver, Michael (1990). *The Politics of Disablement.* Basingstoke: Macmillan.

Overy, Richard (2009). *The Morbid Age.* London: Penguin.

Page, Robert M. and Silburn, Richard L. (1999). *British Social Welfare in the Twentieth Century.* London: Macmillan.

Parker, Roy (1983). The Gestation of Reform: the Children Act 1948, in Bean, P. and McPherson, S. *Approaches to Welfare.* London: Routledge and Kegan Paul.

Parliamentary Papers (1999). *A Century of Change: Trends in UK Statistics since 1900,* RESEARCH PAPER 99/111, 21 Dec.

Parsloe, Phyllida (1972). Through the Eyes of the Probation Officer. *British Journal of Social Work,* 2 (1): 21–6.

Parton, C. and Parton N. (1988). Women, the Family and Child Protection. *Critical Social Policy,* 8 (24): 38–49.

Parton, Nigel (1981). Child Abuse, Social Anxiety and Welfare. *British Journal of Social Work,* 11 (1): 391–414.

Parton, Nigel (1986). The Beckford Report: A Critical Appraisal. *British Journal of Social Work,* 16 (5): 511–30.

Parton, Nigel (2004). From Maria Colwell to Victoria Climbie: Reflections on a Generation of Public Enquiries into Child Abuse. *Child Abuse Review*, 13 (2): 80–94.

Payne, Malcolm (2005). *The Origins of Social Work: Continuity and Change.* Basingstoke: Palgrave Macmillan.

Pearce, Robert (1997). *Attlee.* London: Longman.

Penny, Marian (2010). *Personal interview and correspondence.*

Perry, E.R.B. (2010). *Personal correspondence.*

Pierson, John (2011). *Understanding Social Work: History and Context.* Maidenhead: McGraw Hill, Open University Press.

Pimlott, J.A.R. (1935). *Toynbee Hall. Fifty Years of Social Progress 1884–1934.* London: Dent.

Pincus, Allen and Minahan, Anne (1973). *Social Work Practice: Model and Method.* Itasca, Illinois: F.E. Peacock.

Pither, Julia (2011). *Personal interview.*

Polyblank, Jennie (2011). *Personal interview.*

Pool, Richard [pseudonym] (2010). *Personal interview.*

Powls, Ken, M.B.E (2010). *Many Lives: a Memoir.* Howden: The Adam Press.

Preston-Thomas, Herbert (1909). *The Work and Play of a Government Inspector.* Edinburgh: Blackwood.

Pringle, J.C. (1937). *Social Work of the London Churches.* Oxford: Oxford University Press.

Pritchard, C. and Williams, R. (2010). Comparing Possible Child Abuse-Related Deaths in England & Wales with the Major Developed Countries 1974–2006. *British Journal of Social Work*, 40 (6): 1700–18.

Prokascka, F. (1988). *Philanthropy in Modern Britain.* London: Faber and Faber.

Quirk, Joan (2005). *Comment from Joan Quirk* via Nick Chamberlain of Sevenoaks Age Concern, article no. A4390120. Available at: http://www.bbc.co.uk/ww2peopleswar/stories bbc.co.uk/ww2peopleswar/stories. [Accessed: 29/05/11].

Raphael, Beverly (1986). *When Disaster Strikes: A Handbook for the Caring Professions.* London: Harper Collins.

Rathbone, Eleanor (1905). *William Rathbone.* London: Macmillan.

Read, Fiona (2007). Not 'Ordinary Lunatics': The Ex Services Welfare Society and the Treatment of Shell Shocked Men after the Great War. *Stand To! Journal of the Western Front Association,* 78, January.

Rees, Bronwen (1965). *No Fixed Abode.* London: Stanmore Press.

Rice, Kenneth (1965). *Learning for Leadership: Interpersonal and Intergroup Relations.* London: Tavistock Publications.

Richmond, Mary E. (1917). *Social Diagnosis.* New York: Russell Sage Foundation.

Richmond, Mary E. (1922). *What is Social Casework, An Introductory Discussion.* New York: Russell Sage Foundation.

Rimmer, Joyce (1980). *Troubles Shared: The Story of a Settlement 1899–1979.* Birmingham: Phlogiston Publishing.

Rimmer, Joyce (1995). *How Social Workers and Probation Officers in England Conceived their Roles and Responsibilities in the 1930s and 1940s.* Aspects of the History of British Social Work, New Bulmershe Papers, University of Reading.

Rimmer, Joyce (2011). *Personal interview.*

Roberts, David (1963). How Cruel Was the Victorian Poor Law? *Historical Journal,* 6 (1): 97–107.

Roberts, Robert (1976). *A Ragged Schooling.* Manchester: Manchester University Press.

Robertson, James (1952). *A Two-Year-Old Goes to Hospital.* Scientific Films.

Rockefeller Archive Centre (1985). *Series 16 – Mental Hygiene Programme in England 1927–1947,* Bureau of Social Hygiene Archives. Available at: http://www.rockefeller.edu/archive.ctr/arcman.html. [Accessed: 29/10/11].

Rodgers, Barbara N. and Dixon, Julia (1960). *Portrait of Social Work: A Study of Social Services in a Northern Town.* Oxford: Oxford University Press.

Rolph, S., Atkinson, D., Walsley, J. (2003). 'A Pair of Stout Shoes and an Umbrella': The Role of the Mental Welfare Officer in Delivering Community Care in East Anglia: 1946–1970. *British Journal of Social Work,* 33 (3): 339–59.

Rooff, Madeline (1972). *One Hundred Years of Family Welfare.* London: Michael Joseph.

Rose, Michael and Woods, Anne (1995). *Everything went on at the Roundhouse. A Hundred Years of the Manchester University Settlement.* Manchester: University of Manchester.

Russell, A. (1991). *The Growth of Occupational Welfare in Britain: Evolution and Harmonization of Modern Personnel Practice.* Aldershot: Avebury.

Ryan, Brenda (2011). *Personal interviews.*

Ryan, Pat (1985). Politics and Relief: East London Unions in the Late Nineteenth and Early Twentieth Century, in Rose, M.E. *The Poor and the City: The English Poor Law in its Urban Context, 1834–1914.* Leicester: Leicester University Press.

Sackville, Andrew (1989). Thomas William Cramp, Almoner: The Forgotten Man in a Female Occupation. *British Journal of Social Work,* 19 (2): 95–109.

St Bartholemew's Hospital London Archive (1889). *Minute Book of the Metropolitan Hospital General Committee,* 7 August.

Samaritans. Available at: http://www.samaritans.org/about_samaritans/facts_and_figures/publications.aspx. [Accessed: 02/06/11].

Sandbrook, Dominic (2005). *Never Had It So Good: A History of Britain from Suez to the Beatles.* New York: Little, Brown.

Sedley, S. (1987). *Whose Child? The Report of the Panel of Inquiry into the Death of Tyra Henry.* London Borough of Lambeth.

Seebohm Report (1968). *Report of the* Committee *on Local Authority and Allied Personal Social Services*, Cmnd 3703. London: HMSO.

Sheldon, Nicola (2007). The School Attendance Officer 1900–1939: Policeman to Welfare Worker? *History of Education,* 36 (6): 735–46.

Shorrock, Peter (accessed 2010). *Central Association of Mental Welfare Record and Lancashire County Council Mental Welfare Department record for Amy P [Pseudonym]* with kind permission of Lancashire Archive, Lancashire County Council.

Simey, Margaret (1951). *Charitable Effort in Liverpool in the Nineteenth Century.* Liverpool: Liverpool University Press.

Smith, Marjorie M. (1952). *Professional Education for Social Workers in Britain.* London: Family Welfare Association.

Snell, Henry (1938). *Men Movements and Myself.* London: J.M. Dent.

Sparrow, J. (1978). *Diary of a Student Social Worker.* London: Routledge and Kegan Paul.

Spring Rice, Margery (1939). *Working Class Wives: their Health and Conditions.* London: Pelican.

Standring, Ron (2010). *Personal interview and correspondence.*

Stephens, Tom (ed) (1945). *Problem Families: An Experiment in Social Rehabilitation.* London: Pacifist Service Units.

Stevenson, Olive (2005). *National Life Stories: Pioneers in Charity and Social Welfare.* British Library Sound Archive, C1155/01.

Stewart, John (2006). Psychiatric Social Work in Inter-war Britain: Child Guidance, American Ideas, American Philanthropy. *Michael Quarterly, Norwegian Medical Society,* 3: 78–91.

Stocks, Mary (1960). *A Hundred Years of District Nursing.* London: George Allen and Unwin.

Stocks, Mary (1970). *My Commonplace Book.* London: Peter Davies.

Stroud, John (1962). *The Shorn Lamb.* Harmondsworth: Penguin.

Stroud, John (1971). *Thirteen Penny Stamps; The Story of the Church of England Children's Society (Waifs and Strays) from 1881 to the 1970s.* London: Hodder and Stoughton.

Sunday Times Insight Team (1979). *Suffer The Children: The Story of Thalidomide.* London: Andre Deutsch.

Sutter, Julie (1903). *Britain's Next Campaign.* London: Brimley Johnson.

Syddall, Howard (2011). *Personal interview.*

Thane, Pat (1996). *Foundations of the Welfare State.* London: Longman.

Thompson, Paul (1992). *The Edwardians: The Remaking of British Society.* London: Routledge.

Thorpe, David (1994). *Evaluating Child Protection.* Oxford: Oxford University Press.

The Times (1948). *The Appointed Day,* 5 July, 3.

Timms, Noel (1961). Social Work in Action – A Historical Study (1887–1937). *Case Conference,* 18 (1): 259–63.

Timms, Noel (1964). *Psychiatric Social Work in Great Britain 1939–1962.* London: Routledge and Kegan Paul.

Titmuss, Richard (1950). *Problems of Social Policy: History of the Second World War.* HMSO.

Tomkins, Daniel (1997). *Mission Accomplished: the Story of the First Hundred Years of the Bolton Methodist Mission.* Peterborough: Methodist Publishing House.

Torrie, Margaret (1970). *Begin Again: A Book for Women Alone.* London: Dent.

Totton, Barbara (2011). *Taped interview.*

Townsend, P. (1962). *The Last Refuge.* London: Routledge and Kegan Paul.

Townsend, P. et al. (1970). *The Fifth Social Service: A Critical Analysis of the Seebohm Proposals.* Report from a Fabian Society Conference. Glasgow: Civic Press Publishing.

Victim Support. Available at: http://www.victimsupport.org/About%20us/History%20and%20achievement. [Accessed: 15/10/11].

Walton, R.G. (1975). *Women in Social Work.* London: Routledge and Kegan Paul.

Watkinson, W.R. (1955). *The Relieving Officer Looks Back: The Last Years of the Poor Law in Holderness.* Withernsea: A.E. Lunn.

Waugh, Rosa (1913). *The Life of Benjamin Waugh.* London: Unwin.

Welshman, J. (1996). In Search of the 'Problem Family'; Public Health and Social Work in England and Wales 1940–1970. *Social History of Medicine,* 9 (3): 447–65.

Whelan, Robert (2001). *Helping the Poor: Friendly Visiting, Dole Charities and Dole Queues.* London: Civitas.

Wickwar, Hardy and Wickwar, Margaret (1936). *The Social Services.* London: The Bodley Head.

Williams, H.C. Maurice (1956). Problem Families in Southampton. *The Eugenics Review,* 47 (4): 217–23.

Willmott, P. and Young, M. (1957). *Family and Kinship in East London.* Harmondsworth: Penguin.

Willmott, Phyllis (1992). *A Singular Woman: the Life of Geraldine Aves,* NISW. London: Whiting and Birch.

Willmott, Phyllis (2004). London's School Care Committee Service 1908–1989. *Voluntary Action Journal,* 6 (2): 95–110.

Wolfensberger, W. (1972). *The Principle of Normalization in Human Services.* Toronto: National Institute on Mental Retardation.

Women's Group on Public Welfare (1943). *Our Towns: a Close Up: a Study Made in 1939–1942 with Certain Recommendations by the Hygiene Committee of the Women's Group on Public Welfare.* London: National Council for Social Service.

Woodroofe, Kathleen (1962). *From Charity to Social Work.* London: Routledge and Kegan Paul.

Woodruff, William (2000). *The Road to Nab End.* New York: Little, Brown.

Wootton, Barbara (1959). *Social Science and Social Pathology.* London: Allen and Unwin.

Worth, Jennifer (2007). *Call The Midwife.* London: Weidenfeld and Nicolson.

Wright, Thomas 'The Riverside Visitor' (1892). *The Pinch of Poverty: Sufferings and Heroism of the London Poor.* London: Isbister.

York City Council Minutes 1931/1932, York Library, Y352.

Young, F. and Ashton, E.T. (1956). *British Social Work in the Nineteenth Century.* London: Routledge and Kegan Paul.

Younghusband, Eileen (1947). *Report on the Employment and Training of Social Workers.* Dunfermline: Carnegie UK Trust.

Younghusband, Eileen (1951). *Social Work in Britain.* Dunfermline: Carnegie UK Trust.

Younghusband, Eileen et al. (1959). *Report of the Working Party on Social Workers in Local Authority Health and Welfare Services.* London, HMSO.

Younghusband, Eileen (1978). *Social Work in Britain: 1950–1975.* London: George Allen and Unwin.

Index